The National Trust
SCHOOL OF GARDENING

A treasure chest of gardening
advice and inspiration

The National Trust
SCHOOL OF
GARDENING

A treasure chest of gardening
advice and inspiration

REBECCA BEVAN

Illustrations by Madeleine Smith

For my mother, who inspired my love of gardening

First published in the United Kingdom in 2021 by
National Trust Books
An imprint of HarperCollins Publishers
1 London Bridge Street
London SE1 9GF
www.harpercollins.co.uk

HarperCollins Publishers
1st Floor, Watermarque Building, Ringsend Road, Dublin 4, Ireland

ISBN: 9781911657156

A catalogue record for this book is available from the British Library.

10 9 8 7 6 5 4

Reproduction by Rival Colour Ltd, UK
Printed and bound in Bosnia and Herzegovina

If you would like to comment on any aspect of this book, please contact us
at the above address or national.trust@harpercollins.co.uk

National Trust publications are available at National Trust shops or online at
nationaltrustbooks.co.uk

CONTENTS

INTRODUCTION

The National Trust employs over 500 gardeners who have an extraordinary wealth of expertise. The places they care for vary enormously, from the sweet cottage gardens that once belonged to Beatrix Potter and Thomas Hardy to the huge terraces of Powis Castle and Cliveden. Collectively these gardens span some 400 years of horticultural history, containing formal parterres, water gardens, rose gardens, glasshouses, walled gardens, orchards, meadows and exquisite flower borders. Some are internationally famous and have become a mecca for gardening enthusiasts, while others remain relatively undiscovered.

While National Trust gardeners are at work, they are frequently asked questions by visitors. Some people are keen to hear the stories of the gardens, but many more want to know the names of the plants and how they are cared for. Clearly, even the grandest gardens have much to teach us about our own. Their lawns, borders and kitchen gardens may be a lot larger than ours, but the maintenance techniques are similar, and they contain wonderful plant combinations to recreate, or interesting varieties to grow at home. Garden visiting can also give us inspiration about what makes a garden sing – be it generous planting, winding paths, a welcoming bench in a sunny corner, or the way colour schemes change through the seasons.

Written for gardeners of all kinds – whether keen novices or experienced enthusiasts – this book shares the wisdom of National Trust experts on everything that's relevant to domestic gardens. It is intended to give you the inspiration and confidence to make the most of your garden, while not overwhelming you with rigid rules or unnecessary technical detail. It starts with a chapter on garden-making, be that starting from scratch or simply working out which plants and materials are best in

◀ Hidcote in Gloucestershire, one of the finest gardens in the world, is cared for by the National Trust.

◀ A gardener chats to visitors in the Dutch Garden at Ascott in Buckinghamshire.

◣ Alfriston Clergy House in Sussex, the first property cared for by the National Trust and one of its smallest gardens.

▶ A painted lady butterfly on *Dahlia merckii*.

an existing one. Next is flower borders – a subject close to most gardeners' hearts – with detailed advice on how to choose and combine perennials for great effect. Roses, climbers, shrubs and trees, lawns and meadows, topiary and hedges, fruit and vegetables, cut flowers and greenhouse cultivation all have their own chapters, filled with simple, up-to-date advice on plant selection, maintenance, pruning and training.

Each chapter begins with a brief introduction to the history and cultural significance of our great British gardening traditions. Did you know that wisteria has been cultivated in Asia for over 2,000 years, or that bedding was fashionable long before herbaceous perennials? This is followed by a case study from a National Trust garden where the chapter topic is demonstrated exceptionally well. The Courts Garden in Wiltshire is the perfect place to show the value of topiary and hedges for giving structure and character to a garden, while at Tintinhull in Somerset the container displays are exemplary. Each case study is accompanied by tips from National Trust Head Gardeners, such as which perennials provide the succession of colour in the borders at Packwood House or which cut flowers are best for drying. Finally, each chapter contains several pages of practical advice to help you make this aspect of gardening, or group of plants, work well for you at home. These include concise step-by-step instructions for growing dahlias, taking cuttings, making a wildlife pond, laying a lawn and much more, alongside clear diagrams. Special care has been taken to make pruning instructions as straightforward as possible, with overarching

principles explained to help you to achieve success at home.

National Trust gardeners have long known that their gardens provide valuable habitats for wildlife. Now we know that small domestic gardens play an increasingly important role in boosting biodiversity too. To help gardeners embrace their environmental responsibility, this book offers detailed advice on the species found in our gardens and their needs. Sustainable gardening is also about improving soil health and reducing our dependence on resources such as peat and water. Nunnington in Yorkshire provides an inspiring backdrop for advice on such things, with tips about composting, avoiding slug pellets and even making your own plant labels.

Today we are also increasingly aware of the therapeutic benefits gardening brings us: fresh air, exercise, a shared hobby, a connection to the seasons and the natural world, and a constant source of joy and hope. Never have there been more reasons to dedicate time to gardening. Whether you have been growing for years or are just becoming interested; whether you are creating a new garden, maintaining an established one or renovating an old one, this book has a wealth of information to inspire and guide you. Beautifully illustrated with photographs and original drawings, I hope you will find it an enjoyable read as well as an invaluable reference.

'The most noteworthy thing
about gardeners is that they are
always optimistic, always enterprising,
and never satisfied. They always look
forward to doing something better
than they have ever done before.'

VITA SACKVILLE-WEST

CHAPTER 1
CREATING
A GARDEN

THE ORIGINS OF GARDENING

Human beings have been making gardens for millennia. Early civilisations enclosed parcels of land for safety, selecting only the most useful wild plants to grow inside. Gradually, the concept of the garden evolved to become a protected space where plants were cultivated for food, medicine and also beauty. Some of the earliest gardens recorded are those of the temples and palaces of Ancient Persia and Egypt. These were highly architectural with walls enclosing them, shady pergolas, ponds and paths. Many aspects of their design influenced the layout of Roman villas and Islamic gardens and are recognisable in European gardens today.

Britain has been home to a wealth of gardening fashions, which can still be seen in historic gardens. For centuries ornamental features which we now take for granted, such as lawns, clipped hedges and exotic plants, were the preserve of grand gardens only. Most people used their small plots more practically – for food, herbs and keeping chickens. The construction of suburban villas and terraced town houses in the 18th century changed that, with small versions of fashionable gardening styles beginning to appear. In the 19th century, gardening became a widely shared hobby for country and city folk

SPIRIT OF PLACE

The National Trust looks more than 250 gardens, which span several centuries of horticultural history. National Trust gardeners are acutely aware of the layers of history beneath their feet and of the stories these places have to tell. To care for each garden properly, they research its history and identify the enduring qualities that give it character today.

This approach to understanding a garden's 'spirit of place' can be useful when maintaining and developing your own garden, whatever its size or story. By understanding what makes the place special, you will be set on course to shape it sensitively and to choose wisely from a seemingly endless range of plants and materials.

of all classes. A wealth of gardening books and magazines provided advice on 'how to garden' and horticultural shows across the country gave people the chance to display their gardening prowess.

Today in Britain it is estimated that about 80 per cent of households have a garden and 27 million people are interested in gardening. Our gardens vary hugely in their sizes, soil types and surroundings and we use them for many purposes from cultivating flowers and food to eating outdoors, drying laundry, playing games and keeping pets. They can also be important refuges for wildlife. Some people are lucky enough to learn how to garden from their parents or grandparents. For many others, taking on a patch and tending it is the start of a lifelong hobby, one that brings continual learning and great rewards.

▼ The garden at Hill Top in Cumbria retains the look and feel it had when Beatrix Potter lived there.

MONK'S HOUSE, EAST SUSSEX

At the end of a narrow lane stands a small, unassuming, flint-and-weatherboard cottage known as Monk's House. Stepping up through a simple wooden gate, visitors are met with a surprisingly large and exuberant garden, watched over by the ancient steeple of St Peter's church.

This sense of retreat into an abundant, spacious garden is what drew Leonard and Virginia Woolf to buy Monk's House in July 1919. They had admired it before, glimpsing the orchard and garden over a wall when walking in the village. Leonard recorded in his autobiography that 'the orchard was lovely and the garden was of the kind I like, much subdivided into a kind of patchwork quilt of trees, shrubs, flowers, vegetables, fruit, roses and crocus tending to merge into cabbages and currant bushes.' Virginia wrote of her 'profound pleasure at the size & shape & fertility & wildness of the garden' and told friends 'this is going to be the pride of our hearts; I warn you.'

During their first years at Monk's House, the Woolfs simply tended what was there, learning to prune the fruit trees they were so pleased to inherit and to grow annual flowers and vegetables. Then, as money and time allowed, they began to develop the garden to suit their own tastes, never forgetting the productive haven that they first fell in love with.

They created garden rooms from the flint walls of derelict buildings and laid simple red-brick paths, echoing the brick floors left by the buildings. Millstones, abandoned in the garden by millers who had once owned Monk's House, were sunk into the paths, and statues and pots were bought locally. Leonard loved ponds and designed several, the largest of which was inspired by the shallow dew ponds found on the Sussex Downs.

▼ The steeple of St Peter's Church overlooks the garden.

◀ The entrance to Monk's House from the lane in Rodmell.

▲▲ Flint walls and brick paving are a key part of the garden's character.

▲ Virginia's writing lodge nestled amongst trees in the orchard.

Above all, Virginia and Leonard valued the timeless, rural feel of the location and so, when the opportunity arose, they bought the neighbouring field to protect their privacy and ward off development. The open, grassy terrace they created on the edge of this field gave them spectacular views across the water meadows and out to the Sussex Downs. Soon after, they built Virginia a new writing lodge, tucked into a corner of the small orchard, with a view across to Mount Caburn.

LEONARD'S AMBITION

Like all ambitious gardeners, Leonard's plans were sometimes too grand for the location and Virginia once had to put her foot down about another new greenhouse. After a trip they made to France and Italy, he created an Italian Garden which has quite a different feel to the rest of the space. It may have been this project that caused their great friend Vita Sackvillle-West,

who was creating her own magnificent garden at Sissinghurst, to give them the sage advice: 'You cannot recreate Versailles on a quarter-acre of Sussex.'

Virginia died in 1941, but Leonard continued to garden. During the five decades that he owned Monk's House he became an exceptionally good horticulturalist, trying new plants and techniques. As his love of exotics grew, he built a conservatory at the back of the house. In the 1950s, he even opened the garden under the National Gardens Scheme, allowing visitors to enjoy this colourful retreat away from the world.

AFTER THE WOOLFS

Leonard died in 1969 and in the following decades his garden fell into disrepair. When the National Trust took on Monk's House in the 1980s, the garden was tidied and simplified,

ready for opening the house to visitors. Soon after, keen horticulturalist Caroline Zoob and her husband became tenants of Monk's House. Caroline did a great deal of work in the garden, replacing fruit trees and planting up borders. She did not tie herself to a moment in the garden's history, but was always keen to stay true to Leonard's style which she saw as 'cottage gardening … but with more sophisticated plants'. She was inspired by comments from Virginia's diary, such as 'our garden is a perfect variegated chintz … all bright, cut from coloured papers, stiff, upstanding as flowers should be' and 'never has the garden been so lovely … dazzling one's eyes with reds and pinks and purples and mauves'. Caroline made contemporary plant choices but tried to mix up the colours as Leonard would have done. One of her most successful colour schemes echoed paintings by Virginia's sister Vanessa Bell and her

◀ Soft blue Russian sage is combined with orange crocosmia and brightly coloured zinnias.

▼ Leonard's conservatory at the back of the building, built to house exotic plants.

▲ The door to Virginia's bedroom is surrounded by roses and honeysuckle.

daughter Angelica: soft lilac-blues of Russian sage, campanulas and catmints combined with burnt oranges from crocosmias, daylilies, zinnias and tithonias.

Today the garden is maintained by a National Trust gardener who strives to retain the sense of a cherished private garden bursting with colour and personality. Despite it being open to the public, paths remain narrow and uneven with steps smooth and worn from use; climbing plants encircle windows and signage is kept to an absolute minimum.

CREATING YOUR GARDEN

Few people begin gardening with a blank canvas.
We usually inherit an established garden, often
one that has suffered neglect or does not reflect
our taste. We may live with it for many years
before having the time, inspiration or confidence
to make it our own. Or we might shape it to suit
our needs but find that, as they change over time
and the garden matures, there is room for further
improvement.

Whatever your situation, there are a few key
factors to consider before making big changes.
Firstly, get to know the existing qualities of your
garden. Next, establish what else you need from
it. Finally, develop a clear sense of the style you
want, as this will guide your choices.

The aim is to get the big decisions right first
time, even though not every detail need come
together at the beginning. All gardens are works
in progress, providing endless opportunities for
imagination, experimentation and development.

GETTING TO KNOW YOUR GARDEN

Even in an unloved plot, there are likely to be
some characteristics worth retaining. This could
be a tranquil, sheltered atmosphere; building
materials that fit well with the surrounding
landscape; or the size and shape of a particular
shrub or tree.

To really get to know a garden, you need to
spend a full year watching it as it evolves through
the seasons. Take regular notes and photographs
showing both the features that you like and those
that detract from the effect you want.

Some characteristics of the garden are
permanent and will need to be worked with
while others can be altered as money, time and
inspiration allow.

◄ An elegant bench in a sunny spot
at Peckover in Cambridgeshire.

Sun and wind

The aspect of a garden can strongly influence its character, affecting the way light and wind move around the garden and therefore where features – such as patios, benches and borders – should be situated.

South-facing areas of the garden are usually the most prized as they receive the maximum sun whatever time of year it is, enabling the ground to warm up quickly and the widest range of plants to be grown. However, the overhead sun can be very hot, so seating areas or greenhouses may need shade in the height of summer. West-facing areas are warmed by the evening sun in summer, a gift for anyone who wishes to sit outside after a day indoors. In the colder months the sun will be low in the sky, which makes it shine through plants beautifully but can also mean it is lost early, blocked by neighbouring buildings, trees or hills. East-facing spots receive morning sun, which is always very welcome, but in winter the low-angled beams carry little heat and may not appear above nearby structures, keeping the area chilly. North-facing areas present the biggest challenge as they receive little sun, but even these can be made lush and inviting with the right plants.

The amount of wind that passes through your garden is partly to do with aspect but is also affected by the lie of the land and surrounding buildings. On open hillsides you are likely to find that wind is a permanent feature of your garden but, in most sites, sheltered areas can be created by planting shrubs and trees.

Within a garden there can be huge variability in conditions. One area may be sheltered while another is whipped by the wind or one bed may stay frosty on a spring day long after others are bathed in sun. It pays to get to know these idiosyncrasies before making changes.

Soil type

In the UK we have a range of soil types which hold water, heat and nutrients differently. The most extreme of these will greatly affect what we can grow and therefore the overall design of the garden.

One of the most common soils is made up of a lot of clay. This holds moisture and nutrients well but can be hard

▲▲ A simple table and chairs positioned to enjoy spectacular views out of the garden.

▲ This unique gate provides character to the garden at Hill Top in Cumbria.

to work; it is also cold and wet in winter and slow to warm up in spring. At the other end of the spectrum are free-draining soils which don't easily hold nutrients or water but are easy to dig, never soggy in winter and warm up quickly in spring. These are often naturally sandy, stony or chalky soils but, in urban areas, can be the result of buried building rubble beneath the soil.

Another factor affecting what will grow well in your soil is its pH. Some soils are naturally acidic (with a pH value lower than 7) and ideal for plants like camellias, rhododendrons, heather, blueberries and pieris. Others are very alkaline (with a pH value higher than 7) and suitable for lime-tolerant plants such as ceanothus, lilac and clematis. Fortunately, the vast majority of soils are neutral to slightly alkaline, which a huge range of garden plants enjoy. You can test the pH of your soil with a simple kit, but having a look to see whether your neighbours are growing acid-loving or lime-tolerant plants is usually enough of an indication.

The ratio of sand, silt and clay particles that make up a soil creates its texture. This, along with the soil pH, cannot be permanently altered. The way the soil breaks up or holds water is known as the structure; this can be hugely improved with garden compost, manure and cultivation.

Views from the garden

Views of your immediate surroundings or features in the distance have a big impact on the character of a garden. Neighbouring trees or characterful buildings may be drawn into your garden by leaving openings in your boundary and choosing plants to complement them. Meanwhile, unsightly elements can be screened with the judicious positioning of garden structures, hedges, fences, shrubs and trees.

Hillside gardens with expansive views over rooftops or out to the countryside can be a blessing and a challenge. If the views are attractive, you can position seating to enjoy them and this may shape the layout of the whole garden. You can even frame views of landmarks such as spires or hills by pruning shrubs or trees in your garden or planting new ones. Conversely, if views contain eyesores, trees can be used as screening. You don't always need to plant a large tree on the boundary to act as a screen. Instead, use something smaller and plant it nearer the seating area or window from which you most often look out, to fill the view.

Gardens without views have their advantages too, providing a sense of seclusion which can be a key part of their character. In open or exposed gardens you may even wish to create small, enclosed areas to provide sanctuary.

Existing materials

Paths, walls, fences and other hard-landscaping materials strongly influence the feel of a garden and are visible year-round, forming a backdrop to the planting. Some of these are likely to be permanent features; others may need to be added or replaced.

Most gardens will incorporate several different materials, such as brick, stone, concrete, wood and paint. Try to identify the ones that work best with the house and surrounding environment, so that you can gradually replace or remove those that jar until you achieve a more limited palette. You may find the oldest materials fit best with the area and are worth retaining, even if they are worn and damaged.

When considering your boundary walls and fences, it's always wise to talk to your neighbours. There is a common misconception that homeowners of terraced gardens are responsible for the fence on their left but there is actually no legal basis for this. Occasionally your deeds will specify which boundaries you are expected to maintain but usually an agreement needs to be reached.

Existing plants

Trees, shrubs and hedges offer structure and maturity to a garden which takes a long time to recreate, so do not rush to remove them. Many overgrown shrubs can be pruned hard and brought back into peak condition within a couple of years, whereas removing and replacing them would be hard work, costly and require several years to produce the same effect. (For more advice, see 'Renovation pruning', p.131.)

Climbers and wall shrubs that soften boundaries are especially important and worth keeping, even if they have to be cut back to allow maintenance work to walls and fences. Exposed boundaries tend to look stark and make gardens seem smaller.

The plants that are doing well in your garden provide clues as to which are best suited to your site and soil. Even among the perennials there may be much that is worth keeping and perhaps the suggestion of a colour scheme or planting style

that could be developed. This is far easier and more cost-effective than starting from scratch.

WHAT DO YOU NEED FROM YOUR GARDEN?

How you want to use your garden will dictate much about its layout and the changes you need to make. The features most people want in the sun are seating areas, a laundry line and at least one flowerbed.

If your garden is big enough for a lawn, herb garden, vegetable patch and greenhouse, these also need plenty of sun. Useful components that can go in the shade include bin and bike storage, a shed, log store and compost heap. Think about what needs to be easily accessible from the house (a dining area) and which can be further away (compost). For families, the lawn may need to be big enough for ball games and you might want play equipment too. These could be swapped for a veg patch or more flowerbeds when they are no longer needed.

▲▲ A family garden with a greenhouse, lawn and well-hidden trampoline.

▲ A town garden with structure provided by pergolas, topiary, brick paths and mature planting.

◀ Mature wisteria and clematis engulf a garden boundary.

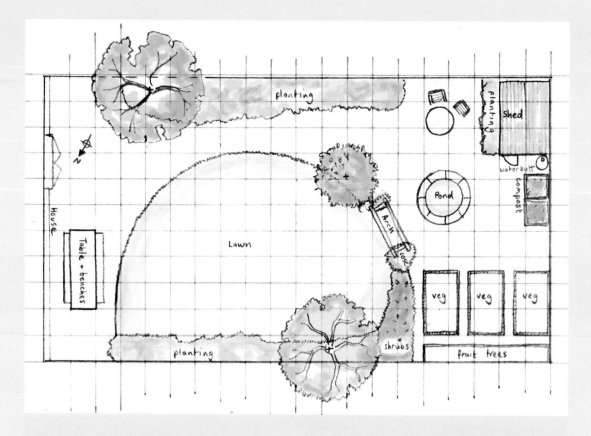

Labels within image: planting, Shed, planting, waterbutt, compost, House, N, Arch, Pond, Lawn, Table + benches, veg, veg, veg, planting, shrubs, fruit trees

Garden planning

Once you have a wish list of the new components you want, it's time to think about how and where to fit them in. At this stage it's useful to draw a scale plan of the garden on graph paper and mark on it the features you plan to keep, such as mature trees and shrubs, a path or shed. If you trace or photocopy this so that you have several copies, you can experiment with positioning possible new features in different arrangements. Remember to think about where the sun shines at different times of the day, which parts are most sheltered, and if there are views to reveal or conceal.

Once you have worked out what you can fit in and where it is best positioned, you need to think about paths. Ideally, paths should lead you along the shortest route to the places you need to go most often. If they don't, you may find the more direct route gets worn across the lawn or beds. If paths curve, ensure it is for a reason, such as

around a pond or tree – all features look best if they have a purpose to them. Any paths that you will use in winter, especially while pushing a bike or wheelbarrow, may need to be paved, especially in wet or shady gardens. Even in a small garden, your paths can create a journey around the space and lead you to a view, feature or bench where you can look out of the garden or back at the house.

If you don't like the idea of creating a masterplan with everything decided in advance, it's fine to let the garden evolve as ideas occur to you. This may, however, lead to a little more reworking of things in the future if you realise, for example, that the optimal place to build a shed might be where you have already erected compost bins. To reduce the risk of such a thing happening, start out with fairly temporary arrangements and wait until you are decided before installing permanent features.

▶ Brick steps lead up through the terraces around Alfriston Clergy House in East Sussex.

▼ Deep borders and a narrow path at Lytes Cary in Somerset.

Hard landscaping

Whether you plan to employ landscapers or do it yourself, take care with the details of design. The materials you use in a garden can either hold the space together or jar against each other and upstage the plants. Every element counts, including paths, patios, fence panels, gates, arches, steps, seats and containers. Suitable materials don't need to be expensive; they just need to blend well with each other. For example, if using gravel, look at various samples to match the colour of existing stonework. When replacing fencing, remember that gardens don't always need solid panels: hedges, trellises and railings can look more appropriate and characterful.

The ratio of planting to hard landscaping is very important. Ideally, paths and paving should take up less overall space than lawns and beds. To achieve this, ensure paths are no wider than needed (30–90cm is usually enough) and that the beds beside them are slightly wider to allow for ample planting. Avoid laying patios up to boundaries or house walls and instead leave planting spaces for vegetation to soften hard surfaces. Think about the permeability of surfaces too. Laying paving on sand rather than cement allows water to drain through and plants to establish in the gaps. If impermeable paving is used, plan drainage carefully, directing water into beds and borders if possible, rather than letting it drain into sewers.

If the garden is sloping and flat areas are needed for seating or lawn, you may want to create terraces to accommodate the changes in level. Brick, stone, sleepers, concrete blocks or gabion baskets filled with stones are all suitable for retaining walls. Concrete blocks are very practical but ugly and so usually need to be rendered or faced with brick or stone. Retaining walls can create a lovely opportunity for flowerbeds above, so when soil is being moved around by hand or mini-digger, do ensure the topsoil is piled to one side and returned to the surface once digging is complete.

FINDING YOUR STYLE

Once you have embraced certain existing features and decided where to position new ones, your garden should be taking shape, either on paper, in reality or in your mind's eye. A style may also be emerging, suggested by your surroundings, the materials you have, and the plants that do well in your soil. Identifying a cohesive style, even if you can't put it into words, is really useful and will guide you when choosing seating, materials and plants.

Gardens in areas with a strong local character may be heavily influenced by their surroundings. Coastal gardens, for example, frequently have rope, decking, brightly painted fences and hardy palms. Gardens on woodland margins look good with wooden seats, ferns and mossy, glade-like lawns. For most gardens, such a clear direction is not provided by the local environment and a style needs be teased out more gently.

Garden visiting is a great way to develop a sense of what's possible and what you like. The National Trust cares for many smaller domestic gardens, but even the largest and most historic may have features that can be translated into your own plot. Many private gardens in your local area are also likely to open occasionally under the National Gardens Scheme and spending time in these can be very inspiring. Flower shows are another place to gather ideas, although it's important to remember that show gardens are temporary and their planting is usually designed purely for a lavish display at one time of the year.

Formal or informal

Gardening fashions are sometimes categorised as formal or informal. Purely informal styles with undulating, daisy-filled lawns, wildlife ponds, curving paths and natural materials are well suited to cottages and country locations. Their reliance on deciduous shrubs and herbaceous plants means they tend to reflect the seasons, harmonising with fields, hedgerows or native trees in the surrounding view.

▶ An informal garden style with a wooden barrel, shabby chic furniture and architectural plants.

▶▶ A lush, green, sub-tropical style garden with large-leaved, exotic-looking plants.

FORMAL FEATURES

Use formal features such as matching urns, standard roses, lollipop shrubs or topiary with caution. They are great for emphasising the façade of a grand-looking building, but can look out of place either side of a modest front door. If the architecture of your house is not especially attractive, use plants to soften it instead. A climber over the porch or a scented, evergreen shrub beside the door can be very welcoming.

They are also easy to manage in a wildlife-friendly way and usually look fine if left untended for a month or two. In urban areas, more formal gardens, possibly terraced, with clipped evergreens, straight paths and uniform blocks of planting can look great and provide a green canvas year-round. Structural gardens such as this need regular hedge-cutting and mowing, but can have quite minimal planting, making them relatively low-maintenance.

For most private gardens, something in between usually works well, with level areas, symmetrical beds and architectural features such as topiary nearest the house, and more sloping ground, larger shrubs, fruit trees and looser masses of planting farther away. However, many wonderful gardens completely break these rules, with large, architectural shrubs close against house walls or swathes of tall grasses and perennials filling the front garden. There is no need to feel restrained by convention.

Plant selection

To create a harmonious garden, resist the urge simply to collect all your favourite plants in one space. Instead, try to choose each plant especially for its spot, factoring in the soil, light levels, flowering time and colour, size and habit. Then filter possible options through the lens of the style of garden you have created or are aiming to achieve.

In gardens with extreme levels of sun, shade or wind, sandy soil or bogginess, the overarching style

▶ Catmint and lamb's ear both thrive in sunny, free-draining conditions and give a Mediterranean feel.

◢ Mexican fleabane growing between paving slabs creates a soft, relaxed look.

may be dictated by the plants that you are able to grow. For example, in sunny, free-draining spots, small, scented shrubs with leaves in shades of grey do very well and naturally go together, providing a Mediterranean feel that suits painted walls and glazed or terracotta pots. In damp, shady spots, plants that thrive are usually deep green and often large-leaved, creating a lush feel that looks great with wood and brick.

In gardens where conditions are less specific or vary across the site and you are able to grow a wide range of plants, it may be harder to visualise and stick to a style. Creating restrictions for yourself can help. For example, if you are aiming for a traditional English country garden with roses and lavender, eschew exotic-looking plants such as palms and phormiums. If you want a bold, modern look, avoid floaty annuals and cottage-garden classics and instead seek out architectural shrubs and perennials. Bear in mind how the same plants can look very different in different contexts. Bamboo or eucalyptus, for example, may be wonderful in a city garden but entirely out of place in the countryside.

Even the most experienced gardeners find it hard to get this right first time. Trying new plants and tweaking combinations each year can be one of the most absorbing and rewarding aspects of gardening.

Garden maintenance

The way we garden also has a huge impact on the spirit of a garden. Regular shaping of shrubs, mowing stripes in lawns and removing all self-seeders from paving makes for a very well-groomed, orderly feel, which is suitable for formal gardens but would take away much of the romance of a cottage garden. Allowing low-growing bellflowers or Mexican fleabane to colonise cracks in paths, daisies to flower in lawns

COTTAGE-GARDEN PLANTS

The relaxed and floriferous cottage garden style suits many gardens. Create it with timeless perennials, shrubs and climbers in blues, pinks and whites.

▲ Monkshood ▲ Peonies ▲ Astrantias ▲ Lupins ▲ Sweet rocket

▲ Bearded irises ▲ Hardy geraniums ▲ Clematis ▲ Aquilegias ▲ Lilac

GARDENING IN SENSITIVE AREAS

As well as letting your surroundings influence your style of garden, it may be necessary to respect them in your plant choices and gardening practices. If your garden borders sensitive natural areas such as native woodland or a stream, it's best to avoid planting highly vigorous species, that are prone to running or self-seeding. Some of these plants have been identified as invasive and are no longer available to buy, but you may need to avoid others, such as goldenrod, sumach and buddleja. In sensitive environments keep a close eye on the spread of all your garden plants: some that are not problematic now might become so in the future if climate change or local conditions allow.

and shrubs or climbers to express their natural forms is a more sympathetic approach suited to most private gardens.

The time you have available for gardening may influence your garden design. Shrubs and lawns require far less maintenance than flower borders and containerised plants. If you're pushed for time but want colour, limit flower borders to one dramatic display near the house. If you have other borders in less prominent places, which you want to fill with flowers, plant large groups of a single, vigorous perennial, such as *Geranium* × *johnsonii* 'Johnson's Blue', catmint, penstemons or Japanese anemones. If you inherit a mature garden, this type of planting may already be established, since a handful of perennials tend to thrive from neglect and swamp out their neighbours, creating a very low-maintenance scheme for you to look after.

CHAPTER 2
FLOWER BORDERS

THE POPULARITY OF PERENNIALS

Colourful borders, filled with perennials which mingle well and flower year after year, are what many of today's gardeners most enjoy and aspire to create. But such schemes have not always been fashionable and the range of suitable plants was once very limited.

Only a few border-worthy perennials are native to Britain; the rest have arrived as a result of centuries of trading. First came species from Europe, North Africa and the Middle East. These included mallows, peonies, hellebores and bearded iris, brought for their culinary or medicinal use as much as their beauty. Then, as traders travelled further afield from the 16th century onwards, they brought back many more of today's stalwarts, including agapanthus from South Africa, *Phlox paniculata* from Eastern America and *Bergenia cordifolia* from Siberia.

These hardy perennials were of great interest to plant collectors and botanists but they rarely took centre stage in fashionable gardens, where shrubs, trees and showy exotics were far more appealing. It was not until the late 19th century that they gained in popularity, championed by garden writer William Robinson, who led a move away from Victorian tastes towards a more natural style. Robinson and his friend Gertrude Jekyll recommended combining perennials in deep borders to create long-lasting displays which changed during the summer months.

The 20th century saw the art of borders finessed and the creation of many of Britain's best-loved flower gardens, including Hidcote, Sissinghurst and Tintinhull. As gardening became an increasingly popular hobby, both amateur and professional gardeners took great interest in growing and breeding perennials and combining them into borders. Styles have varied over the decades, from tightly structured arrangements to relaxed schemes with lots of self-seeders, using gentle pastel shades and hot, bold colours. Today Robinson's ideals of naturalistic planting are being taken even further with a fashion for mixing tall, architectural perennials among ornamental grasses to create meadow-like effects.

▶ Sunny borders in high summer at Mottistone on the Isle of Wight.

HERBACEOUS PERENNIALS

A perennial is any plant that lives for three or more years and doesn't become woody. The majority are herbaceous, meaning all their top growth dies off in autumn, leaving only their roots in the ground over winter with some buds at the soil surface.

Traditionally, herbaceous borders used only herbaceous perennials, but successful schemes can include evergreen perennials, shrubs, annuals and exotics for extra flower power. In today's small gardens we want our borders to perform year-round, so mixed schemes with evergreens for winter structure, bulbs for spring colour and grasses for autumn effect are often the solution.

Perennials best suited to most borders are hardy ones that can survive in the ground through cold, wet winters. These usually originate from Northern Europe or similar latitudes in the south, such as New Zealand and southern Chile, or mountainous areas like the Alps or Himalayas. But there are also many plants from South Africa, South America and the Mediterranean that can thrive in warm, sheltered British gardens, provided the soil drains freely.

PACKWOOD HOUSE, WARWICKSHIRE

The flower borders at Packwood House in Warwickshire have become famous for their unique style and sensitive colour combinations. When Head Gardener Mick Evans took over 20 years ago it was a garden dominated by huge topiary and large areas of lawn with just a few relatively unremarkable borders. Bringing a wealth of experience from wonderful gardens such as Sissinghurst and Powis Castle, Mick set about rejigging the borders and adding new ones, each with their own distinctive character.

The son of an artist, Mick went to art college,

so sensitivity to colour is in his blood. Mick learnt the importance of harmonising his planting with existing features in the garden and surrounding landscape when he was a trainee at Sissinghurst in the 1970s. His mentors taught him to see the opportunities provided by every detail, from orange lichen on stone to the tone of a render on a wall. Here at Packwood, the deep plum colours in his double borders chime beautifully with a copper beech in the distance and create a rich contrast to the grey render of the house. Meanwhile, the silver foliage picks out the silvery tones of the oak window frames and lead downpipes. Mick advises thinking of and viewing

◀ Packwood House viewed from the borders.

▼ The Double Borders in August.

the house as 'the heart of the garden, from which everything emanates'.

THE DOUBLE BORDERS

Upon entering the main garden through an archway, you are greeted by the Double Borders. These flank a central path running up from the house to the topiary garden. They are 36m long and 2m deep, but their style could easily be recreated in a smaller space.

For permanent structure they contain architectural *Yucca recurvifolia*, *Stipa gigantea* and cardoons, spaced evenly, precisely opposite each other on either side of the path. This is unusually formal for the 'mingled' planting style that Mick uses at Packwood, but it helps to create structure and rhythm. Beneath this framework is a mingled planting of herbaceous perennials, each positioned singly rather than in traditional groups, but repeated many times to create a matrix of colour.

Looking along the borders closely, it is possible to see that they are both divided into four sections, each with one yucca, one stipa and one cardoon and the same selection of perennials beneath. The structural plants are placed in the same position within each section, but the perennials are arranged more randomly to create a loose, mixed carpet of colour and texture.

The borders have six phases through the year, providing interest from spring until autumn.

MARCH/APRIL

The low pulmonarias and hellebores are in flower. Mick uses *Pulmonaria* 'Diana Clare', with its very silvery leaf and violet-blue flower, and a variety of richly coloured hellebores, including *Helleborus × ericsmithii* with its metallic-sheened leaf.

APRIL/MAY

A dramatic show of purple alliums emerges from the foliage of the perennials. Mick is not a huge fan of tulips (although he does use them in the garden), but loves the alliums for their reliability and vivid purple blooms.

MAY/JUNE

The matrix of perennials – what Mick regards as the 'supporting acts' – is in bloom. These include astrantias, thalictrums, sanguisorbas, geraniums, salvias, echinops and *Cirsium rivulare* – purples, blues and burgundy set off by the constant silvers of artemisias and cardoons.

JUNE

Midsummer is when the tall, elegant flowers of the ornamental grass *Stipa gigantea* emerge, adding a new dimension to the border, providing movement and, as Mick says, 'glistening in the sun and rain'.

JULY

Next come the graceful angel's fishing rods (*Dierama pulcherrimum*), quickly followed by purple loosestrife (*Lythrum virgatum* 'Dropmore Purple'). While dieramas can be hard to establish, Mick highly recommends purple loosestrife for anyone gardening on moisture-retentive soil because the plant is both reliable and long-flowering.

AUGUST–OCTOBER

Towards the end of summer, the loosestrife and 'supporting acts' continue to work hard, providing ongoing colour as the grasses fade to a lovely biscuit colour and give a strong autumnal feel.

Despite the open position of these borders, with no shelter from a nearby wall or hedge, they do not require staking because the main perennials are all relatively low. The closely planted, mingled style means that less upright plants can rest on their neighbours.

The biggest challenge comes from keeping balance on each side of the path, as certain plants do better on the east- or west-facing sides. Dividing is also critical for keeping balance in the borders and preventing spreading plants such as *Campanula takesimana* 'Elizabeth' swamping less vigorous ones such as the dieramas. Mick also needs to pull out alliums regularly after flowering, as they multiply quickly and can become too dominant.

◀ Lush planting engulfs the raised terrace in high summer.

▼ Loose planting in the Yellow Border, also in summer.

midsummer onwards, with red salvias, orange leonotis, purple osteospermums and pot marigolds coming into full flower. Mick likes using long-flowering, brightly coloured bedding plants in this way, as they create noticeable repetition for many months.

He admits to some accidents in this border. He never intended the bright-red oriental poppy *Papaver* 'Beauty of Livermere' to flower at the same time as the yellow shrub *Piptanthus nepalensis,* but in some seasons they do and, with so much green foliage around, he feels he can just about get away with it. 'Green is the glue in a garden,' he says.

THE YELLOW BORDER

Over the years, Mick has increasingly come to value the loose, naturalistic style and it is in the Yellow Border that he expresses this approach, adding wild flowers such as corncockles and allowing the border to develop a 'hedgerow feel' by the end of summer. He loves it when the *Clematis tangutica* climbs off the wall and tangles its way through the tall plants at the back, covering them with fluffy seed heads just like old man's beard (our wild clematis) in late summer. Sometimes he winces when his team have to weed the paths and he is prone to leaving more and more self-seeded verbascums or heartsease along the edges.

The Yellow Border is the first to be cut back in early autumn, giving Mick and his team time to mulch with garden compost and plant out wallflowers and fresh tulips for colour in the following spring. Many more annuals are then added in spring, including *Cerinthe major.*

THE TERRACE BORDERS

Leading on from the Double Borders is a raised terrace planted with a riot of hot colours which look dramatic against the red-brick gazebos at each end. The Terrace Borders contain many annuals, biennials and tender exotics, which are planted out in spring among the perennials. It is a highly intensive way of gardening, designed to wow visitors throughout the summer.

These borders are at their quietest in spring and early summer, when the Double Borders are peaking, but become increasingly colourful from

DESIGNING BORDERS

Many gardeners inherit established borders and improve them over time by adding and removing plants until there is interest for many months of the year and all the neighbouring plants look good together. It's also possible to create new borders this way, adding plants as you discover them and then rejigging their positions over the years until everything combines well. However, for quicker results and far fewer wasted plants, careful planning, design and planting of an entire border is well worth undertaking.

LAYOUT, SITE AND PROPORTION

The traditional borders of grand houses were long and straight, running alongside or either side of a path, inviting those using the path to enjoy the whole effect at a distance and then appreciate the individual combinations close up. In smaller gardens, borders are also best placed along a path, steps, lawn or patio, from where they can be admired, but they need not be long or straight and can instead follow the curve of a path or surround the perimeter of a lawn. It is common for borders to be backed by a wall, hedge or fence, but they also look great between paving and a lawn so that they can be viewed from either side.

Wherever you site your border, proportions are important. Large trees or buildings can dwarf narrow borders, whereas deep borders allow for majestically tall perennials which will really own the space. For borders beneath a wall, fence or hedge, aim to make them as deep as the boundary is high: so a 2m fence would suit a border that is 2m deep or more. Similarly, if your border runs beside a path, you will find it looks best if it is at least as wide as the path and preferably far wider.

Some say that within a border the tallest plants should be only as tall as half the depth of the border, but in most small gardens we need to break

▲ Generous borders make a narrow path very inviting at Hidcote in Gloucestershire.

these rules if we want to accommodate statuesque perennials such as 2m-tall *Rudbeckia laciniata* 'Herbstsonne' or *Thalictrum flavum* subsp. *glaucum*. Opting for big and bold plants in a small space can even make it appear larger.

CHOOSING PLANTS

There are many factors to consider when choosing plants for a border and even experienced gardeners spend hours deliberating. Success depends on knowing the height, shape, flowering time, foliage and spread of many different plants and being able to picture them together, not just in summer, but as they change through each month and over the years. Initially this will require lots of research, notes and drawings but, as your plant knowledge grows, it will get easier and even more enjoyable.

If you are new to this, focus on plants that fit the style and colour scheme of your garden and flower at different times during the summer. For a typical border, aim to have at least two different plants in bloom from late spring until early autumn. Finding suitable plants for the start and end of this period will take the most research; the intervening months are easy.

Right plant, right place

Stick to plants suited to the border's soil and aspect in order to avoid wasting money and effort on plants that will never thrive in that site. Many common border plants, such as hardy geraniums, persicarias and catmint, tolerate a wide range of soil conditions while others depend on free-draining soils, which are never soggy over winter, or deep, rich soils, which do not dry out in summer. Most perennials like a sunny site (over six hours per day in summer for true sun-lovers), but a good number tolerate or even enjoy light shade because it keeps them cooler, in soil that has more moisture. If the garden has demanding conditions, such as deep shade or heavy clay soil, your choices are more limited but there will always be something that will thrive.

LONG-FLOWERING BORDER PLANTS

▲ *Agastache* 'Blackadder' (July–October)

▲ *Anemone × hybrida* 'Honorine Jobert' (August–October)

▲ *Anthemis tinctoria* 'E. C. Buxton' (June–August)

▲ *Campanula lactiflora* 'Prichard's Variety' (June–August)

▲ *Euphorbia cornigera* (May–August)

▲ *Geranium* Rozanne (June–October)

▲ *Geum* 'Totally Tangerine' (late May–August)

▲ *Knautia macedonica* (July–September)

▲ *Nepeta racemosa* 'Walker's Low' (June–September)

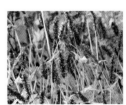

▲ *Persicaria amplexicaulis* 'Fat Domino' (August–October)

Flower colour and form

Combining colours is a skill, which comes easily to some people but takes time for others to develop. The colour wheel can be a useful reference.

Generally speaking, the pastel shades of the outer circle of the wheel all go well together, while some bolder colours from the inner circle can clash. Contrast can be created by combining colours from opposite sides of the wheel, while harmony often comes from blending neighbouring colours.

It can help to restrict the colours in a border, even just by leaving out one, for instance bright yellow or bright pink, both of which can cause clashes. It's also useful to be aware that bright colours tend to leap into the foreground while soft colours (blue, lavender, mauve, subdued pinks, apricot yellows) recede into the distance.

Almost as striking as colour are the shapes of the flower heads, which create a sense of rhythm through the border. Choose a mix of forms, including spikes (as in *Salvia nemorosa*) and flat umbels (as in yarrow). Studying the details of flower shapes and how they are carried above or among neighbouring foliage can help you to create some wonderful plant associations.

Foliage

If you can factor in another consideration when choosing plants, think about their foliage as this provides the framework of your border. There are innumerable differences in colour, texture and shape that can achieve lovely contrasts and combinations. At the very least, try to distribute distinctive foliage, such as the silvers of artemisias, *Stachys byzantina* and cardoons, or the strap-like leaves of ornamental grasses, daylilies and crocosmias, fairly evenly through your borders.

The longevity of foliage is also very variable. Plants such as daylilies and *Phlox paniculata* have lush mounds of leaves long before their flowers form, providing an excellent foil for

▲ The contrasting foliage of ligularia, fennel and crocosmia is combined to great effect.

▼ An autumn border with sedum, asters and veronicastrum foliage.

spring bulbs and early flowers. Others, such as *Ceratostigma plumbaginoides,* have foliage that does not appear until late spring so early bulbs may be needed to fill the space first. Many perennials, including *Veronicastrum virginicum* and *Euphorbia cornigera,* have leaves which look attractive late in the season while others, such as penstemons, hold theirs all year. Conversely, a few species, including delphiniums and oriental poppies, fade to nothing after flowering so it's worth ensuring that they have a neighbouring plant able to fill the gap.

ARRANGING PLANTS IN A BORDER

The key to arranging plants is grouping them so that they have space to grow but appear to knit together, with every angle showing an attractive combination. This is usually achieved by planting

▲ Iris, sedum and geraniums are repeated in this simple border at Great Chalfield Manor in Wiltshire.

▲ Foxgloves spike up through the Rose Garden borders at Sissinghurst in Kent.

perennials in interlocking clumps of different shapes and sizes.

It's crucial to fight the temptation to have just one plant of each type you like dotted through your border. Instead try to buy at least three small plants of any one type and either create a group with them or repeat them at intervals through the border. Groups are especially important with small plants, especially those with small leaves near the front of a border, which would otherwise get lost entirely.

Creating rhythm

Repetition of plants with similar forms creates rhythm and a sense of balance. In a large border, different plants can provide rhythm at different times. In a small border, it may be easier to rely on one or two long-lasting, structural plants. Good choices include *Euphorbia characias* subsp. *wulfenii* with its distinctive flowers and evergreen foliage, or sedum *(Hylotelephium spectabile)* with its fat, glaucous foliage and neat flower heads, which persist for many months. For small, low-maintenance gardens you can create highly successful borders by limiting yourself to just three different plants and repeating them three times or more.

Playing with height

It is traditional to tier borders by positioning low plants at the front, medium-sized ones just behind and the tallest at the back. If you are aiming to do this, for plants such as bearded irises, which have flower spikes held far above low foliage, it's best to consider the height of the foliage when you're deciding where to place them – the flowers last only a few weeks. Many experienced gardeners play around with heights by interspersing groups of medium-sized plants with dramatic spires of taller plants such as foxgloves or verbascums. This creates a more natural look.

Drawing up a plan

Most people find a plan useful in helping to visualise their scheme. You don't need to be a great artist; just follow these simple steps. Work from a list of plants you have already chosen, or simply draw shapes to represent clumps and then research plants of the appropriate height, flower colour and flowering time. If you're drawing the plan by hand, always use a pencil – the process will inevitably involve tweaks to get a plant selection and layout that you are happy with.

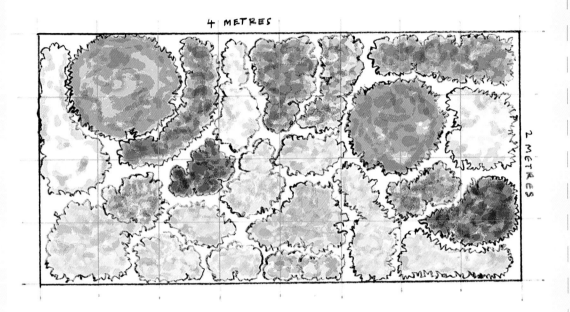

STEP 1 Measure the border and draw it as an outline on graph paper.

STEP 2 Draw the outlines of any existing plants to be kept in the border.

STEP 3 Draw circles to represent new, individual shrubs or large feature plants.

STEP 4 Add groups of rhythm plants (which you are going to repeat), perhaps also marking which are evergreen for winter structure.

STEP 5 Fill in the gaps with other groups of plants intended to harmonise with their neighbours. Try to make each group form a slightly different shape, interlinking with its neighbouring group to avoid bare ground.

With your groups marked on graph paper, you can begin to work out how many plants are needed to create them (usually between 1 and 5 for a small group or 3–7 to fill a square meter). Buying a number of small plants is better than a few large ones, allowing you to create your groups more easily.

PLANTING BORDERS

The best months for planting up a border are September and October, or March and April. The advantage of early autumn is that the ground is still warm, allowing plants to settle in and put down new roots before winter. It is also convenient because most bulbs can be planted at this time. On heavy soils, leave planting of fussy grasses and fleshy-rooted perennials, such as red-hot pokers and agapanthus (which both originate from South Africa), until spring as they will need to establish large, healthy root systems to be able to tolerate winter wet and cold.

In reality, most of us are tempted to buy plants year round, especially in late spring and summer when they are in flower. These should be kept well watered and planted as soon as possible, ideally when the soil is fully moist on a day after rain. They will usually do fine, provided that they are kept moist for their first few weeks and don't get swamped by neighbouring plants.

PREPARING THE SOIL

Thorough soil preparation will make all the difference to the health of your plants, how quickly they fill out, and how well they are able to withstand dry spells in summer. You can improve soil when creating a new border or emptying and replanting a section of an established one.

Dig the soil over to at least one spade's depth, thoroughly removing all weeds as you go, some of which may have very deep roots. To improve the structure and fertility of the soil, add well-rotted manure or garden compost. Spread a 5–10cm layer over the soil surface and fork it in. Finish by walking gently over the surface to firm the soil and remove large air pockets. You can then rake it roughly level before planting.

PLANTING

It's a good idea to set out the plants in their pots on the soil and review their positions to get a sense of the groups they will form and whether you have left enough space between them. Position the shrubs and taller feature plants first, followed by plants you are going to repeat for rhythm, and then fill in the gaps with the smallest plants. Take comfort that even the most experienced designers tend to move plants around at this stage and the finished border often differs from the original drawing!

PLANTING BULBS THROUGH BORDERS

Bulbs are great in borders, spiking up gracefully through other plants' new foliage to give a spring display and then being hidden after flowering as the border plants take over the show. Plant bulbs in autumn for spring flowering, spacing them unevenly in drifts between perennials for a natural effect.

Alliums, narcissi and crocuses will all come back reliably year after year, while many tulips need to be replanted annually. Since finding space for new tulips each autumn can be tricky, look out for varieties which have a good reputation for coming back, such as the Darwin hybrids and fresh white 'Spring Green'.

Once you start planting, work carefully, getting the biggest things in first as they will cause the greatest disruption to the soil level. Plant most to the depth that they were in their pot; any that have roots showing on the surface can go a little deeper. Firm large shrubs and grasses in with your feet, but use your hands for firming around perennials. The aim is to remove any large air pockets without overly compacting the soil.

MAINTAINING BORDERS

Borders vary greatly in their maintenance needs, depending on the range of plants used, their vigour and how well suited they are to the site and soil. If you're short of time and need to keep maintenance to a minimum, look for plants that tolerate drought, don't flop without support and can be reined in with relatively infrequent dividing.

For the best borders, factor in a few hours every week for checking them over; pull out weeds as they appear and keep an eye on any thuggish perennials so that more delicate plants get their chance to shine. To make this easy to do in deep borders, stepping stones can be placed here and there and, if your border is backed by a hedge, leave a gap for hedge-cutting.

Many improvements, such as moving or dividing plants, can't be done at the time of year when you spot them and it's easy to forget your ideas a few weeks later when the border has changed. It's a good idea to take photos and make notes of what is and isn't working through the spring and summer so that you can take action when the time is right.

WEEDING

The key to minimising weeding is good soil preparation before planting, checking over new plants before adding them to your border and mulching to reduce annual weeds. It is, however, inevitable that some weeding will still be needed – and there will be lots if you inherit a mature border that has experienced neglect at some point.

▲ A gardener working in the border at Hidcote in Gloucestershire.

Here are some key things to consider:

- Weeding is best done with a hand fork; a hoe or large fork is likely to damage perennials.
- The key time to tackle weeds is in spring, when annuals are germinating and perennial weeds are starting to appear. Keeping on top of weeds at this time of year really pays off, preventing them from outstripping and weakening your favourite plants or becoming entangled with them.
- Choose days when the soil is moist so that annual weeds will easily pull out by hand and the soil around perennial weeds can be gently loosened with a hand fork, enabling all their roots to be lifted out.
- If you have borders in which plants self-seed, such as aquilegias, foxgloves and love-in-a-mist, work slowly to try to learn what these seedlings look like and leave a few where you want them.
- If you have bindweed or other pernicious weeds which continually wrap around border perennials, you can lift the affected plants in autumn, thoroughly remove the bindweed from around their roots and from the soil and then replant.

◀ **Hedge bindweed (*Calystegia sepium*)** is a pernicious perennial that twines around other plants. Its roots are white and succulent and can go very deep. Dig it out with a fork wherever possible or, if borders are full, just use a hand fork to loosen the soil and pull out as many roots you can. Do keep a close eye on borders with bindweed in them.

◀ **Celandine (*Ficaria verna*)** is a pretty perennial that can cover borders, although it dies back in summer and doesn't do neighbouring plants any harm. Its quick spread is caused by small root tubers and bulbils above ground that break off easily. If you want to rein it in, weed out carefully with a hand fork as early as possible in spring.

◀ **Willowherbs (*Epilobium* spp.)**, of which there are several species, crop up in the disturbed ground within borders. These perennials can be hard to remove once established but pull out easily when young. Some species are great for moth larvae, so if you can tolerate a patch of them in a quiet corner, that would be ideal.

◀ **Herb robert (*Geranium robertianum*)** is an annual wild geranium, which often colonises shady parts of the border. It has attractive foliage, red stems and pretty pink flowers which can be useful to fill gaps, so leave it be and then pull it out when it gets in the way of something nicer.

◀ **Hairy bittercress (*Cardamine hirsuta*)** is an annual that is easy to remove by hand. Do this as soon as you see it, otherwise the flowers quickly turn to narrow seed pods which explode, spreading the seed far and wide.

◀ **Ground elder (*Aegopodium podagraria*)** is a perennial which was introduced by the Romans as a food plant. It can be lovely in a verge but in borders it is highly competitive and weakens neighbouring plants. Dig out as much of its white spreading roots as possible, using a hand fork.

SUPPORTING PLANTS

Look inside the borders of your favourite National Trust gardens and you'll often see a network of woven branches or ironwork supporting the soft, fleshy growth. This is needed because herbaceous plants grown close together can get very tall and lax as they jostle for space. Some will support others but a few, such as delphiniums and sweet rocket, are prone to falling over in midsummer and ruining a display. This is especially true in windy gardens.

Getting the timing of staking right is crucial. It's easy to look at a border in spring and see the nice mounds of foliage and early flowers and think all is under control; then suddenly there is a surge of growth and, by early summer, heavy-headed plants such as peonies have sprawled wide, smothering their neighbours. Staking then is rarely successful as it's hard to get in among the plants and almost impossible to prop them up in a way that looks natural.

There are lots of plant supports on the market. Some of the best create a frame over the top of a plant, allowing stems to grow through it and be supported invisibly. This can also be done using posts or strong canes, with string criss-crossed between them to form a grid or mesh stretched tautly across the top. Alternatively, if you have access to birch or hazel in winter you can cut and dry the flexible stems for weaving together around plants. Structures need to be about two-thirds the eventual height of the plant so that they provide robust support to the stems but are hidden by foliage before the plants come into flower.

Not all plants need staking, especially tough ones grown on poor, sandy soil. If you don't want to build supports until it's really necessary, you can wait a year, propping plants gently as needed and making notes on which ones will need support the following summer.

▲ Twigs woven together provide support for lax perennials.

LIFTING AND DIVIDING

Most perennials need regular lifting and dividing to stop them taking over a border or to keep clumps looking fresh and healthy. The optimum time is usually when a clump has been in the ground for three to six years. There is a handful of perennials that resent disturbance and therefore should be lifted and split only if absolutely necessary. They include hostas, peonies, Japanese anemones and rodgersias.

Autumn is the ideal time to divide most perennials and, in mild weather, you can continue doing this through winter. A few plants, such as eryngiums, red-hot pokers, angel's fishing rods and many of the ornamental grasses, are better divided in early spring so that they have a growing season to recover before the cold and wet winter returns.

Other exceptions include bearded irises, which have rhizomes that respond well to being split in summer after they've flowered, and spring-flowering pulmonarias and primulas, which can be split in mid-spring straight after flowering, provided the ground is moist.

When refreshing a section of the border, lift all the congested clumps out using a fork and spade. It's fine to slice through some as you go if they are too hard to dig up as one clump. Lay all the plants on a tarpaulin (or opened-up compost sack) nearby in order to keep the grass and paths free of mud. Plants can be divided up on the tarpaulin and the best bits laid out on the border for replanting after the soil has been forked over and enriched with compost or manure.

Dividing by hand
Many plants such as achilleas, astrantias, epimediums and hardy geraniums can be lifted and gently prized apart into sections, each with at least one obvious growing point and a good handful of roots.

Dividing by fork
Large clumps of perennials with matted or fleshy roots – including daylilies, red-hot pokers, agapanthus and grasses – can be split apart by using two forks back to back. Some may tear, but you should be able to retain enough sections with healthy roots and growing points.

Dividing by spade
Sometimes established root balls can become woody or congested and may need to be sliced apart, with either a knife or sharp spade. Do this on a firm, level surface. Dispose of any badly damaged roots and select chunks with plenty of healthy roots and growing points. The strongest new plants will come from the edge of the clump – the middle tends to be bare and woody and is best put on the compost heap.

CUTTING BACK

Some spring-flowering perennials, such as hellebores, pulmonarias and epimediums, put on a flush of new leaves after flowering so it's a good idea to cut the old leaves off altogether when they start to look ragged. Perennials that flower in midsummer, such as catmint (*Nepeta*), *Alchemilla mollis* and many geraniums, may look quite messy afterwards and benefit from being cut back as the flowers fade, to promote the growth of a nice new mound of foliage. Time this right and some, such as *Geranium* 'Orion' and *Nepeta* 'Six Hills Giant', will flower again. It's usually possible to tell which plants will respond well to this treatment because they are the ones that, as they begin to sprawl open, send up neat new shoots from the middle.

In autumn it used to be traditional to go through herbaceous borders and cut all the top growth back as it went brown. Borders would then be mulched and left bare for winter. These days, many more people value the structure provided by stems standing through autumn and winter, as well as the habitats they can provide for overwintering insects. Plants such as echinaceas, phlomis and eryngiums have

▼ Winter structure provided by sedum, phlomis, verbascum and other perennials.

THE CHELSEA CHOP

You can pinch back a number of perennials in early summer to encourage them to branch and produce more flowers on shorter stems or to delay flowering. This practice is sometimes called the Chelsea chop because, traditionally, nurseries that hadn't sold their plants by the end of May (after the RHS Chelsea Flower Show) did this to ensure that they could keep plants in pots looking neat and compact for sale later in the year.

It works really well for perennials planted out in borders including heleniums, asters, monardas, rudbeckias, sedums and *Phlox paniculata*. The optimum time is when the plant has reached about a third to half of its eventual height. Simply use a finger and thumb to snap off up to 5cm of each soft, fleshy tip, just above a strong pair of leaves. You can even chop half a clump to get flowers from the same plants over a longer period.

dazzlingly architectural forms and, backlit by winter sun or laced with cobwebs, they can be a feature for months after the flowers have faded. They also act as markers in the border for where your plants are during winter dormancy and both the stems and seeds provide valuable resources for wildlife. If you choose to take this approach, aim to cut back either between late February and April. February is best for showing off bulbs, but later is better for overwintering insects and other garden wildlife.

Whether cutting back in autumn or spring, choose a day when the soil is not saturated so that you aren't compacting it as you tread in among the plants. Many stems will easily snap or pull out (especially if you have left them through the winter) but, if you need to cut them, take care not to damage any fleshy growth at the base. Leave evergreen perennials such as penstemons

(which are best cut by half in March) and evergreen grasses like *Sesleria autumnalis* (which need not be pruned at all).

MULCHING

Mulching entails adding a layer of organic matter to the soil surface around plants and letting the worms and weather mix it in. Once a border is planted this is the best way to feed the soil and improve its structure and moisture-holding capacity.

A 5–10cm deep mulch of garden compost or well-rotted farmyard manure every one to three years is all most borders need. Extra fertiliser is rarely necessary. Mulching is best done in autumn or early spring, soon after you've cut back the plants. The mulch will exclude light from the ground to stop weed seeds germinating and help trap in moisture and warmth. Avoid mulching very dry or frozen soil since it can prevent the soil from

FILLING GAPS FOR SUMMER COLOUR

However well you plan a border, it's inevitable that a few gaps will appear during the spring, either because new plants are yet to fill their space, a plant has failed to return after winter or because biennials such as forget-me-nots and wallflowers have been weeded out after flowering. These gaps provide a fantastic opportunity to add quick-growing annuals or tender perennials for extra summer colour. Tall cosmos or cleomes are ideal for placing individually in fairly small gaps here and there, while a cluster of nemesias or marigolds is better for a bigger space near the edge of a border.

Take extra care with any plants newly planted in early summer as they may struggle to thrive among well-established neighbours and may need watering and protection from slugs.

re-wetting or thawing properly. As well as burying weed seeds, mulching can cover the seeds you want and prevent nice things popping up, so if your border is full of annuals that self-seed, mulch a little less frequently.

Spreading bark chippings or gravel over borders also holds in moisture and excludes weeds but it doesn't feed the soil. Save gravel for Mediterranean-themed dry gardens where it serves the useful purpose of keeping the crowns of plants dry. Avoid bark chippings except under low-maintenance woody plantings, as they should not be incorporated into the soil and are awkward to work around. Fine, composted bark is a better option and makes a useful mulch.

IRRIGATION

Newly planted perennials need to be kept moist for six weeks or so. However, routine watering of established borders throughout summer is not a sustainable practice and National Trust gardeners try to avoid this, even in historic gardens. Established plants in healthy, well-prepared soil that is mulched every few years should have deep roots and be able to survive a number of weeks without rain. In a prolonged drought, flowering may stop and foliage may look faded but plants are rarely killed altogether.

If your plants aren't coping well in short, dry spells, consider deeper mulches and replanting with plants more suited to your soil and site. Only the toughest plants can cope in dry positions such as at the base of a hedge or under the roots of a big tree.

If you do need to irrigate a border, do it thoroughly and no more than once a week. This is far better than little and often, which encourages plant roots to stay at the surface and makes them more vulnerable to drought in the long run.

▲ Reliable perennials such as phlox thrive in this border at Barrington Court in Somerset.

◀ Mulching borders thickly with garden compost adds nutrients and locks in moisture.

CHAPTER 3
ROSES

AN ENDURING PASSION

Our love of roses dates back centuries and spans the globe. Roses feature in the art and literature of Ancient Greece, Rome, Egypt, Persia and China, where they were celebrated for their beauty and symbolism as well as being used in perfume and medicine. The first roses popular in Europe were the damasks and the gallicas, introduced to Britain by returning Crusaders. Roses were so prized that they became the emblem of the Royal Houses of England in the Middle Ages, although the original 'red' rose of York – like all roses in Europe at this time – was pink, not red.

During trading expeditions in the late 1700s, Europeans discovered roses in China that had been cultivated there for centuries. Some of these flowered more than once and had deep red or bright yellow blooms. The first imports were delicate and usually struggled in British winters but were soon crossed with hardier roses. The resulting repeat-flowering hybrids fuelled a fashion for collecting roses that spread across Europe. During the Victorian era endless hybridisations took place, using varieties from China and the Middle East as well as new species found in the wild. Many rose gardens were created during this period, both in private gardens and public parks.

In the 20th century a new breed of roses was developed. Valued for their sculpted, repeat-flowering blooms, upright habit and wide range of colours, these modern 'hybrid tea' and 'floribunda' roses soon took centre stage and, by the 1970s, they graced almost all our gardens and parks.

Fashions have changed again in recent decades. Old roses, such as those collected by Graham Stuart Thomas at Mottisfont in Hampshire, have become popular and rose breeders have developed a new generation of hybrids which combine the best qualities of modern roses with the scent and voluptuous blooms of their predecessors.

▶ The Rose Garden at Mottisfont in Hampshire.

ROSE TYPES

- **Old roses** were popular up to the end of the 19th century. They include gallicas, albas, moss and damask roses and centifolias (which have one main flush of flowers), as well as Portlands, Bourbons, hybrid perpetuals and hybrid musks (which repeat-flower). Most have a relaxed habit and are referred to as shrub roses.

- **Modern roses** became popular in the 20th century: hybrid teas have large, sculpted single flowers; polyanthas and floribundas have clusters of flowers. Modern roses have neat, upright habits and are often called bush roses. Modern breeding has also given us compact roses, including patio, miniature and ground-cover types.

- **Climbing and rambling roses** are usually grouped together. Ramblers have lax stems and usually flower once in early summer, with small blooms carried in clusters. Climbers are less vigorous, have stiffer stems and tend to repeat-flower with larger blooms.

- **Species roses** are wild roses such as *Rosa rugosa*, *R. moyesii* and *R. glauca* and their cultivated forms. Many make wonderful, natural-looking garden plants, although they can be very vigorous and thorny. They have shrubby habits and are also referred to as shrub roses.

- **English roses** are modern hybrids, developed by rose-breeder David Austin to combine the charm of old roses with the reliable, repeat-flowering nature of modern ones. They are sometimes referred to as modern shrubs and can be treated much like old roses.

HINTON AMPNER, HAMPSHIRE

The wonderful Arts and Crafts garden at Hinton Ampner was created by amateur gardener Ralph Dutton (1898–1985) for himself and his family. It is a garden divided into rooms by topiary and tightly clipped hedges with soft, romantic planting in between. Ralph's first experience with roses was when he filled one of the garden rooms with tea roses for his mother. These were prized for their scent but were slightly tender and hated the cold, wet clay of the Hampshire

garden. His next experiment was far more successful: he created a Long Walk of topiary columns with groups of hardy shrub roses planted in between to provide wafts of fragrance for those walking past. This Long Walk has been restored in recent years and is planted with a billowing mass of roses in pinks, purples and cream.

The current Head Gardener John Wood has worked in the garden for 20 years. His love of roses began at Mottisfont, where he helped with the National Plant Collection of pre-1900 Shrub

Roses, but it has further blossomed during his time at Hinton Ampner. John grows a wide range of roses, including modern hybrid tea roses, unusual species and huge ramblers. He is a fan of the old-fashioned, showy hybrid perpetuals. These fell out of favour in the 20th century because their large, heavy flowers often drooped on their delicate stems. Some are also prone to disease, but John believes many are worth growing. John lives in a rose-clad cottage near the garden where he is on hand to tend to the plants. There he experiments with raising a few new roses from seed and taking cuttings of any rarities.

TIPS FROM THE HEAD GARDENER

As a member of the Historic Roses Group, John has a good grasp of rose names and genealogy. He knows, though, that such expertise is not essential for success with roses in your own garden.

He is keen for people not to be nervous about pruning: roses can be pruned any way you want, even with hedge trimmers. You won't kill the plant and you will always get flowers. He says that, in general, the harder you prune a rose, the stronger it will regrow, though usually with fewer, larger flowers. This particularly suits modern roses. Old roses fare better with lighter pruning as they can't carry huge, heavy flower heads and look better with a more natural shape and many, slightly smaller flowers. John encourages gardeners to watch how each rose responds to pruning. If it gets a light trim and becomes bare at the base with all its flowers up top, harder pruning is needed in future.

John and his team prune most of their roses in midwinter. Beds are then tidied up and a thick layer of garden compost is laid as a mulch. In spring, as the roses come into growth, John scatters some organic fertiliser beneath them. The team used to spray their roses with fungicide but now John thinks it makes little difference and

▲ *Rosa* 'Adélaïde d'Orléans' covers a small arch in the walled garden.

◀ Roses at the end of the Long Walk.

that the key to healthy plants is regular mulching. He also believes growing roses among other plants helps to reduce disease.

UNUSUAL ROSES AT HINTON AMPNER

Hinton Ampner is a great place to visit in midsummer to see huge roses rambling through trees. One of the biggest is *Rosa brunonii*, which John thinks may well have been planted by Dutton himself. There are also 'Kiftsgate', 'Rambling Rector' and the delightful 'Wedding Day' with its apricot-coloured buds opening to simple white flowers with yellow centres, and then fading to pink. These enormous roses light

▲ *Rosa longicuspis* var. *sinowilsonii*.

◥ *Rosa banksiae* 'Lutea'.

▲ *Rosa moyesii* 'Geranium'.

up the yews they scramble over and require no maintenance at all.

Growing against the house are two other ramblers: *Rosa banksiae* 'Lutea' (yellow flowers) and *R. banksiae* var. *normalis* (white flowers). These have smothered much of the house in just seven years. They flower in late spring and, now that they have filled the space, John manages them by removing much of the strong, new growth produced after flowering to leave the older, twiggy growth to carry the flowers in the following year.

In a shrub border gracing one of the terraces, two large, thorny roses jostle for space with other ornamental shrubs: *R.* 'Cantabrigiensis' with charming yellow flowers and *R. moyesii* 'Geranium' which carries deep red blooms followed by flagon-shaped hips. The single, open-centred flowers of these species are great for insects, allowing them to access the nectar and pollen at the heart of each rose.

John's favourite rose at Hinton Ampner is Wilson's rose (*R. longicuspi*s var. *sinowilsonii*), which has huge, glossy leaves that are coppery-red when they first emerge. It grows to over 10m tall, so John admits it is not a plant for most gardens.

JOHN'S RECOMMENDED ROSES

John Wood, Head Gardener at Hinton Ampner, is a rose connoisseur and highly recommends the following varieties for growing at home.

▲ **'Roseraie de l'Hay'** is a scented, double rugosa rose with large crimson flowers. It is disease resistant and, like all rugosas, it can be pruned hard to keep it neat, or allowed to form a big shrub with multiple, smaller heads.

▲ **'Sally Holmes'** is a tall, repeat-flowering shrub rose which has single, creamy-white flowers that are very popular with bees.

▲ **'Summer Wine'** is a modern climber with glossy foliage and strongly scented, semi-double, coral-pink blooms.

▲ **'Gypsy Boy'** is a Bourbon rose with purple-red blooms, which does very well at Hinton. Its long, vigorous but quite lax stems mean it can even be trained over a balustrade as a short climber.

▲ **'Climbing Étoile de Hollande'** is a modern climbing rose which is very disease-resistant and has beautifully scented, deep crimson flowers.

▲ **'William Lobb'** is a nice old moss rose, which can be grown as a tall shrub or trained up into an apple tree. It has heavily scented, double, deep wine-purple blooms.

▲ **'Scharlachglut'** is a semi-climbing shrub rose that produces one flush of bright scarlet flowers and forms amazing, orange-red hips.

▲ **'Ghislaine de Féligonde'** is a very good rambler that will grow happily on a short pillar, has few thorns and never gets blackspot. Flowers start out apricot and fade to white.

▲ The apricot-pink blooms of *Rosa* 'Phyllis Bide' compliment the paintwork at Smallhythe in Kent.

CHOOSING ROSES

When choosing roses, the main factors to consider are the height you'd like the plant to reach, the flower colour needed to complement your scheme, and whether you want one spectacular flush of flowers or a scattering throughout the summer. Once you have found roses that meet your criteria, you can focus on the details of each rose's flower – its shape, scent and hue.

If bright colours and a neat habit are what you want, you may be drawn towards bush roses. If scent and romance is more important, you are more likely to pick an old rose or English rose. If you are looking for a rose to plant within a border, shrub roses of all kinds are a good choice since they combine especially well with other plants.

When choosing climbers and ramblers, bear in mind that their height can really vary. If you only want to cover a shed or the lower storey of a house, choose a short climber rather than setting yourself up for a constant battle with a rambler. For a standard garden fence, a modern shrub rose trained flat against it might be better than a climbing rose.

THE POWER OF THE ROSE

Roses are one of those plants that many people grow entirely for their flowers. Over the centuries, rose-breeding has given us blooms and scents to suit every taste.

Rose scent

Stopping and smelling roses whenever you can will reveal how much their perfume varies, from deep and rich to light and fresh, with notes of different oils, spices and fruits.

Damask roses are generally credited with providing the classic old-rose smell and are the most important species used to produce rose water, attar of roses and essential oils in the perfumery industry. Many other roses have this traditional fragrance, including the gallica hybrid 'Charles de Mills' and the rugosa hybrid 'Roseriae de l'Hay'.

Bourbon roses are prized for their fruity notes. 'Louise Odier' has one of the strongest fragrances while 'Madame Isaac Péreire' is said to have a raspberry scent, which makes it useful in jams.

Moss roses have a unique fresh, green smell, not from their petals but from the hairs on their flower stalks, while musk roses emit a musky smell from their stamens.

The late David Austin has done much to capture the scent of old roses in his breeding programmes, having recognised that many modern roses had little or none. Roses such as 'Constance Spry', the first rose he bred, have a delicious myrrh smell, while 'Gertrude Jekyll' has a classic old-rose fragrance and 'The Poet's Wife' is rich and lemony.

Some modern roses can also smell sweet: try hybrid teas 'Fragrant Cloud' and 'A Whiter Shade of Pale', or floribundas 'Fragrant Delight' and 'L'Aimant'.

BUYING BAREROOT ROSES

In summer it is tempting to buy roses growing in containers when you see them for sale. Generally, these will do fine if planted into moist soil and kept well watered. However, professionals prefer

ROSES FOR SHADE

All roses do best in a sunny position, but a handful will tolerate more shade, and they are really useful if you want to grow a rose against a north- or east-facing wall. Here are some examples.

▲ **'Albéric Barbier'** is a very tall rambler with semi-evergreen foliage. The creamy-white flowers are fairly large, appearing in a mass in early summer and sometimes again later in the season.

▲ **'Félicité Perpétue'** is a large rambler with semi-evergreen foliage. The small, pinkish-white flowers appear only once in summer but are carried in generous, hanging clusters.

▲ **'Madame Alfred Carrière'** is a large, repeat-flowering climber with scented, creamy-white flowers that have a pink blush.

▲ **'Goldfinch'** is a medium-sized rambler with almost thornless stems. The warm yellow flowers are highly scented, making it a fabulous addition to most gardens.

▲ **'Ballerina'** is a medium-sized shrub rose with small, pink, single flowers which are held in big, eye-catching clusters. It repeat flowers throughout the summer.

▲ **'Maigold'** is a tall climber with large, orange-yellow flowers which are highly fragrant. The main flowering season is early summer but it may produce more blooms intermittently through the season.

▲ **'Mermaid'** is a very tall climber which flowers reliably all summer. The yellow blooms are large and single with deep yellow centres and can be highly attractive to bees.

▲ **'Souvenir du Docteur Jamain'**, a repeat-flowering shrub, is available in climbing form with sumptuous red flowers.

to make a note of the flowers they like and hold off buying until autumn or winter. At that time of the year roses can be ordered as 'bareroot' plants. Bareroot roses have been grown in the open ground and are lifted while dormant and sent out with their roots wrapped up. This method means that the plants usually have large root systems and have experienced minimal stress, so they tend to establish well. They are usually cheaper to buy and also have the advantage of reducing our dependency on plastic plant pots.

During the dormant season, some garden centres sell bareroot roses that have been lifted from the open ground and potted up. These are fine, provided they have been kept moist and their roots have not been cut back hard to fit the pot, but they should be avoided towards the end of winter when they may have been out of the ground for too long.

ROSE REPLANT DISEASE

Are you planting a rose where one has just been removed? Many gardeners have experienced a condition known as 'rose replant disease' or 'soil sickness', in which roses fail when planted on the spot from which another was removed. It is not fully understood, but using plenty of good compost and a scattering of mycorrhizal fungi can usually avoid the problem. If you want to be safe, you can also dig a really large pit for your rose and fill it with soil from another part of the garden. Some people even plant the rose in fresh soil in a cardboard box placed within the planting hole: this way the roots are protected from coming into contact with the original soil for a couple of years until the box rots and the roots break through, by which time the risk should have passed.

Rose flower forms

The shape of a rose can vary more than you might expect, with some changing greatly in character from bud to mature bloom.

FLAT flowers are single or double and open, with the centres showing. This is the form of most wild roses.

POINTED layers of petals spiral around, forming a high centre. This is typical of a hybrid tea before it is fully open.

ROUNDED layers of overlapping, evenly sized petals form a bowl shape.

QUARTERED folds of petals appear to be in four sections; this is a highly prized feature of some old roses.

CUPPED flowers are usually double with petals curving around the centres.

URN-SHAPED a classic rose shape, similar to the pointed hybrid-tea type, but with a flat top.

ROSETTE layers of partly overlapping, but unevenly sized, petals form a flattish rosette.

POMPOM masses of small petals form rounded flowers, usually borne in clusters.

ROSES IN CONTAINERS

A number of shrub and bush roses will tolerate growing in containers for a few years, but Portland roses and patio roses are usually the most successful. As with any plant that is likely to stay in the same pot for many years, choose as large a container as you have space for and use a peat-free, loam-based compost rather than a typical multipurpose one.
It is never a good idea to plant a climber or rambler in a container as the root system needs to be really extensive and kept consistently moist to support all the top growth.

Miniature roses are often sold in pots for growing indoors, but they need a really sunny (yet not too hot) spot and will need to be moved to a cold place for at least six weeks in winter if they are to stay healthy and flower the following year.

PLANTING ROSES

Roses tolerate everything except the thinnest of sandy or chalky soils, but they do best in deep, rich, clay soils, which retain plenty of moisture. This allows their long taproots to grow down deeply and support strong, healthy top growth.

If you are planting against a wall or fence that is dry at the base, position the rose about half a metre away so that it is more likely to benefit from rain. If planting one at the foot of a mature tree, position it about 1m away where you can find a pocket between the roots. You'll then need to provide some canes for support until it reaches into the tree.

To give your rose the best chance of establishing successfully, dig the planting area deeply and incorporate some well-rotted manure or garden compost into the hole. Many National Trust gardeners also sprinkle mycorrhizal fungi in granular form over the roots, as it is thought to help the new roots capture more nutrients and water. Mycorrhizal fungi occur naturally in undisturbed soils where they attach themselves to plant roots in a symbiotic association, often improving the roots' performance.

PLANTING DEPTH

Ensure the graft union (the swollen area where the rose was grafted onto its rootstock and from where the branches originate) is either at soil level or buried up to 5cm beneath it. If the graft union is above the soil and the rootstock is exposed to light, it can increase the likelihood of unwanted suckers growing from beneath the graft. For roses bought in containers, this may mean planting deeper than they were in the pot.

CUTTING BACK AFTER PLANTING

If planting in the dormant season, hybrid tea, floribunda and rambling roses should be pruned hard after planting to encourage plenty of new stems from the base. Cut down stems to about

10cm for hybrid teas, 20cm for floribundas and 40cm for ramblers. If planting during the growing season, just trim lightly and then cut back harder the following winter.

This hard pruning is not advisable with shrub roses, patio roses, miniature or climbing roses, as it may disrupt their natural growth habits. With these roses, it is better to simply cut back any damaged or very spindly stems.

UNDERPLANTING ROSES

Today very few small private gardens have dedicated beds for roses. Instead we like to mix our roses into our borders. This looks gorgeous and has many practical advantages, including keeping the soil weed free and deterring pests.

It makes sense not to position herbaceous plants right underneath roses, where they might compete for nutrients and water, but the spaces between them can be filled with a wide range of complementary plants, including campanulas, peonies, foxgloves and sweet rocket. Vigorous ground-cover plants such as lady's mantle, catmint, geraniums and violas work especially well at the front of a border, flowering at the same time as the roses. Many have the added advantage of being perfect for mixing into bouquets.

PRUNING ROSES

Pruning roses is done to avoid the build-up of old wood and get the maximum number of flowers. There are two main approaches: one is to cut all stems very hard, stimulating new, upright growth which will form flowers at its tips; the other involves removing a few older branches altogether, leaving others to produce flowering side shoots. The former technique is used only on hybrid teas and floribundas; all other roses benefit from lighter pruning.

WHEN TO PRUNE ROSES

Like most deciduous shrubs, roses are usually pruned when they are dormant. At most National Trust gardens, rose pruning starts in December and continues until early March when the roses come into growth. Pruning in autumn or early in a mild winter is a mistake as it can stimulate buds to burst in a mild spell and the resulting shoots may then get killed by frost and not regrow. The only pruning that can be done in autumn is trimming the longest stems of tall plants in windy sites, so that they are not battered by gales. These stems will be shortened further at pruning time in winter.

Once-flowering ramblers and shrub roses can be pruned in summer. This involves removing flowered stems to help focus energy into the new growth

GOOD PRUNING PRACTICE

- Have clean, sharp secateurs, loppers and a pruning saw to hand. Wear a long-sleeved top and thick gloves.
- Always cut just above a bud because it is where new growth will come from. Cutting anywhere else will cause the stem to die back to the bud, leaving an ugly brown stub of wood. Buds can be quite inconspicuous in winter, especially on thick stems.
- Try to choose a bud that is facing outwards so that the new stem grows out in this direction. Continually doing this will create a bush with an open centre, which is for good air circulation, rather than one with branches crossing through the centre.
- Try to do a sloping cut that allows rainwater to drain off, away from the bud.
- As you are pruning, look out for any dead, unhealthy or damaged shoots and always cut them out. Very thin, spindly growth can be cut back hard to encourage it to regrow more strongly.

which will bear the following summer's flowers. In big rose gardens, it can be a good way of spreading the pruning tasks across the year, although it does mean losing some of the hips.

PRUNING HYBRID TEAS AND FLORIBUNDAS

Hybrid tea roses are very easy to prune. Simply cut all stems down to 5–20cm off the ground. You can leave more if you want, but most of the new growth will come from the top, leaving a bare leg at the base.

Floribundas will also respond well to this hard pruning, but for maximum flowering leave shoots about 20–30cm long.

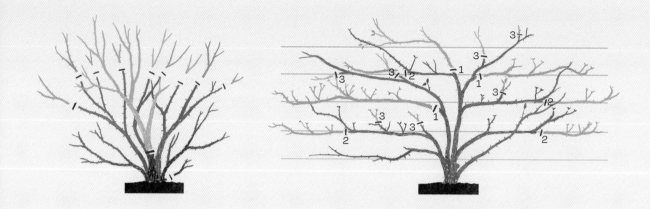

PRUNING SHRUB ROSES (OLD, SPECIES AND ENGLISH)

These need a more gentle, considered approach as they vary in vigour and habit, depending on their parentage. Some can be cut hard like modern roses (see previous page), but the resulting stems may be long and lax and not able to support the heavy flower heads. If this happens, just give them some support and prune less hard the next year.

For repeat-flowering shrub roses (including Bourbon, hybrid perpetual and English roses), the best approach is to trim young plants very lightly. For plants that are three years old or more, cut all stems back by about a third and remove one or two at ground level to encourage new growth from there (see diagram above left).

For once-flowering shrub roses (including species roses and old roses such as albas, centifolias, damasks and gallicas), you will get many more flowers by leaving the rose at the height it wants to be and simply removing a few old stems from the base each year.

PRUNING CLIMBERS AND RAMBLERS

For the first few years, there is no need to prune these roses – just tie in new branches as horizontally as possible to form a nice fan shape or, if they are growing up a pillar, train them around it.

Once plants have begun to fill their space, regular pruning involves a mixture of cutting out whole branches and tying younger ones into their place (see 1 above); shortening branches back to strong shoots which can then be tied down (see 2 above); and trimming any overlong side shoots on the branches you are keeping (see 3 above). With vigorous plants (e.g. ramblers) there will be lots of branches to remove, and this may require untying the whole plant from its framework first.

If you have a windy garden, it is wise to tie in long shoots loosely in autumn to prevent them from snapping off in gales. They can then be pruned or trained into the framework as needed in winter.

Ramblers growing through trees or smothering garden buildings need no pruning.

PRUNING PATIO, POLYANTHA, GROUND-COVER AND MINIATURE ROSES

All these roses are compact and so usually don't need regular pruning to retain their sizes and shapes. Things to look out for are disproportionately long, upright stems ruining the shape of the plant (shorten them down within the framework of the plant), spindly growth (cut back to a short stub to encourage stronger regrowth) and a build-up of old, congested wood in the centre (which can be prevented by removing a few old stems each year once the plant is mature).

MANAGING SUCKERS
AND VERY LONG SHOOTS

Roses are grafted onto rootstocks and these can sometimes send up suckers from the base. These long shoots are usually thornier than the rest of the rose with smaller leaflets. Cut them out completely, ideally just below the surface.

Old roses may also produce very long stems, which are part of the plant but are out of proportion with it, spoiling the shape. Left unpruned, they will usually arch over and flower the following year. If you have plenty of space, you can leave them or tie them to a frame but, if you prefer to keep your rose bush-shaped, simply cut them back to within the framework in winter.

REGENERATING OVERGROWN ROSES

If you inherit a rose that is too big for its space, or very congested with old woody stems, you can simply cut the whole thing down in winter, back to about 30cm. All types of roses will respond well to this treatment. You then can go on to manage the regrowth in future years, according to whether it is a modern rose, old rose, species rose, climber or rambler.

SUPPORTS FOR RAMBLERS
AND CLIMBERS

Roses are not self-clinging and will require supports if they are to cover a vertical surface such as a fence or wall. Once they are up into a tree or on the roof of a shed or pergola, it is less important to tie them in as they can scramble over a horizontal surface.

For walls and fences, trellis is an option but wires are ideal as they are unobtrusive, can cover large areas cheaply and can be taken down at pruning time if needed, enabling the rose to be untangled from them. If you do this, let the whole rose drop to the ground, retrieve the wires and put them back up tightly. The rose can be pruned on the ground and tied back branch by branch to create a new framework.

Wires need to be positioned about 30cm apart, with a vine eye every metre to stop them sagging under the weight of the rose. Flat vine eyes that can be hammered into mortar are often used, but screw-in ones, used in conjunction with a drill and wall plugs, tend to give more secure fixings.

Some old shrub roses, such as damasks and centifolias, have especially lax stems and heavy blooms so may benefit from support. A permanent metal frame or temporary support of stout stakes and strong string around the plant is suitable. Other roses, including hybrid perpetuals and Bourbons, respond well to having their stems pinned down to the ground all around the plant, to form a spider shape, where space allows.

ROSE HIPS

Many garden roses including *Rosa rugosa* (seen above) and *R. moyesii* have spectacular hips, which add interest to the border in autumn and winter. The smaller hips, such as those on our native briar roses and dog roses, are popular with birds and small mammals. To enjoy the hips, you can leave pruning of ramblers until winter and delay all pruning as late as possible. To get hips on repeat-flowering roses, deadhead to promote new flowers up until late summer and then leave the last few flowers to form hips.

DEADHEADING

For repeat-flowering roses, deadheading is well worth doing to encourage the plant to produce as many flowers as possible. Ideally, don't just snip off the bloom but cut back the stem to a healthy new bud, from which the next flowering shoot will form. For the quickest emergence of a new flowering shoot, just cut to the uppermost bud but, if you want to enhance the plant's shape, you can cut the stem shorter.

For floribundas, it is best to wait until all the blooms in a truss have faded and snip the whole truss off at once. There may not be an obvious bud just beneath it to cut back to, in which case cut lower down where there is a leaf or junction with another stem.

◥ Remove spent rose flowers when their petals fall.

◤ Rose Macmillan Nurse with very glossy, healthy foliage and flowers.

KEEPING ROSES HEALTHY

The key to minimising problems with pests and diseases is keeping your roses free of stress and growing strongly. It may be useful to think of blackspot and mildew in roses as being similar to the common cold. You can try to avoid coming into contact with the germs, but it's almost more important to boost your health to help ward off infection.

The main health-boosting strategies for roses are annual mulching and pruning to ensure good air circulation. At the first sign of infection, foliar sprays can also help to fend off disease.

FOLIAR SPRAYS There is a wide range of products available for controlling pests and diseases on roses. Many, however, have limited efficacy once a disease has got established and some are harmful to beneficial insects like bees and ladybirds. If you do decide to use a product to treat a fungal problem, it is best to choose a fungicide designed purely for that purpose rather than one also containing an insecticide. The most popular products with National Trust gardeners are seaweed-based plant invigorators, garlic sprays, rose tonics and compost teas, all of which are thought to act as foliar feeds and are helpful ways to fight off fungal infection.

WATERING Established roses have long roots, which can usually find moisture deep in the soil, even in dry spells. Frequent sprinkling or irrigation systems on rose beds just keeps the surface of the soil wet and encourages rose roots to stay at this level, making them vulnerable when drought does come. It can also promote fungal diseases. So keep your watering to newly planted roses and water thoroughly, but not more than once a week in dry weather. Roses in containers will need more watering.

AIR CIRCULATION Roses in dense plantings or enclosed spaces are particularly prone to fungal diseases as the still air allows for a build-up of spores. Ensure roses are not planted too close together, do not have other plants growing through them and are pruned to allow airflow between branches.

MULCHING A 10cm layer of well-rotted manure or garden compost laid over the soil beneath roses after pruning will add nutrients, improve soil structure and lock in moisture. It will also bury the spores of fungal diseases, which might otherwise overwinter at the base of plants and reinfect them in summer.

FEEDING If you have beds dedicated to hungry modern roses, the best time to feed them is in spring when they are actively growing. There are many specialist rose fertilisers on the market but most National Trust gardeners find that a scattering of pelleted chicken manure is sufficient.

COMMON PROBLEMS

There are a number of pests and diseases common to roses. It's worth noting that most of them are specific to roses, so you don't need to worry about them spreading to or from other plants.

Blackspot

Leaves develop spots and then turn yellow and drop off, with a bad infection stunting the growth of the plant. Limit the spread of this disease by removing infected leaves as soon as they are seen and trying a foliar treatment. In winter, you can break the disease cycle by collecting up fallen leaves and disposing of them, and then mulching around the rose to bury fungal spores.

DISEASE-RESISTANT ROSES

Some rose varieties are especially tough and can shrug off mildew and blackspot while a neighbouring rose becomes completely defoliated. Disease-resistance is often listed in catalogues and on plant labels. Famously healthy roses include 'Gertrude Jekyll' (English), 'Buff Beauty' (hybrid musk), 'Silver Anniversary' (hybrid tea), 'Mountbatten' (floribunda) and all rugosas.

Rose rust

Remove infected leaves showing orange pustules as soon as they are spotted and try a foliar treatment. Most mild infections are unlikely to cause any long-term damage, but if your rose is badly affected each year, consider replacing it with a more disease-resistant variety.

Rose powdery mildew

Mildew can attack leaves, shoots and flower buds, making the plant unsightly and reducing its vigour. Trim off badly affected shoots, apply a foliar treatment to the rest of the plant and drench the plant roots with water if the weather is dry. If mildew reoccurs annually despite mulching and pruning, it may be best to replace the rose with another plant more suited to the site.

Flower balling

In wet weather, flower buds can become sodden and when the outer petals dry in the sun they can stick together, preventing the bud from opening. Some roses with very delicate petals are particularly susceptible to this, but it's not infectious so simply deadhead and hope for better weather.

Aphids

Green- or pink-coloured aphids may feed on flower buds and new leaves from mid-spring onwards and sometimes leave a sticky residue. Most healthy roses can accommodate a few aphids, which provide a food source for other insects and small birds. If the infestation appears to be affecting the health of your rose, try squashing them by hand or using an organic insecticide based on pyrethrum, plant oils or fatty acids. The last two are the least likely to affect larger insects such as ladybirds, which will be feeding on the aphids. Try to spray before or after the rose is in flower to avoid harming bees and other pollinating insects.

Sawflies

Roses are vulnerable to a number of different sawflies, which lay their eggs on rose leaves, mainly in summer. Damage ranges from pale patches on the surfaces of leaves (slug sawfly) or rolled-up leaves (leaf-rolling sawfly) to defoliated plants (large rose sawfly). Although bad infestations can slightly weaken a plant, they will soon recover once the caterpillars have matured so it is best to tolerate them as they provide a good food source for birds. There are also no organic pesticides that are effective against them. If you cannot bear the damage, picking off leaves with eggs or larvae and squashing them can limit it.

LEAF-CUTTING BEE

Semi-circular notches taken out of rose leaves may look like a problem, but actually are a sign of something wonderful happening in your garden. Leaf-cutting bees cut out leaf sections to line their nests. They do this for only a few weeks of the year and the damage will not cause any long-term harm to your rose. Pick off the leaf if you find the notches unsightly.

CHAPTER 4
LAWNS & MEADOWS

LAWN BASICS

A lawn is simply a mix
of grasses kept short with
regular mowing. Many
different grass species thrive
in our temperate British
climate with its regular rain
showers and fairly even
temperatures. They respond
well to mowing because,
unlike most plants which
grow from their tips, grasses
grow from their bases.

Although immaculate,
weed-free and bright green
striped turf is often held
up as an example of the
'perfect lawn', there are
actually many different
types of lawns suited
to different situations.
A family garden needs
grasses which are resilient
and hard-wearing enough
to withstand year-round
ball games, while a cottage-
garden lawn suits less
vigorous grass, and often
includes clover and other
wild flowers.

THE EVOLUTION OF LAWNS

The word lawn derives from the medieval word *launde*, meaning an open, grassy glade in woodland. Such glades were naturally occurring: they developed when native grasses covered the ground in a sunny clearing and were grazed by wild animals.

Some of the earliest man-made lawns were the grasslands around castles, kept clear of trees so that guards could see people approaching. By the 17th century, most large private homes also had lawns around them, giving a sense of space and grandeur. To create the impression of seamless parkland sweeping up to the house, a ditch, or ha-ha, was often built – sheep and cattle would graze on the far side of this while nearer the house the lawn would be cut with a scythe. A wide expanse of perfect lawn became a status symbol for those who could afford to employ a man to scythe it.

In 1830 the lawnmower was invented, making grass management far easier and bringing lawns within reach of owners of more modest homes. Designed by Edwin Beard Budding in Stroud, Gloucestershire, the lawnmower was a huge success and a few decades later was being mass-produced at an affordable price. Soon anyone who could spare the space for an open area of neat grass was doing just that and by the middle of the 20th century every self-respecting British homeowner with a garden had a lawn.

Today our lawn obsession could be said to be waning, as those with small plots prefer to fill the space they have with more exciting plants. However, for those who do have lawns, they serve multiple purposes, including play, relaxation, a backdrop to their borders, or simply an attractive, low-maintenance way to fill open space. Many traditional gardeners take pride in creating a perfect green centrepiece; others favour something looser and more natural.

LYTES CARY MANOR, SOMERSET

Lytes Cary is a medieval manor house set in low-lying Somerset farmland. The current gardens were designed in the early 20th century in the Arts and Crafts style. Garden 'rooms' are linked together by narrow paths framed by hedges. They include the Sunken Garden, Pond Garden and Apostles' Garden, in which large topiary shapes sit on short grass. There is also a Croquet Lawn stretching from the house, with views of the meadows beyond.

▲ The Sunken Garden.

▶ The Apostle Garden.

Since lawns are an essential feature – setting off the stone paths and buildings, the colourful planting and dark yew topiary – they need to look good all year round. This is no mean feat: the soil at Lytes Cary is heavy clay and shallow, meaning it is dry in summer, cold in winter and prone to waterlogging. Added to this, the garden – which was originally designed for a family of three – now receives an abundance of visitors, meaning the turf is subject to much wear and compaction.

MAINTAINING THE LAWNS

To tackle the challenging conditions at Lytes Cary, Head Gardener Damian Mitchell implements a strict lawn-maintenance regime. This begins in early autumn, once the grass has recovered from summer drought and is beginning to grow again. It starts with a close mow of all the lawns and then machine scarification to remove the huge amounts of moss and thatch generated over the year – up to 8 tonnes are lifted from the 0.8ha of lawn. Scarification is followed by aeration, using a machine which can either spike the turf or be fitted with hollow tines for the most compacted areas (see p.90). Hollow-tining removes a core of earth from the turf and the resulting holes are filled in with a mix of 30 per cent loam and 70 per cent sharp sand, which is shovelled on and brushed in by hand. This top dressing is expensive, but Damian sees how the sand helps to improve drainage and retain structure and so he ensures that all parts of the garden receive this treatment at least once every four years. After aeration, any lawns that seem bare are over-seeded with a grass seed mix containing lots of hard-wearing ryegrass. Autumn lawn care ends with a granular autumn feed to keep the grass healthy over winter.

Mowing is done intermittently through the winter when grass is barely growing but, once the soil warms up in spring, it is needed frequently. By May the team are often mowing twice a week and have gradually reduced the settings so they are cutting lawns short. They use a rotary mower with a roller because it is lighter than a cylinder mower and therefore less likely to compact the soil.

Since the grass is under pressure in summer, Damian feeds it frequently, using seaweed-based liquid and granular feeds. The granular feeds are always applied in the rain so that they wash straight down to the roots, where they are needed. In hot, dry conditions, as growth slows down, the team stop fertilising and reduce mowing so that the grass is left slightly longer, making it more resilient to

▲ Mown path through the established wildflower meadow.

drought. This has the added benefit of allowing the white clover to flower and provide food for bees. Damian likes clover in his lawns because it stays green in summer and he feels it is more appropriate for this ancient, rural location than perfect, weed-free grass. He uses no weedkillers, so that all the grass clippings can go in the compost heap. If problem weeds such as docks and dandelions do appear, volunteers are quick to weed them out.

THE MEADOWS

Two meadow areas help the garden to blend into its surrounding farmland. One of these is made by simply allowing the grass to grow long. Paths are then mown within it and deckchairs placed out for visitors. The grasses here are very tall and vigorous and there are no wild flowers among them yet, so Damian is working on cutting regimes and introducing seeds and small wildflower plants.

The other, much older, meadow area is located under the pear and medlar trees. Here the sward is a magnificent mix of grass and local wild flowers, with masses of snake's head fritillaries planted along the edges of the path and camassias added throughout for a show in spring. This meadow is left to grow from when the first bulbs show in winter until about late summer, when it is cut and baled. Deciding when to cut is always a balance between letting all the flowers set seed and not leaving the grass standing too long so that it flops over and smothers neighbouring plants. After the summer cut, Damian ensures both areas are mown regularly for the remainder of the year to let light and air get into the sward.

▲▲ Volunteer Bob Dawson mows over 1,000km each year at Lytes Cary.

▲ Deckchairs invite visitors to sit amid the long grass.

CREATING A LAWN

Most of us inherit well-established lawns and our efforts are focused on keeping them healthy and beautiful. If you have the opportunity to create a new lawn from scratch, there are a few things to consider that will help you to achieve the look and durability you want.

The shape of a lawn can have a big impact on the design of a garden, especially in winter when its outline is clearly visible. Rectangular, square and circular lawns with neat, clearly defined edges suit formal gardens and give great structure year-round. Informal gardens are generally more suited to unevenly shaped lawns, which create the effect of a natural, grassy clearing between beds.

In big gardens, extensive lawns look nice broken up into different areas with the furthest partially obscured from view by planting, tempting visitors to explore. It's best to avoid complicated shapes which are difficult to mow. Grass paths need to be at least the width of your lawnmower so you can easily mow them. If narrow grass paths are used frequently in winter and prone to wear, sink stepping stones into them for added stability.

For areas of lawn running alongside paving and borders, lawn maintenance will be much easier if you can comfortably mow up to edges without having to leave a gap that then requires strimming, edging or weeding. This usually means ensuring paths or edging stones are level with the turf so that the mower can pass over them, cutting the grass right up to the edge. Flat edging stones around beds will also allow border plants to splay over onto them instead of suffocating patches of grass or getting in the way of the mower.

SITE PREPARATION

You can sow lawns from seed or lay them using turf. Either way, the area will need to be dug over and weeds, roots and large stones removed. Unlike

▼ Stepping stones laid in turf avoid tracks being worn through it.

preparing borders for planting, it's not necessary to dig in organic matter as this will just rot down and make the ground uneven. If the ground is often soggy, digging to relieve compaction may help. You can also incorporate sharp sand into the surface but, if the problem persists, it might be better to consult an expert who can advise about installing drainage.

After digging, rake the ground over and then tread it down gently before raking again to level off uneven areas. Do this up to three times to create a really smooth surface, raking out any stones that you unearth. If you have time, leave

◀ Borders edged with level paving make for easier mowing and prevent plants smothering the grass.

the ground for a couple of weeks to settle and hoe off any weeds that appear. This is especially worth doing before sowing grass seed in spring, otherwise weeds may well germinate among the grass.

SOWING LAWNS FROM SEED

Establishing lawns from seed is easy and affordable, but requires patience as you'll need to wait about three months before using the lawn. The best time to sow seed is either early autumn when the soil is still warm or spring when it has begun to warm up.

ALTERNATIVES TO GRASS

For tiny areas of green, grass is impractical as it will be awkward to mow. In this situation low-growing camomile or thyme can work well. They are not very resilient to being walked on but create a compact, green covering that needs trimming only once a year. With camomile it's best to go for the low-growing, non-flowering variety *Chamaemelum nobile* 'Treneague'; for thyme, choose a creeping type with beautiful summer flowers, such as *Thymus serpyllum* 'Snowdrift'.

▲ A healthy green sward thrives in this partly shaded garden.

Starting from seed gives you the opportunity to choose the right grass types for your site. Widely available lawn-seed mixes include a general-purpose mix suitable for most lawns; a fine mix for formal areas; or a shade-tolerant mix for north-facing gardens overhung by trees. If you think you might need a different mix specially formulated to suit your site or to match existing turf, you could contact a specialist grass seed supplier for advice.

Seed packets recommend how much seed is needed per square metre (usually about 70g). To get a sense of how thickly to scatter it, mark out one square metre and experiment with that first. Mix up the seed thoroughly before sowing, as smaller-seeded species can fall to the bottom. It's a good idea to scatter half the seed in one direction and then the other half in the other direction for even coverage. There are machines which distribute seed if you have a large garden.

Lightly rake in the seed, but don't worry if a lot remains on the surface. To prevent birds from eating it or cats from disturbing the soil, cover the area with netting until it germinates. This should take between one and three weeks, depending on the weather. The ground needs to be kept moist while the seed is germinating. This usually happens naturally from morning dew or rain showers, but if you're unlucky and get a dry spell, water with a sprinkler attachment on a hose every two or three days. Netting left covering the grass after it germinates is a useful reminder that delicate new grass seedlings shouldn't be walked on.

You won't need to mow until the grass reaches 5cm or so, which, with autumn sowing, may not be until the following spring. Keep the lawnmower blades on a high setting for the first few cuts.

Lawn-seed mixes

There are three main grass types used in lawn-seed mixes in the UK. Fescues (*Festuca* spp.) and bents (*Agrostis* spp.) make up fine lawns as they are

LEVELLING A LAWN

If your lawn is uneven following landscaping work and you want to level it precisely, you can do this in small areas without any specialist equipment. Make marks on a series of short pegs, each mark exactly the same distance from the peg top, using a brightly coloured permanent pen or tape. Position the first peg in a corner of the area you want to level, knocking it in until the coloured line is where you want the level of the soil to be. Then place more pegs at regular intervals using a long spirit level (or plank with a spirit level on it) between each pair to ensure the peg tops are level with each other. Rake the soil so that it comes up to the marker lines on each peg; if necessary, add or take away soil to get the area level.

attractive and tolerant of close mowing. Perennial ryegrass (*Lolium perenne*) is used for many back garden lawns as it is more hard-wearing. A typical lawn seed mix will include a combination of these species and often a little smooth meadow grass (*Poa pratensis*). Ryegrass is very green, fast-growing and quite coarse, so mixes made predominantly from it require frequent mowing and can look wrong in some settings, especially if they are used to fill a gap in an old lawn.

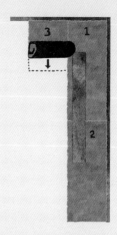

STEP 1 Begin with a smooth, level surface. Starting in one corner, place the first piece of turf and unroll. Position the next one immediately below it, with the short edges touching, and unroll. Use your hands to flatten out any edges that are curled back, so that the two turves butt up against each other tightly. Continue until you have one length of the lawn done.

STEP 2 Place boards on the turf you have rolled out and stand on them while you begin to lay the next row. Cut the first piece of turf in the second row in half with a sharp knife so that the joints end up being staggered like brickwork. Put the leftover cut section to one side to use later.

LAYING LAWNS FROM TURF

Using turf is more expensive than growing a lawn from seed, but it gives you a lawn that you can walk on within three weeks. It can also be laid at almost any time of year, provided the weather is not very hot and dry, or cold and frosty. Choice is often limited to hard-wearing amenity grass mixes with ryegrass, so if you want fine turf you will need to shop around. Turves are usually 60cm wide and around 1.5m long and come rolled up and stacked on a pallet. Always order them to be delivered as close as possible to the date you plan to lay them and check that they will be freshly lifted from where they're growing. When the turf arrives, check it over for weeds and signs of mould. It can stay stacked for 1–2 days. If you can't use it all by then, spread it out grass-side up and water it or leave it in the rain.

INSTANT LAWNS

There is, of course, the option of artificial grass. Although this does create a low-maintenance green covering, it is not recommended for domestic gardens. The texture and smell are nothing like real grass, it lacks beneficial insect life and, as the plastic degrades, there is a risk it may pollute the soil. Artificial grass also needs to be kept clean and it can get uncomfortably warm in hot weather. If your garden is too small for a lawn or you don't want to spend time mowing, gravel or paving – greened-up with low-growing plants – can be just as nice as grass.

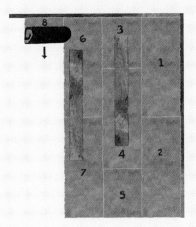

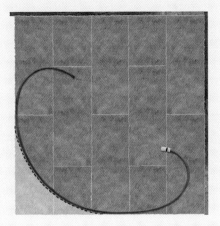

STEP 3 Continue until you have covered the whole area, repositioning boards so you can avoid walking on the new turf. If at any point you need only a small section of turf to finish a row, shorten the penultimate piece, which you have already laid, to give you space to finish with a larger section (which is less vulnerable to drying out).

STEP 4 Once you have laid all the turf, use boards, a rope or hose to mark out the perimeter of the lawn and cut the turves back to it.

Once the turf is laid (see above) it's best to water it thoroughly with a sprinkler attachment on a hose. Hopefully rain will follow but, if you hit a dry spell, irrigate every few days for the first three weeks so that it does not dry out.

The first cut should be made when the grass has grown to around 5cm, which may take between three and six weeks. Keep the blades set fairly high for the first few cuts and avoid walking on it for as long as possible.

MAINTAINING LAWNS

All lawns benefit from regular mowing and some annual maintenance, but a relaxed approach which tolerates moss, weeds and a mix of species is, of course, a lot less work than trying to achieve a perfect green carpet.

MOWING

Typical garden lawns are usually kept to 3–5cm in height; fine lawns are even shorter. Of course you won't be measuring your grass and instead just need to grab any opportunity to mow it when it's starting to look a little ragged and the weather is dry. If your mower has different cutting heights, start in spring on one of the highest settings, dropping down over the season as the growth rate increases and you are having to mow more often. If the weather becomes hot and dry, raise the blades again. Generally speaking, not more than a third of the length of the grass should be cut in one go, so if you go away or experience prolonged wet weather and your lawn gets out of control, set the cutting height higher again rather than cutting it short all in one go, which is bad for both your mower and your lawn.

◀ Edging shears are the best way to keep lawn edges tidy.

EDGING AND RAKING

After mowing, you'll usually be left with a few ragged edges that have escaped the blade. To avoid this, it's easiest to trim them with sharp, long-handled edging shears or a lightweight strimmer before you mow. That way the mower will collect up the clippings. Every now and again it may also be necessary to re-cut edges with a half-moon edger or sharp spade as creeping grass species will often find their way into the border. Use a plank on straight edges to get a nice neat line.

In autumn, mowing may collect up fallen leaves, but if a leaf layer has formed and you don't need to mow, clear them up with a grass rake – the humid conditions they create are not good for turf. Put the leaves in the compost or in a separate leaf bin to rot down and make leaf mould (see 'Making Leaf Mould', p.249).

Varying the height of grass in spring and summer by not close-mowing everywhere can look great and save you both time and fuel. Try leaving areas furthest from the house longer and mow tempting pathways through them that lead to a bench or deckchair. You don't have to let grass grow really long and meadow-like so that it needs strimming – even just leaving patches for a few weeks between cuts will be enough to allow daisies, clover and a few dandelions to bloom.

Provided that your lawn has not been recently treated with weedkiller, lawn clippings are great for the compost heap, adding nitrogen and moisture and helping other materials to break down more quickly. If your lawn produces masses of clippings, adding them all in one go can suffocate a compost heap. Put some to one side to add later when other ingredients have been generated.

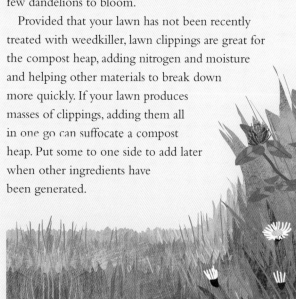

CHOOSING A LAWNMOWER

Lawnmowers have either rotary or cylinder blades. Rotary mowers are suitable for most lawns, but a cylinder is best for bowling greens and perfect swards made of fine-leaved grasses. If you want neat stripes, you'll need a mower with a roller on the back. Cylinder mowers always have rear rollers and tend to make the best stripes, but some rotary models have them too. If you are going for a rotary mower and don't mind about stripes you have the choice between a wheeled or hover type. Hover mowers are great for uneven ground, slopes and lawns without edging, but you don't have any control over the cutting height and the finish is not always as neat as from a wheeled mower with different height settings.

Mowers can be electric plug-in types or petrol- or battery-powered. Plug-ins are usually very light and affordable but trailing a cable can be infuriating, especially on larger lawns. For small, fairly flat lawns, a cheap and sustainable option is a manual mower. Most mowers have a grass-collection box, although the option to let clippings fly (as you get with a mulch mower) can be useful for returning nutrients to the lawn in summer.

LAWN STRIPES

Stripes are created by flattening the grass as you mow in one direction and then turning and mowing alongside the first stripe in the opposite direction. For clear stripes, you need a rear roller on your mower but faint stripes may be created simply from the different directions in which you cut. Stripes look most effective on straight, formal lawns, usually running down the garden, leading the eye to the furthest point. The best technique is to go around the edge first and then begin going up and down, turning within the cut perimeter. Align your mower so that there is a tiny overlap between each row, with no uncut grass escaping between them, and try to maintain a dead straight line. For healthy turf, roll each line in the opposite direction from the last time you mowed so that it doesn't get permanently flattened one way. Fine-turf aficionados even brush their lawns with a besom to get the grass to stand up before being cut.

SCARIFICATION AND AERATION

If you only do one thing to your lawn besides mowing, it should be scarification. For most lawns this is far more important than feeding or weed control. Scarification involves raking your lawn firmly with a metal spring-tined rake to remove some of the moss and dead grass (known as thatch) that has built up. This lets air, light and water get to the grass roots. It's quite a workout but well worth the effort. The best time to do it is autumn as the moist conditions aid grass recovery, but it can also be done lightly in spring.

If your lawn seems compacted from years of use and one autumn of scarification doesn't instantly yield better results, it may be worth aerating it. Autumn is also the best season to do this, when the ground is moist. Work systematically across the lawn, pushing a garden fork down into the turf as far as it will go and then leaning back on it to open up fissures in the soil. These holes can be left over winter and will soon become invisible. Aeration is very hard physical work and for large lawns it will be necessary to hire a mechanical aerator. For compacted turf, a mechanical aerator can be fitted with hollow tines which take plugs of soil out of the lawn for a longer-lasting impact.

TOP DRESSING

Top dressing is a mix of materials designed to scatter over lawns but also a term used to describe the action of doing this. Products for dressing turf are usually composed of sharp sand and fine soil. If spread in a fine layer after scarification and aeration, top dressing fills pits on the lawn surface. Some proprietary products have fertilisers added and many contain peat, which should be avoided as it is a finite natural resource. It is possible to make your own top dressing using sieved soil and sharp sand and, if you have any, leaf mould is an excellent addition. Be aware that 'lawn sand' is a very different product from the sharp sand in top dressing and is intended mainly for killing moss.

LAWN REPAIRS

Lawns often develop dips in them from wear and tear or animal damage. These can easily be fixed in the spring or autumn. Use a spade to cut a cross over the offending area, lift and fold back each of the four cut corners of turf, leaving about 10cm of soil attached. Fill the hole with crumbled soil from elsewhere, firm it gently and then fold the turf back and tread it down. Lumps in lawns that catch your mower can be fixed in a similar way: peel back the turf and dig out surplus soil or buried stones.

Bare patches can be easily fixed with a little grass seed sown in warm, moist conditions in early autumn or spring. A thin lawn with multiple patches can be over-sown completely to thicken it up. Do this in early autumn, after scarification, and use about half the rate of grass seed recommended for sowing a new lawn.

FEEDING AND IRRIGATION

It's tempting to irrigate lawns in dry spells to keep them looking green, but this is not a good use of water; grass is well adapted to going dormant and then bouncing back to life when the rain comes. In severe droughts, many National Trust gardeners have to let their lawns turn brown and crispy, knowing water is better saved for people, animals and preserving rare plants.

If you do need to water a lawn, once in a week should be enough, done in the evening so that the least amount evaporates and the turf stays moist overnight. Use a sprinkler attachment and leave it running for about 20 minutes. Avoid very regular but brief sprinkling: this just wets the surface and encourages lawns to have shallow roots, making them more vulnerable in the long run. Augers are available to take plugs from the soil and investigate how deep grass roots are, if there is compaction, and how far moisture is percolating (irrigation should ideally wet the top 10cm).

Most average family lawns do not need fertilising. If you do need to give weak turf a boost, one feed in mid-spring using a granular lawn fertiliser should be enough. Many lawn feeds contain herbicide or moss killer, but choose these only if you want to eliminate weeds and moss. Avoid feeding the lawn unnecessarily – too much nitrogen can make lawns vulnerable and excess nutrients will leach through the soil and could contaminate water courses.

MANAGING TURF PROBLEMS

Many lawn problems are a matter of perception and mainly only an issue for those wishing to achieve the perfect sward. If you have been lucky enough to inherit a very old lawn with wild flowers and possibly even rarities such as waxcap fungi or orchids, it is best to embrace them and not use herbicides or invasive procedures.

LAWN WEEDS

Lawn weeds are generally native plants that are low-growing enough to survive in short, mown grass. Regular lawn maintenance is the best way to ensure they do not dominate. Some are very specific to certain conditions and changing these – if you can – will deter them. Field woodrush, for example, only thrives in a wet lawn, so installing drainage will solve the problem and is more sustainable than regular herbicide use.

Occasional hand-weeding with a slim trowel or daisy grubber is very effective in removing the worst offenders, such as dandelions, plantains and docks, which have deep roots and large leaves that can ruin the look of a lawn. Make sure that you remove the whole root and then firm the disturbed turf back down.

If you do decide to use a weedkiller on your lawn, it will target all broad-leaved species, including harmless daisies and clover, but be ineffective on grass-like weeds, such as annual meadow grass and woodrush. Take care to follow the instructions on the packet; more than one application will usually

◀ A spring-tined rake is ideal for scarifying a lawn.

▼ Dandelions can be a nuisance in lawns but their pretty flowers provide food for insects.

be needed. Some broad-leaved weeds, such as slender speedwell and mind-your-own-business, are also resistant to herbicide. Regular scarification, forking out and resowing will be needed for these. For a few weeks after using weedkiller, try to mow lawns regularly and let the clippings fly rather than collecting them up for the compost. If you do have to collect them, put them in the general waste rather than your compost or green waste bin.

Moss

A small amount of moss in lawns does no harm and can feel nice underfoot. The presence of excessive moss is usually a sign that something is wrong. Common causes are shade from overhanging trees, compaction, poor drainage, lack of fertility or mowing too short for the type of grass. Autumn scarification and spiking followed by a spring feed will usually make a huge difference and is highly recommended before resorting to moss killer.

If shade is the problem and cannot be resolved, consider allowing moss to form a green alternative to turf in areas where grass refuses to grow.

If you do decide to use moss killer, it will turn the moss black and you will then need to rake it out. This may leave your lawn rather bare prior to reseeding and, if you haven't fixed the long-term problems so that the new grass can thrive, the moss will return.

PESTS AND DISEASES

Pest and disease problems usually appear as discolouration, holes or mounds in your lawn and investigation to discover the cause is needed.

Discoloured patches on lawns

Leatherjackets and chafer grubs feeding on grass roots can cause brown patches and birds are often seen pecking at these areas. There are no suitable pesticides for this and the grass will usually green up again when the grubs go deeper into the soil or emerge as adult beetles. If absolutely necessary, a biological control called *Steinernema feltiae* can be watered onto the lawn in warm, moist conditions in the hope it will kill the grubs.

Patches can also be caused by fungal diseases such as lawn rust and red thread. There are a very limited number of fungicides available for gardeners and the best techniques for resolving problems are improving drainage, scarifying and aerating, mowing regularly and feeding only in spring.

Other reasons for dry patches include thin, dry soil over buried rubble or tree roots (this usually appears in dry summer weather and disappears in moist conditions) and dog urine (particularly from female dogs). Urine scorched areas are usually round with bright green margins.

Mounds on lawns

Mounds that appear on lawns could be caused by earthworms, moles or ants. Small piles of fresh, slimy-looking earth are worm casts – a sign that you have a healthy population of worm species that live in burrows. Like all worms, they are good for your garden soil and there are no longer any treatments approved for killing them. Smaller piles of very fine soil on lawns are more likely to be caused by harmless ants nesting under the turf. To ensure mounds do not get flattened by mowing and create muddy patches in which weeds can establish, brush them apart on a dry day before you mow.

Moles can be a bigger problem, as they create larger mounds with tunnels running underneath lawns. Moles are territorial and damage is usually caused by one individual. Trapping and killing or relocating the mole is unpleasant and usually ineffective as a new mole will move

into the territory. Some people report success with repellents and sonic deterrents. If you can tolerate the damage, you'll probably find it mainly occurs in late winter and early spring and, if the mounds are tidied up, the lawn will have recovered by the time the good weather comes and you want to use it.

Holes in lawns

Holes appearing in autumn, winter and early spring are usually caused by badgers, birds or foxes digging for leatherjackets and chafer grubs close to the soil surface. This can cause much damage but usually stops before mid-spring, so it's possible simply to repair lawns before you want to start regularly using them. Infestations of grubs are quite sporadic so problems may not reoccur each year.

Reposition any damaged turf and tread it back down as soon as possible, if necessary filling in dips beforehand with soil from the border. To deter badgers, try filling in holes in fences, but foxes are usually impossible to keep out.

ENCOURAGING WILD FLOWERS

Meadows are mixtures of wild flowers and grasses, which were traditionally left to grow long before being cut for hay or grazed down. Meadows are very biodiverse but over 90 per cent have been lost in the UK during the last 70 years, due to development and changes in farming practices.

In larger gardens and orchards, meadow areas look fabulous while also providing food sources and hiding places to a wide range of creatures. They can be established on bare ground or created from lawns by reducing the vigour of the grasses and altering mowing regimes to encourage wild flowers.

CONVERTING LAWNS TO MEADOW

Old country lawns made up of a mix of species may easily be converted into meadow, either by stopping mowing in spring and summer to see what happens or by close-mowing lawns to reduce their vigour for a year or two and then introducing wildflower seeds and plugs. One of the first plants to introduce is yellow rattle, which weakens grass, helping other species to get established. Autumn is the best time to sow most wildflower seeds, as this is when they would naturally be shed from their seed pods; many also need winter cold to stimulate germination in spring.

With more vigorous, modern lawns containing a lot of ryegrass, it can be hard to weaken the grass enough to let other species flourish. Sometimes the best choice is to remove the turf and topsoil and start again with more nutrient-poor conditions and a seed mix suited to your soil. When choosing seed mixes or wildflower plugs, try to find ones that are designed for your soil type and, if possible, also made from seeds collected from meadows in your area, to preserve local variation. Many specialist wildflower suppliers can advise you on the best mix.

It is also possible to add non-native garden plants to meadows. The most popular of these are bulbs such as daffodils and camassias for a display in spring before the grass gets tall. If your grass isn't too vigorous, it may also be fun to experiment with other tough ornamental perennials, such as meadow cranesbill (*Geranium pratense*) and ornamental forms of yarrow (*Achillea millefolium*).

Maintaining meadow areas

Newly sown meadows should be cut several times in their first year to encourage plants to thicken up – do this every couple of months on the highest lawnmower setting. Once established, cutting can be infrequent, with timing dependent on the species you want to encourage.

◀ Ox-eye daisies in the meadow in June at
The Courts Garden in Wiltshire.

▼ Long grass and May flowers in the orchard
at Hidcote in Gloucestershire.

Meadows that include spring-flowering bulbs, primroses and cowslips should not be cut from Christmas until they have grown up and flowered. Once the flowers finish, they should be given time either to die back naturally and go dormant (bulbs) or to set seed (primroses and cowslips). After this, the meadow can be scythed or strimmed down from June onwards and kept short with regular mowing for the rest of the year. Meadows managed in this way have the advantage of looking quite tidy and useable for much of the summer.

Meadows supporting traditional summer-flowering plants – such as ox-eye daisies, knapweed, scabious and betony – can be mown on a high setting until early April (provided there are no spring flowers) and then left to grow, flower and set seed until early August. At this point they can be scythed or strimmed down and then mown a few times during the autumn to let light and air into the sward. Meadows like this look great under fruit trees and will be cut by the time you need to get in and pick fruit. If you do need to pass through them, simply mow paths where they are required.

With all meadow areas, the long grass from the first cut can be left to dry for a few days and shaken out to ensure seed has dispersed, but should then be raked up and composted so as not to add nutrients to the sward. All subsequent mowings should be collected with a grass box on the mower. Occasional hand-weeding of thuggish plants such as docks, thistles and nettles will be needed on both new and established meadows.

FLOWERING LAWNS

If you want a flower-rich lawn but not long meadow grass, there is another option. The flowering lawn is a new idea, which embraces low-growing plants adapted to survive mowing, such as yarrow, selfheal, red clover, bird's foot trefoil and daisies. Many of these spread by runners and readily send up flower heads on very short stalks. They can be grown together amongst less vigorous grasses to create a sward which is colourful and good for pollinators, but still suitable for mowing every few weeks, and for walking and lying on. Flowering lawns can be established using specialist seed mixes and turf, or you can introduce suitable plants to existing swards. It's wise to do some research into the species likely to do well in your garden as not all mixes will succeed.

CHAPTER 5
POTS & BEDDING PLANTS

USING BEDDING PLANTS IN CONTAINERS

Bedding plants can be annuals (which germinate, mature, flower and die in one year) or biennials (which germinate and grow in one year and flower and die the next). However, the vast majority are tender perennials and shrubs, which are grown from cuttings, allowed to flourish for a season and then usually thrown away. Good bedding plants for containers need to be reliably long-flowering and have neat, uniform habits, which are often dwarf or trailing.

There are two main seasons when bedding is planted: in spring for a summer display (summer bedding) and in autumn for a spring display (winter bedding). Most gardeners can use the same containers to plant both a summer and winter scheme, as the first will finish just in time to plant the second and vice versa. There is a huge range of summer bedding plants to choose from. Some, such as nasturtiums, pot marigolds and sweet alyssum, are hardy and can withstand spring frosts, but most are tender and can't be planted outdoors until the risk of frost has passed, usually at the end of May. The range of winter bedding is more limited but there is usually something available to add a splash of colour through the winter months and plenty more that will come into its own in early spring.

A BRIEF HISTORY OF BEDDING

The British love of bedding began over 150 years ago when the construction of large, heated glasshouses enabled professional gardeners to grow vast quantities of tender plants for bedding out in summer. Species were selected for their bright colours, abundant flowers or ornamental foliage. Popular choices were pelargoniums, originally from South Africa, and petunias, heliotropes and *Salvia splendens* from South America.

Classic Victorian bedding in country houses and public parks involved large structural specimens underplanted with a mass of flowers and surrounded by a low border of edging plants. Schemes were usually neat and symmetrical with bold colours, especially patriotic red, white and blue. Palms, bananas and other exotics became popular and new trends evolved, including carpet bedding – the use of small, tightly clipped foliage plants to create detailed patterns.

As glasshouses became smaller and more affordable at the end of the 19th century, the bedding boom began to reach domestic gardens. Amateur gardeners soon learnt to cultivate a range of tender plants, which they proudly displayed in their back lawns and borders. The bright colours and instant effect that bedding plants provided ensured their popularity throughout the 20th century, and the rise of garden centres gave people access to an ever-wider range of plants without the need to grow their own.

Today, most gardeners want their flower beds to be filled with more permanent plants for year-round interest, so bedding plants are mainly used in pots, window boxes and hanging baskets. But for anyone who loves a showy bedding scheme, many can be admired in historic gardens and public parks.

◀ Traditional bedding at Tatton Park in Cheshire.

TINTINHULL, SOMERSET

The garden at Tintinhull was created by Phyllis Reiss, a shy amateur gardener who was friends with the 20th-century horticultural luminaries Vita Sackville-West and Margery Fish. It has a formal framework of garden rooms filled with loose, bold and colourful planting. After Reiss's death, garden designer Penelope Hobhouse took on the tenancy and was deeply inspired by the garden, developing her planting ideas there. She used many containers which, she wrote, would 'give any garden a feeling of luxury'.

Today Senior Gardener Helena Hewson plants up the containers at Tintinhull, experimenting with colours and forms that harmonise with each of the garden rooms. It's a task she loves, although she does sometimes feel the weight of the past – as though her predecessors are watching.

In the sheltered courtyard where visitors first enter Tintinhull, there are several large stone and terracotta pots which Helena plants with *Canna indica*, *Helichrysum petiolare* and *Pelargonium* 'Shottesham Pet'. All three plants are tolerant of this hot, sunny site and the large, luxuriant canna foliage looks great against the stone building. Helena believes Penelope Hobhouse, who has written much about plant shape and form, would approve of this simple scheme with its bold, contrasting foliage.

CEDAR COURT AND EAGLE COURT

Leaving the courtyard, you enter Cedar Court through an arch and are greeted by a large stone trough, originally a wellhead. It is planted with a tender shrub, *Abutilon* 'Boule de Neige', surrounded by peppermint pelargoniums (*Pelargonium tomentosum*). Against the wall are four square pots, each filled with a white-flowered cup-and-saucer vine (*Cobaea scandens*), which smother tall tripods and usefully hide some ugly pipework. Either side of a bench are more pots of pelargoniums, including deep red 'Lord Bute', delicate, silver-leaved *P. sidoides* and scented *P. quercifolium*. Helena is happy when she sees people rubbing the plants' leaves to release the fragrant oils.

Cedar Court leads into Eagle Court, an enclosed garden at the front of the house. Against the house wall are some large pots filled with foliage that perfectly complement the honey-coloured hamstone, streaked with purple and flecked with lichen. The plants in these include copper and gold × *Heucherella* 'Brass Lantern', golden-leaved *Carex oshimensis* 'Evergold' and single-flowered *Dahlia* 'Bishop of Dover'. Helena believes that Phyllis Reiss and Penelope Hobhouse would have appreciated how these unsophisticated, widely available plants come alive in the right setting.

Either side of the steps leading to the front door, Helena has grouped pots of varying sizes filled with a mix of different

▲ Tibouchinas and other plants form a collection on the steps in Eagle Court.

plants. Her favourites include clear-blue, daisy-flowered *Felicia amelloides*, an old-fashioned but reliable plant which Phyllis Reiss would almost certainly have grown, and *Salvia discolor*, a more adventurous choice with silver leaves and jet-black flowers. Towering above these are two *Tibouchina urvilleana*, grown as tall standards with bare stems.

THE POOL GARDEN

In the Pool Garden – an iconic feature of Tintinhull which Reiss designed as a memorial to her nephew – are four giant terracotta pots placed at each corner of the rectangular pool. These feature in books and photos dating back through the 20th century and have always been planted up according to the fashions of the time. Nowadays, Helena favours large, purple-leaved cannas surrounded by *Salvia cacaliifolia*, pelargoniums and *Helichrysum petiolare*. She chooses not to use bright colours here as there is already enough drama provided by the famous hot and cool borders either side of the pool.

Helena recommends scented-leaved pelargoniums for growing in pots: they are tolerant of heat and drought and irresistibly tactile. She and her team of volunteers propagate all their own pelargoniums from a collection that they keep in the greenhouse. They take cuttings in September and again in spring, if needed. The small greenhouse contains an area which is heated for rooting the cuttings. Once they are rooted and growing, they are moved into a slightly cooler area, heated to 8–11°C. In spring they are put into unheated cold frames until the frosts have passed and they can be planted out into their summer positions.

◥ Magnificent pot displays are lit by sun in the Pool Garden.

CHOOSING AND SITING CONTAINERS

The design, materials, size and arrangement of containers can really alter a space so you may need to experiment with different options to find out what suits your garden. Calm, formal areas look good with pots made of matching materials, arranged very deliberately, while more informal gardens can accommodate a mismatch of containers, grouped wherever space allows. If possible, try to harmonise pots with the existing materials of the garden: unglazed or pale-glazed terracotta is a safe bet for complementing wood, stone and brick. Bright glazes can give a fun, Mediterranean feel against rendered walls but will need bold plants that aren't easily upstaged.

New terracotta (ideally frost-proof) pots can look very orange, but they soon weather. Terracotta-coloured plastic is an affordable alternative and can blend in with older materials, especially if it is partially hidden by foliage or surrounded by other pots. Lovely stone and metal containers can often be found in reclamation yards and there are also light, frost-proof fibreglass ones designed to give a similar look. Wooden planters such as half-barrels, window boxes and square 'Versailles' pots are also popular.

However nice your pots, the plants should be the stars of the show. Key to this, as a general rule, is to ensure that the plant mass is always as big or bigger than the container. Most small spaces look better with one large pot that can accommodate a decent specimen plant, rather than small pots dotted about, which can get rather lost. Bigger pots also have the advantage of drying out less quickly if you are away during a sunny weekend and can't water them. If you only have small pots, grouping them into collections can create the sense of mass needed to make an impact. The advantage of groups of plants is that individual pots can be moved into the display when they look their best and hidden out of sight when their plants go over.

▲ A blue-glazed pot complements these tiled steps, creating a Moroccan theme.

POSITIONING POTS

Pots tend to look good positioned in corners, beside doors, archways, pergolas, benches and steps, or when marking or defining a spot. Groups of containers are a nice way to cover a disused doorway or fill a view from a window. Really big individual planters can also be used to create a focal point in a small garden, while flat-backed, wall-mounted pots are useful for greening up vertical surfaces, as are shelves or stands filled with pots positioned against walls or sheds.

Avoid positioning containers in windy sites as this will cause plants to dry out quickly. Most bedding plants like sunny places but a few — such as bacopas, mimulus, fuchsias and begonias — will thrive in light shade. Placing pots near or against south- and west-facing walls can mean plants are kept warm by heat reflected off or trapped in the brick and stone, so this is ideal for tender exotics. Walls can prevent rain

▲ A collection of pots grouped together makes real impact on this decking.

▶ Repetition of the same tulip combination gives this group of pots maximum impact.

falling onto pots, so you may need to water them more often. The location of taps and water butts may also influence where you position pots, as you will probably be watering daily in summer.

PLANTING SCHEMES FOR CONTAINERS

The affordability and temporariness of bedding plants makes it easy to experiment with new combinations each year. Some gardeners aim to create schemes that harmonise with nearby borders. For others, seasonal container displays are an opportunity to introduce new colours and textures to change the look of an area. A striking effect for a terrace or balcony is to fill a number of pots with the same selection of bedding plants so that together they form a collection. You don't need exactly the same combination in each pot, but some repetition between them will draw the eye from one to another and feel harmonious. For example, if your palette were burgundy verbenas, purple petunias and heliotropes combined with silver foliage, the smallest pot could simply contain a purple heliotrope or rich burgundy verbena surrounded by tiny, trailing silver-leaved dichondras, while the bigger pots could have silver-leaved senecios among verbenas and trailing petunias.

Although most of us want our pots to be bursting with colour, bold flowers close together can easily clash. To overcome this, choose complementary colours such as pastels, which always go well together, and aim for a mix of different flower shapes with some plants chosen purely for their foliage. There are many bedding plants that have been bred to have fabulous silver, gold, lime-green or glossy leaves. It's also best to choose a mix of plants of different heights and habits, including some that are upright and some that are trailing. Many species used for bedding – including pelargoniums, verbenas and lobelias – are available in upright, spreading, semi-trailing or fully trailing forms, so check when you are buying. Plants that trail elegantly are especially important for hanging baskets and window boxes.

BUYING BEDDING PLANTS

The advantage of buying bedding plants in flower (rather than growing your own from seeds, cuttings or plugs) is that you can plan your combinations easily and they look good right away. The disadvantages are of course the cost and the likelihood that you will be acquiring lots of unwanted plastic pots. Garden centres in the spring are tempting places, but it's important to resist buying your bedding plants until mid-May unless you have somewhere frost free to start them off. Autumn brings further enticements – with bulbs aplenty and winter bedding such as daisies, primulas and pansies. While many of these plants will be in bloom, it's worth noting that flowering is likely to stop in the coldest months before starting again in spring.

The bedding-plant industry releases new plants all the time so you will probably discover different ones each year. Naming can be confusing, with many plants sold under

◀ *Dichondra argentea* **'Silver Falls'** has delicate, very shiny, brilliant silver leaves and trails elegantly.

◀ *Glechoma hederacea* **'Variegata'** is a tough, variegated plant which is often referred to by its former name *Nepeta*.

◀ *Lobelia erinus* **Cascade Series** has a cloud of tiny flowers, which don't need deadheading.

◀ *Pelargonium peltatum* is a classic trailing plant, often known as ivy-leaved geranium, and is available in many different colours and forms.

◀ *Petunia* **Surfinia Series** is a range of reliable, cascading petunias often known as surfinias.

PERENNIALS IN CONTAINERS

Many shrubs, perennials and grasses also have a place in containers. Some of the longest flowering include everlasting wallflowers, dwarf penstemons and shrubby salvias. Either mix them with bedding plants in large containers or provide them with containers of their own to stand among pots of bedding plants. Most will need annual repotting into fresh compost and regular liquid feeds to keep performing. Perennials well-suited to container growing which need less frequent repotting and feeding include lavender and rosemary (both of which love sun and tolerate drought), hostas (which can be kept far more slug-free in pots than in the ground) and agapanthus (which flowers best when squeezed into a container). For those with a greenhouse or conservatory to overwinter tender plants, exotics with dramatic foliage such as cannas, aeoniums and *Melianthus major* are really effective surrounded by floriferous bedding plants.

trade names rather than true cultivar names. For example, petunias bred for specific purposes may be labelled surfinias – or even supertunias! Most bedding plants have been selected for their compact natures, ideal for pots and baskets, but often rather squat and unnatural-looking for borders. For instance, the majority of cosmos for sale in garden centres are dwarf types, whereas a tall cultivar such as 'Purity' will look far lovelier in a border. These may need to be grown from seed or ordered from a catalogue.

A healthy, pot-grown bedding plant will be sturdy, with short internodes (spaces between the leaf nodes) and no yellowing, signs of mould, mushy growth or dead leaves. If you tip it out of the pot, healthy white roots will be visible, ideally not yet circling the inside of the pot too much (indicating they are becoming trapped for space). Most bedding plants will need to be hardened off (acclimatised to outdoor conditions) before being planted out, this is because they have been grown in greenhouses and usually kept in very protected conditions.

PLUG PLANTS

A cost-effective option for buying bedding, if you have a frost free greenhouse, is to order tiny plug plants online. This will also give you access to a far wider range than you will find in gardens centres. Pot them up individually as soon as they arrive and grow them on until it's time to plant them out. If you don't have a greenhouse, a very sunny windowsill, conservatory or porch can be suitable.

GROWING BEDDING PLANTS

Bedding can be grown from seeds or cuttings, and some shrubby or tuberous plants can be overwintered and used again. Seed sowing of bedding plants takes place in September, January, February and March. Cuttings are best done in July, August or September.

Hardy annuals such as clary sage and biennials such as wallflowers are very easily grown from seed. Some need a heated propagator but many will germinate on a sunny windowsill or in a greenhouse. Follow instructions on the seed packet to ensure that you sow them at the optimum time, pot up the seedlings individually when needed and move them outside as soon as possible. Some – such as nasturtiums and candytuft – can be sown directly into the ground in spring.

Tender annuals such as cosmos, nemesias and lobelias can also be sown from seed, but usually require more warmth to get them going, so a heated propagator is definitely worth investing in. Once they have germinated and have been potted up individually, they will need a warm, sunny place to grow on until they can be hardened off and planted out at the end of May. A greenhouse is best as plants grown in the house tend to get long and leggy from too much warmth and too little light.

OVERWINTERING TENDER PLANTS

Many tender plants used as bedding, such as fuchsias, salvias, *Helichrysum petiolare* and pelargoniums, are long-lived in their natural habitats and can be overwintered in the UK provided that they are kept dry in a bright, frost-free greenhouse. However, they are also easy to propagate from cuttings in late summer; the resulting plants take up less space in the

BEDDING PLANTS FOR BEES

Many bedding plants have been bred to be double-flowered for drama or sterile in order to encourage them to repeat-flower. This means insects either can't reach the centre of the flower or don't find pollen and nectar when they get there. If you want pots buzzing with life in summer, choose dahlias with open centres, verbenas, zinnias, cosmos, calendulas and salvias. For spring, crocuses, wallflowers and forget-me-nots are fantastic food sources.

▲ Propagation of bedding plants in the greenhouse at Hinton Ampner in Hampshire.

greenhouse and usually make more compact and floriferous plants the following year. If taken from July to early September (and ideally placed in a heated propagator), cuttings should put down roots in about six weeks and can then be overwintered in a slightly warm greenhouse (minimum 5°C is usually enough). They will then put on much more growth in spring, ready for planting out once the risk of frost has passed. (For more details on taking cuttings, see p.210 'Taking cuttings under glass'.)

Tender plants used for bedding that are worth overwintering include dahlias, chocolate cosmos and tuberous begonias. They can be kept in their pots if the compost has been allowed to dry out, but it's usually safer to lift the roots, dry them out

▲ Pink and white pelargoniums, brilliant blue lobelia and trailing variegated ivy.

◤ Deep pink osteospermum with white trailing verbena and pale blue lobelia.

◤◤ A dazzling corn marigold with lime-green tobacco plants.

and then pack them in fresh, very dry compost. Either way, remove all the top growth first and store the tubers in a dry, frost-free place, ideally with some light and air circulation. In March they can be potted up, watered sparingly to moisten the compost and brought back into growth somewhere warm and sheltered, prior to planting at the end of spring. (See also 'Growing Dahlias', p.232.)

PLANTING UP CONTAINERS

Whichever container you use – whether it was originally designed for plants or not – it needs to have drainage holes at the bottom. To stop compost falling out of large holes, place a stone or piece of broken pot over each hole. No other crocks, stones or gravel are needed to aid drainage (unless you are planting something like a cactus which needs grit mixed into the compost).

Fill all your pots three-quarters full with peat-free compost. A multipurpose one is suitable for all bedding plants. Shrubs and perennials planted in a pot for a few years do better in loam-based compost that will retain its structure for longer. Fresh compost is always needed for seasonal displays so don't be tempted to reuse any – it won't have enough nutrients left and is better spread on beds as a soil improver. For spring planting, some gardeners mix in a slow- or controlled-release fertiliser, but if you don't want to buy another product, there's no need: compost has plenty of nutrients and you can add more from organic liquid fertiliser during the summer. Water-retaining granules can be helpful in hanging baskets, but are not essential.

Before planting a container, it's worth positioning all your plants in it to get a sense of how the whole display is going to work. For most schemes, you will want the pots to look good from all angles, but for window boxes on ledges or balconies you will probably favour one viewpoint. Once you are happy, start by planting any central feature plants and then add the smaller upright and trailing ones. Plants can be squeezed in a lot closer than they would be in a border, but still need some compost between them and plenty beneath to grow into. Firm plants gently

PLANTING A HANGING BASKET

STEP 1 Most hanging baskets are open-sided and need to be lined to keep the compost in. There are lots of different liners available which can easily be cut to fit.

STEP 2 Once lined, half-fill your basket with peat-free, multipurpose compost. Cut three or five holes in the sides, evenly spaced around, and gently poke the root ball of a trailing plant through each of them (this is easiest with very small plants).

STEP 3 Fill the rest of the basket with compost and plant the semi-trailing types around the edge and one or more upright ones in the centre. Firm the plants in and top up the compost until it is 2–3cm below the rim, then water thoroughly. Ideally keep the basket in a sheltered, frost-free place until the plants are doing well, before hanging it up in its final position.

and top up with compost, ensuring that none of the leaves or stems are buried and there is a little gap between the top of the compost and rim of the pot, to give space for watering.

BULBS FOR SPRING COLOUR

Bulbs have long played a role in bedding schemes. Traditionally in grand houses and parks, summer bedding would be taken out in autumn, soil would be lightly cultivated and a mass of bulbs planted for a spring display, often with wallflowers or forget-me-nots on top of them. These bulbs and biennials would then be lifted after flowering, just in time to plant summer bedding. A similar rotation can be carried out in pots. You can remove summer bedding plants just as the first frosts arrive, usually

▲ White tulips and burnt orange wallflowers fill a trough in the Tower Garden at Tatton in Cheshire.

in October, and the pot filled with fresh compost and bulbs. Tulips are ideal, as most need replacing annually, while other bulbs such as crocuses, *Iris reticulata*, daffodils, snowdrops and grape hyacinths will come back year after year so may be best given their own containers. Short, compact, early and mid-season tulips are particularly suitable – tall ones are vulnerable to being knocked over by wind, while the late ones are sometimes still flowering when it's time to get the summer bedding plants in.

In large containers, you can also plant winter bedding such as pansies, wallflowers or forget-me-nots on top of the bulbs to flower alongside them in spring, but in small containers this competition can affect the quality of the bulb display. Some gardeners successfully mix different kinds of bulbs within a pot, planting the biggest ones deepest and the smaller ones closer to the surface. A neater effect is to fill each pot with one type of bulb and group the different pots together so that the whole scheme lasts from the first irises or daffodils in February until the last tulips in May. Keep pots containing freshly planted or dormant bulbs covered with netting – they can be popular with squirrels and mice.

When bulbs finish flowering they need to be left to die down naturally, so you can either move the pots out of sight or lift the bulbs and replant them in the garden. Alternatively, grow them in plastic pots that fit inside your display pots so that when flowering ends you can lift them out and leave them in a corner of the garden to die down while you use the display pot for summer bedding.

BEDDING PLANT MAINTENANCE

Bedding plants are undeniably high maintenance, especially summer schemes planted in late spring just as droughts tend to arrive. Bedding in the ground will need regular watering for six weeks until it is well established, while plants in

WINTER INTEREST

Most of the bulbs and bedding planted in containers in autumn don't really come into their own until the spring, so if you want interest right through the winter it's worth planting pots especially for that purpose. Evergreen grasses, hellebores, heucheras, euphorbias, winter-flowering heathers, winter kales and cabbages, variegated euonymus and ivies are all ideal. Shrubs such as skimmias are also nice, but are an expensive choice for something that might be thrown away in spring. Small winter-flowering bulbs such as *Iris reticulata* and snowdrops will cohabit well with these plants, but it's best not to include large spring bulbs because they may struggle for light and moisture.

containers will need care throughout the summer. Check each pot by pushing your finger into the compost. It's fine for the surface to be dry, but if there's no moisture below your first knuckle, it needs to be watered. This might be every day or even twice a day in hot, dry weather. Even when it has rained, watering may be needed, as the dense canopy of foliage covering pots and baskets often prevents water from reaching the compost. If you go away during the summer, it's always a good idea to move pots and baskets into a group in the shade and stand some in shallow trays of water. This way, if you get a neighbour to pop in to water your plants, the job will be less onerous.

The other most time-consuming task used to be deadheading, but modern breeding has done much to produce plants that keep flowering regardless of whether their spent flowers have been removed. Nonetheless, you will find that many plants – such as dahlias, pelargoniums, osteospermums and traditional petunias – are more floriferous and look tidier if you pick off the faded blooms at least once a week. This can be an enjoyable job, especially if pots are on a sunny terrace. Pinching with fingers is usually sufficient, but some gardeners like to use scissors or specially designed snips. You can also take this opportunity to trim back overly vigorous plants if they are swamping their neighbours.

To get the maximum flowering display, it's a good idea to feed summer bedding plants at least twice between early July and the end of August using a liquid feed diluted with water. This is not needed with winter bedding, which grows slowly and can get enough nutrients from the compost.

DEALING WITH PROBLEMS

Most bedding plants are relatively free of pests and diseases. Slugs and snails can be a problem on tender new plants, especially dahlias, and so pots should be checked over regularly to remove any that are hiding in rims or underneath. Plants permanently in pots can be prone to vine weevil. The adults are only mildly annoying – cutting notches in leaves – but larvae living in the compost can damage roots, so check the root balls when repotting (or if unexplained wilting occurs), knocking off the old compost and removing any fat, white grubs that are visible.

The main threat to bedding plants is frost. If you can't resist planting out your summer schemes before the end of May, have some fleece on standby to cover plants if freezing conditions are due overnight. In autumn, pots will need attention as soon as the first frosts are forecast. Most summer schemes can be left to be hit by the frosts and then disposed of (or cut back, lifted and stored), but those containing exotics such as fleshy aeoniums or bananas are best lifted

▲ Pots abound in this charming garden, filled with geraniums, petunias, scaevolas, busy lizzies, marguerites and lobelias, as well as shrubs and perennials.

before they get hit. Some perennials in containers, including *Melianthus major*, lemon verbenas and shrubby salvias, may not need to go into the greenhouse if you can find a dry, sheltered spot for them with plenty of winter sun. For pots that will spend winter exposed to rain, lifting them up onto bricks or 'pot feet' can help drainage and avoid frozen water cracking the pots, especially if they stand on very smooth, flat surfaces.

LOW-MAINTENANCE DISPLAYS

An easy, drought-tolerant summer display can be created using cacti and succulents, which look charming grouped together in small pots and troughs. Some, such as aeoniums and echeverias, need to be grown under glass and put outdoors only in summer but others, including sedums, sempervivums and saxifrages, are surprisingly hardy. Compost mixes for these should be gritty to help them drain easily and the pots can be quite shallow.

CHAPTER 6
CLIMBERS

CLOTHING OUR GARDENS

The pleasing combination of a rigid man-made structure softened by climbing plants has been a feature of gardens for as long as we have been making them. Over 2,500 years ago, Persian gardens were enclosed by walls, creating shelter and providing a canvas for climbers. Plant-clad pergolas shading walkways featured in Ancient Egyptian gardens, Roman villas, Islamic gardens and medieval monasteries. Trellis also goes back millennia; it was used by Ancient Egyptians to train vines and brought to England by the Romans.

In Britain, the first climbers used in gardens would have been our natives: ivy, honeysuckle and briar roses. Wild clematis, known as traveller's joy, is too vigorous for training, but in the 16th century prettier and more manageable species of clematis were introduced. Next came the poet's jasmine, a sweetly scented climber, which had been cultivated for centuries across Persia and Asia, and, at the very end of the century, the passion flower arrived from South America. These new imports soon became a feature of gardens, often trained on arbours over seats.

In the 19th century, climbing roses became hugely popular and some of today's other best-loved climbers were introduced, including *Wisteria sinensis*, a native of China that had been celebrated there for over 1,000 years. Victorian nurserymen also began to hybridise different species of clematis, developing wonderful varieties such as 'Jackmanii' which remain popular today.

The Arts and Crafts movement made good use of all the climbing plants that were available, especially wisteria and rambling roses. The garden rooms of this era had walls and pillars to be clad with climbers, combining strong structural features with soft, romantic planting, a look which epitomises great British gardens today.

▶ Climbers smother a pergola in the Sunk Garden at Mount Stewart, County Down.

TYPES OF CLIMBER

Most climbers originate from woodlands where they sprawl over, cling to, or twine around other plants in order to reach up into the canopy for more light to initiate flowering. Species have evolved different mechanisms to enable them to do this, such as tendrils, twining stems and clinging, adventitious roots which grow from the stems.

Climbers can be evergreen or deciduous and either long-lived, with a permanent woody framework, or herbaceous, dying back to the base each year. Some climbers from subtropical places, such as cup-and-saucer vine (*Cobaea scandens*) and black-eyed Susan (*Thunbergia alata*), are perennials in their natural habitat, but are grown as annuals in Britain as they cannot withstand our winters.

Climbers are invaluable for covering garden structures and softening boundaries, needing only a small planting space in a border to fill a much greater expanse above. In small gardens, we often share climbers with our neighbours as these plants tend to find their way into the optimum position for flowering. Their adventurous habit and generous nature make them ideal for cottage gardens and other relaxed, informal planting schemes.

▲ *Rosa* 'Madame Alfred Carrière' growing on the South Cottage at Sissinghurst.

▲ Climbing hydrangea surrounds the gate into the Rose Garden.

SISSINGHURST CASTLE GARDEN, KENT

Before writer Vita Sackville-West had even taken possession of her new home at Sissinghurst Castle, she planted the climbing rose 'Madame Alfred Carrière' against the front of the South Cottage and, over the course of the following three decades, almost every wall in the garden was to be clothed in climbers.

Vita and her husband Harold Nicolson bought the derelict property in 1930 and immediately set about turning the collection of ancient buildings into their family home, creating a romantic garden, which is now one of the most famous in the world. The mellow brick walls make the perfect backdrop for climbers and today a huge range of them are present in the garden. Some are originals from Vita's time; others were planted subsequently by the many talented gardeners who have worked at Sissinghurst.

THE TOP COURTYARD

Entering the walled Top Courtyard in midsummer, you are greeted by a delightful combination: a tender yellow 'Mermaid' rose growing beneath a window with *Clematis* 'Minuet' rambling through it, and an unusual shrub, *Indigofera pendula,* arching above them both, its long, wisteria-like flowers hanging in front of the panes. The contrasting foliage and flowers, and sense of profusion, is thrilling. Earlier in the season, *Clematis patens* 'Manshuu Ki' flowers through *Wisteria floribunda* to create an equally fabulous pairing.

The south-facing wall is strung with pig wire, which has rusted to become almost invisible against the brick and makes an excellent frame for three different, summer-flowering clematis: 'Perle d'Azur', 'Madame Julia Correvon' and 'Étoile Violette'. They are well-established, vigorous plants, which are cut back to their bases annually and have their new growth fanned out to ensure that they smother the

quinata), *Clematis* 'Elizabeth' and a Banksia rose. All have found their way up the tower with minimal support and the chocolate vine is now ascending a ladder attached to the very top!

THE ROSE GARDEN

Stepping through a gate in a wall clad with a climbing hydrangea, you are engulfed by the Rose Garden, which Vita envisaged as 'a tumble of roses and honeysuckle, figs and vines'. The walls drip with sweet-scented *Trachelospermum asiaticum*, *Solanum laxum* 'Album' and various clematis and honeysuckle. Inside the beds are wigwams of sweet peas, carefully chosen to harmonise with the permanent planting and add height above the perennials. Most eye-catching of all in this sea of colour is *Clematis* 'Perle d'Azur' trained to form a huge fan on an east-facing wall, completely smothering it in large blue flowers.

wall, rather than race to the top of it. This is fiddly work, but the gardeners are not too wary of snapping the delicate stems – they soon regrow.

Other walls hold more delights: classic climbers such as floriferous *Solanum crispum* 'Glasnevin' and generous climbing roses as well as unusual additions that benefit from the shelter, including porcelain berry (*Ampelopsis brevipedunculata*) with its quirky pink and blue fruit. Standing guard above them all is the iconic Elizabethan Tower where Vita did most of her writing. This is hung with chocolate vine (*Akebia*

▲ The walls of the Rose Garden are draped in climbers and wall shrubs.

THE COTTAGE GARDEN

The Cottage Garden is a riot of bold colours, very different to the rest of the garden: yellows, copper, orange and fiery red. To complement this scheme, annual climbers Spanish flag, Chilean glory flower and orange sweet pea 'Henry Eckford' are trained up hazel poles. These annuals are raised under glass each spring and planted out into the warm, sheltered garden where they grow quickly to add colour at eye-height. In a hot, sunny position against the wall of the cottage, a lax shrub called *Abutilon megapotamicum* is used as a climber. Vita loved this species with its tiny, red and yellow, lantern-like flowers and here it is made all the more dramatic by an underplanting of orange and red African daisies and marigolds.

WHITE-FLOWERED CLIMBERS

Even the cool and refreshing White Garden is bursting with blooms and each of the white flowers has a different quality to it. *Rosa* 'Mulliganii' smothers the pergola while *R.* 'Cooperi' clothes a nearby wall, both of them providing a flush of single flowers with warm yellow centres. Peeping out among the display is delightful *Clematis* 'Kaiu' with nodding, pink-tinged, light grey bells, and the reliable everlasting pea *Lathyrus latifolius* 'Albus'. On a cool wall against the Priest's House is an evergreen that thrives in shade: *Pileostegia viburnoides* has large panicles of creamy-white flowers that light up dark places.

Along the Moat Walk are two large white wisterias, original plantings by Vita and Harold. *Wisteria brachybotrys* f. *albiflora* 'Shiro-kapitan' begins to bloom first but *Wisteria floribunda* f. *alba* 'Shiro-noda', a white form of the classic Japanese wisteria, has far longer and more elegant racemes. They take one gardener two days to prune, tiptoeing between the thick mossy stems, which lie on top of the Moat Wall like a huge sleeping python.

◀ Orange sweet peas complement the colour scheme in the Cottage Garden.

◣ *Rosa* 'Mulliganii' covers the pergola in the famous White Garden.

◣◣ White wisteria growing along the Moat Wall.

▶ Solanum crispum 'Glasnevin' grows alongside climbing rose 'Blossomtime' in the Top Courtyard.

WALL SHRUBS

Scattered throughout the garden are shrubs trained against walls, softening the boundaries and adding to the sense of sprawling profusion. These include evergreens such as myrtle, started as a cutting from Vita's wedding bouquet, glossy *Garrya elliptica*, *Ceanothus* 'Puget Blue' and a huge *Magnolia grandiflora*. There is a peach on a sunny wall, a morello cherry on a shadier one and there are a number of figs, grown for their lush architectural foliage. Japanese quince also do well here: *Chaenomeles × superba* 'Knap Hill Scarlet' is an original planting of Vita's.

◀ Some clematis have highly attractive, fluffy seed heads which persist into winter.

to think only about flowers though – the appeal of most climbers is in their foliage which can vary hugely in shape, colour and size. Those with glossy leaves tend to reflect light while those with lime green or variegated leaves can add great contrast to a border. Many climbers also have fantastic autumn colour and a few form attractive berries or seed heads which provide interest long after the flowers fade.

HARDINESS

Warm south- or west-facing walls increase the options for what you can grow, creating a microclimate for sun-lovers, such as trumpet vines (*Campsis radicans* and *C. grandiflora*) and star jasmine (*Trachelospermum jasminoides*). If you have a sheltered north- or east-facing spot, unusual climbers that like shade but dislike prolonged cold, such as *Stauntonia hexaphylla* and *Berberidopsis corallina,* may thrive. If your garden is reliably frost-free, you could try tender species such as evergreen *Holboellia latifolia, Sollya heterophylla* or *Lapageria rosea.*

CHOOSING CLIMBERS

The range of climbing plants suited to most British gardens is not limitless. If you tailor your searches to species suitable for your soil and the amount of sun that they will receive, ruling out all those that are not reliably hardy, your options will be fairly clear. You will narrow them down even further by deciding if you want a deciduous or evergreen climber and whether it needs to be self-clinging or can be given supports. If you opt for popular species such as clematis or roses, the hardest decision will be choosing between the many different cultivated varieties, each with its own distinctive colour and flower shape. Try not

SIZE AND VIGOUR

In most gardens it is best to avoid rampant climbers, such as the potentially invasive Russian vine (*Fallopia baldschuanica*) or the extremely vigorous rose 'Paul's Himalayan Musk'. Slightly more manageable rambling roses, such as 'Albertine', and fast-growing climbers, such as *Clematis armandii* and *Lonicera henryi,* can often be accommodated, but are best grown over large structures where you do not need to rein them in. Even *Clematis montana,* jasmine and common honeysuckle really need walls, fences or pergolas of 2m or above. Wisteria also prefers lots of space, but careful pruning can keep it compact.

◀ **Chinese magnolia vine (*Schisandra rubriflora*)** is an unusual deciduous species with small, waxy red flowers.

◀ ***Hydrangea seemannii*** is an evergreen and slower-growing climbing hydrangea, which needs a sheltered position.

◀ **Chinese Virginia creeper (*Parthenocissus henryana*)** has pretty foliage and good autumn colour, will grow in shade and is more manageable than other *Parthenocissus* species.

◀ **Oriental bittersweet (*Celastrus orbiculatus*)** is vigorous with wonderful, yellow autumn foliage.

◀ **Chocolate vine (*Akebia quinata*)** is semi-evergreen with lobed leaves and purple-brown flowers, which are followed by unusual purple fruits.

◀ ***Hedera colchica* 'Dentata Variegata'** is large-leaved and boldly variegated. Ivies are great for wildlife when they reach flowering size.

◀ ***Clematis* 'Frankie'**, like many clematis, will grow in partial shade. This spring-flowering type likes free-draining soil.

◀ **Climbing hydrangea (*Hydrangea anomala* subsp. *petiolaris*)** is a lovely, deciduous, lacecap variety with clusters of small, white flowers and oval leaves.

◀ **Common honeysuckle (*Lonicera periclymenum*)**, like most honeysuckles, will grow in partial shade; it has nectar-rich flowers that are great for moths. 'Graham Thomas' is a nice, creamy-yellow flowered variety.

◀ ***Pileostegia viburnoides*** is very shade tolerant, but slow growing, with leathery leaves.

To cover typical garden fences, look for species that are naturally short, can be cut down annually or will respond to being tied down horizontally. Many shrubs can also be trained against a fence and kept at under 2m.

CLIMBERS ON HOUSE WALLS

In some circumstances, climbers on house walls have been known to trap moisture and cause damage to masonry or render. This is mainly an issue if houses are constructed of soft brick or have soft mortar, or if climbers are left unmanaged and send shoots under tiles, timber cladding or gutters. Self-clingers are a particular nuisance, sending small adventitious (stem) roots into mortar and render; many of these roots are left behind when the plant is cut back and may require scraping off. Erecting wires for non-clinging climbers also has disadvantages, as this requires holes to be drilled that may act as entry points for moisture.

Despite these issues, many home-owners consider the aesthetic benefits of a climber well worth the risks. Some even benefit from the insulating properties of climbers growing on windy east- or north-facing house walls. If you decide to go ahead, ensure that you can access the wall to keep the climber in check. If you are adding wires, use screw-in vine eyes with wall plugs and drill into the mortar only, to avoid damaging the masonry.

PLANTING CLIMBERS

The base of a fence or wall is often drier than elsewhere because rain may not reach it (this effect is known as a rain shadow). For this reason, it's best not to plant climbers right underneath it, but 30–50cm away. If the ground is full of rubble, species such as passion flowers, which enjoy very free-draining conditions, may thrive but, for most others, it's wise to dig out the rubble and top up the planting area with topsoil from elsewhere in the

▲ Honeysuckle, roses and clematis smother the walls of Monk's House in East Sussex.

CLIMBERS FOR GARDEN FENCES

A number of clematis can be kept suitably small including *Clematis* 'Arabella' (shown above), which is short with a scrambling rather than climbing habit, *C. cirrhosa* var. *balearica*, which is evergreen and flowers in late winter and *C.* 'Helios', which can be cut to the ground annually and has yellow flowers late in summer.

Everlasting sweet peas such as *Lathyrus latifolius* 'Rosa Perle' are also a good option as they are herbaceous, with new growth starting from the base each year. Most honeysuckles are very vigorous but *Lonicera periclymenum* 'Rhubarb and Custard' is a fairly compact variety. Glossy, evergreen star jasmine (*Trachelospermum jasminoides*) is another option – it can grow to several metres tall but horizontal training and annual clipping will keep it in check. For roses, steer clear of vigorous climbers and ramblers. Instead try a short climber such as *Rosa* 'Blush Noisette' or opt for a shrub rose and simply fan out the stems against your wall or fence.

garden – ideally with some well-rotted manure or garden compost mixed in.

Most climbers don't mind being planted in among other plants if they have a good section of wall or fence to themselves. In fact, the shade cast by neighbouring foliage at ground level can be good for species such as clematis, which like their roots to be kept cool. Make sure your planting hole is at least three times the size of the pot the climber has been grown in.

Plant most climbers in the ground at the same depth as they were in their pots. The exception to this rule is clematis, which responds well to being planted up to 8cm deeper. If the root ball looks congested, use your hands to tease it apart in order to encourage the roots to spread out. After planting, always remove any ties and canes that are binding the plant together and fan the stems out. Canes can be reused to help guide stems up to the supports if necessary.

PLANTING THROUGH PAVING

All climbers do best when planted in the ground, where the roots have room to extend, rather than being confined to a container. For this reason, it's best to leave planting space beneath walls and fences when you are laying a patio. If you need a climber to cover a structure on an existing patio and there is no open ground, lift a paving slab if possible, dig out any hardcore or builders' sand underneath and plant the climber in there. As it establishes, the climber should send roots underneath the patio where it is cool and moist, enabling it to grow far bigger and more healthily than if it were constrained by a pot.

If you have no choice but to plant in containers, choose the biggest pots you can find and ensure that they can drain freely. Then opt for species that are tolerant of container growing, such as *Trachelospermum jasminoides*, compact clematis and annuals for a summer display. Use loam-based compost for permanent plantings and be prepared to water and feed frequently.

SUMMER-FLOWERING ANNUAL CLIMBERS

These tender climbers can be bought as small plants in spring or raised in a greenhouse and hardened off ready for planting at the end of spring, when all risk of frost has passed. Plant in large troughs or well-prepared border soil and keep well watered for the first few weeks. They will grow fast, so have supports in place and tie the stems in to guide them upwards.

▲ Black-eyed Susan
(*Thunbergia alata*)

▲ Canary creeper
(*Tropaeolum peregrinum*)

▲ Chilean glory flower
(*Eccremocarpus scaber*)

▲ Yellow sweet pea
(*Lathyrus chloranthus*)

▲ Morning glory
(*Ipomoea purpurea*)

▲ Cup-and-saucer vine
(*Cobaea scandens*)

▲ Purple bell vine
(*Rhodochiton atrosanguineus*)

▲ Spanish flag
(*Ipomoea lobata*)

▲ Sweet pea
(*Lathyrus odoratus*)

SUPPORTS FOR CLIMBERS

Most climbers have twining stems (which can twine clockwise or anti-clockwise), tendrils (which may grow from the stem or leaves), or clinging, adventitious roots and pads. These different habits influence how we use the plants and what kind of support they need.

Species of climber that produce clinging roots from their stems include ivy, climbing hydrangea, pileostegia and schizophragma, while all parthenocissus species have tiny adhesive pads. Most of these climbers need little or no support and are ideal for climbing up tall walls with no wires or trellis on them.

Twining plants (such as akebia, jasmine and honeysuckle) and those with tendrils (such as sweet pea, passion flower and vines) need frames, wires or trellis to wrap around. Twiners are more likely to go neatly up vertical supports, whereas those with tendrils usually need lots of horizontals and more tying in to guide them. Many species with tendrils need to be deterred from clinging to themselves or neighbouring plants, as do some twiners, such as wisteria, which can twist around its own stems and become permanently entangled.

Some climbers, such as roses and *Solanum crispum*, have no clinging mechanism and tend just to sprawl over other species, sometimes with the help of thorns. These are often referred to as 'scandent' in habit and have long, flexible stems which need very regular tying in. Always attach these climbers to the front of their supporting wires or trellis rather than allowing them to squeeze behind supports; that way you will be able to untie and rearrange stems as needed.

TRELLIS, WIRES AND TWINE

Trellis is commonly used on top of walls and fences to extend their height, giving more space for climbers as well as creating more privacy between you and your neighbour without adding a solid barrier. Trellis can also be used to line the inside of fences and walls, providing sufficient support for almost every type of climber. As well as standard square trellis, it is possible to find designs suited to particular gardens, including cottage-style diamond lattice or modern slats. Whichever you use, take care to fix it securely so that climbers can be left to smother it with no risk of collapse or the need to cut them back for repairs. It's best to screw the trellis onto thin batons attached to the wall

or fence, so that it sits a few centimetres proud, allowing for air circulation and ease of twining or tying.

If lining walls and fences with horizontal wires instead, space them 30–45cm apart with the lowest wire no more than about 50cm from the ground. Use at least 2mm-thick galvanised wire; it is hard to manipulate but far longer-lasting than plastic-coated garden wire. To get a taut wire, it may be worth investing in tensioning hooks or bolts, which will also allow for future tightening. There are several models available. Some are only suitable for screwing through wooden posts. Others attach to the ends of wires and can be hooked onto vine eyes set in a wall. As with trellis, wires should sit a few centimetres out from the wall or fence. If a climber has a permanent woody framework, tie the thick stems in position against supports with soft plastic-coated wire or strips of fabric. These should be checked annually to ensure that they are not becoming too tight as the stems thicken. All other stems can be tied in using natural twine; this does only last a year, but that is usually sufficient.

WALL SHRUBS

Plants suited to growing against fences and walls are those which can be trained to form wide, fairly flat structures and will flower despite having their outward branches regularly shortened. It is possible to experiment with many shrubs, but known successes include:

- *Abeliophyllum distichum*, an early-flowering, white forsythia, suitable for very warm, sheltered walls.
- *Azara microphylla*, an evergreen tree, which bears delicious, vanilla-scented flowers.
- *Camellia sasanqua* 'Plantation Pink' which, like many camellias, can be trained as a wall shrub if you have an acid soil. However, it is hard to keep slim.
- *Chimonanthus praecox*, a slightly tender, early-flowering, fragrant shrub, which needs to be planted against a south-facing wall to thrive.
- *Cotoneaster horizontalis*, a very shade-tolerant and hardy shrub, with a very flat, architectural structure, which carries berries and has good autumn colour.
- *Euonymus fortunei* 'Silver Queen', a neat, evergreen shrub tolerant of deep shade, which has attractive, white variegation and a slightly climbing habit.
- *Fuchsia magellanica*, which tolerates light shade, and is easy to train with masses of flowers in late summer.
- *Garrya elliptica*, a large, evergreen shrub with glossy foliage and long, silky catkins.
- *Ribes speciosum* (shown above), an ornamental currant, which is easy to grow and train, with bright red, fuchsia-like flowers.
- *Vesalea floribunda*, a lovely shrub, which needs a sheltered, sunny spot. (Formerly called *Abelia floribunda*.)

PRUNING CLIMBERS AND WALL SHRUBS

A handful of perennial climbers, including climbing nasturtium, everlasting sweet pea and golden hop, are herbaceous; their top growth dies back in winter and can be removed altogether. New shoots will arise from the base the following year.

All other perennial climbers retain their stems that often become thick and woody and from which they shoot each year. Without management these climbers can naturally climb very high, becoming bare at the base with most foliage and flowers carried at the top. Pruning is designed to prevent this and give you flowers and foliage lower down, where you want it. With many climbers this involves developing a framework of permanent branches and then cutting back anything that extends beyond where you want it. Deciduous climbers are usually pruned in winter and evergreens in spring, but it sometimes pays to factor in flowering time to avoid cutting off

▲ Well-trained climbers on walls, trellis and a pergola provide seclusion in this courtyard garden.

potential flowers. As with pruning shrubs (see 'Pruning shrubs', p.147) this may mean delaying the pruning of spring and early summer flowering plants, such as *Chimonanthus praecox* and winter jasmine, until immediately after they have flowered.

CREATING A FRAMEWORK

After planting, stems are fanned out to cover a fence or wall. Self-clinging species can then be left to establish naturally over the next few years, while others need their new shoots tied in to fill in gaps. Unwanted growth can be cut out or shortened.

The wider you are able to make the framework, the more space you will have to tie in branches and the bushier your climber is likely to appear. If plants grow vertically, they will reach the top of the structure more quickly and if the tips are cut,

they are likely to grow vigorously from that point, getting rather top heavy. If training a climber up a pillar or arch, twine main stems around the verticals to slow their vigour and encourage bushiness and flowering side shoots. If you only want bushiness and flowers on top, as is often the case with pergolas, you can let them go straight up the verticals and then fan them out horizontally over the top.

SHORTENING EXCESS GROWTH

Once the framework is established, stems growing out from the fence or wall (known as laterals) that are not needed can simply be shortened annually. This can be done either by carefully cutting each stem back with secateurs to form a short spur, with two or three buds along it (spur-pruning), or by simply trimming all the laterals as needed, possibly even using shears.

Spur-pruning is suitable for wisterias, climbing roses, *Actinidia kolomikta*, bougainvilleas, trumpet vines, grapevines and crimson glory vine (*Vitis coignetiae*), as well as wall shrubs like winter jasmine (*Jasminum nudiflorum*), fuchsias, ceanothus, pyracanthas and Japanese quinces, which will all flower on short spurs growing off the main framework.

Trimming as needed will work for *Akebia quinata*, climbing hydrangeas, jasmine, ivy, honeysuckle, passion flowers and *Trachelospermum jasminoides*. It's best to keep the laterals at least 30cm long, ideally with some fairly young growth on them, as less may reduce flowering. If the plant is a tangle of stems – often the case with honeysuckle and jasmine – take care not to chop through any of the main framework accidentally.

REPLACEMENT PRUNING

Once climbers exceed the space available to them, rather than continually cutting them back to the same point, it is best to remove some whole stems, tracing them back to a lower side shoot and cutting just above it. You can then tie in the side shoot to fill the gap you have created. The same approach is useful for cutting out bare sections of plant and replacing them with younger shoots. This is common practice with climbing roses. *Solanum crispum*, which quickly becomes bare at the base, is best managed by occasionally cutting out whole stems at the base to stimulate new lower growth which can be tied in a few months later.

Rambling roses, Japanese wineberry (*Rubus phoenicolasius*) and semi-climbing fruits, such as tayberry, loganberry and blackberry,

PRUNING WISTERIA

Wisteria is the classic choice for forming a very neat framework and pruning to short spurs.

STEP 1 After flowering in spring, allow new shoots to develop naturally until summer (try to resist shortening them if they are in your way as this will affect flowering).

STEP 2 In July or August, shorten new shoots so they have five or six leaves. This will tidy up the plant and allow light in to ripen the shoots. At this point in summer, growth will have slowed and so there should be minimal regrowth from now on.

STEP 3 In December or January, shorten the same shoots again, back to two or three buds. These lowest buds are usually the fattest ones, which are going to form flowers in spring.

can have all their old fruited stems cut out annually and all the new young stems tied in their place to make a new framework. If you do this in summer after flowering or fruiting, you can easily see which are the old stems and which are the new.

Mid- to late summer-flowering clematis are best cut back to the base altogether at the end of winter, so that a new framework of stems forms each year and they never get thick, woody and bare. These clematis, like herbaceous climbers, are good for scrambling through other plants, as cutting them down completely makes them easy to tidy up.

RENOVATION PRUNING

A handful of plants, including *Clematis montana* and *C. armandii*, are best given plenty of space, initially trained to fan out the stems and then left largely unpruned. New shoots will form on top of old growth and may become a tangle of stems, but you will usually get a very impressive display of flowers. After seven years or more, if the plant has

far outgrown its space and developed a very bare base, it can be cut hard down to about 60cm. For *C. armandii*, this can be done in spring immediately after flowering. For *C. montana*, you can wait until flowering has finished in late spring – but it is better to sacrifice a year of flowers and do it at the end of winter to give the plant a whole spring and summer to grow and recover. Within six weeks of hard pruning, new shoots should begin to develop and these can be tied in to form a new framework.

Many other climbers tolerate renovation pruning like this. The most resilient species include ivies, climbing hydrangeas, jasmines and even wisteria. New growth will be vigorous, but the plant may not flower profusely for a few years.

Mature climbers can be a great place for birds to make nests, so do check them carefully before renovation pruning during the bird-nesting season, which starts at the end of February and runs right through until the end of July.

COMMON PROBLEMS

The range of pests, diseases and disorders that attack climbers varies greatly, depending on the species. Tender climbers are prone to weather damage while woody shrubs may be affected by many of the same issues as ornamental shrubs.

COLD-WEATHER DAMAGE

Evergreen climbers that originate from milder climates than the UK may suffer in harsh winters, with wilting or browning of foliage. This can simply be left until plants are in active growth in late spring and trimmed off. *Trachelospermum jasminoides* tends to turn reddish in cold winters, but usually regains its deep green colour in summer.

Deciduous climbers from milder climates may come into leaf in warm spring weather and then their fragile new buds may be frosted off in cold snaps. *Actinidia kolomikta* and its even more tender cousin, the kiwi fruit (*Actinidia deliciosa*), are especially prone to this, which is why they are best planted in sheltered spots. If new growth does appear and harsh frosts are forecast, protect them with fleece. If buds are frosted off, growth will be checked but plants are rarely killed altogether.

PESTS AND DISEASES

One of the most common diseases to affect climbers is powdery mildew, often a sign that a plant is under stress during drought, so water well and prune out the worst-affected shoots. If problems recur each

▲ Powdery mildew on *Akebia quinata*.

CLEMATIS PRUNING

The wide range of clematis we grow in our gardens is the result of decades of plant breeding, using many different species as parents, so their growth habits really vary. For convenience, their pruning needs have been grouped into three distinct approaches. If you don't know which type of clematis you have, leave it for a year to see when it flowers.

GROUP 1 covers the early-blooming clematis (including late spring-flowering *Clematis montana*) that flower on shoots produced in the previous year; they need no regular pruning.

GROUP 2 comprises mainly large-flowered clematis that bloom in late spring and early summer on the previous year's growth and sometimes again in late summer on new growth. Prune lightly after the first flush, shortening shoots that have flowered and removing any that are dead. If they have not become too entangled and have enough space to keep growing, they can be left unpruned.

GROUP 3 includes clematis that flower from mid- to late summer on new growth; they can be cut down hard to about 30cm and will send up lots of new shoots from the base. Do this in February as the plant starts to shoot.

MANAGING HONEYSUCKLES

Our native honeysuckle (*Lonicera periclymenum*) is great for wildlife and can be found in a variety of forms, including early, pink-flowered 'Belgica' (often known as early Dutch honeysuckle), late, pink-flowered 'Serotina' (late Dutch honeysuckle), and creamy-yellow 'Graham Thomas'. Non-native relatives include perfoliate honeysuckle (*L. caprifolium*), vigorous evergreens (*L. japonica* and *L. henryi*), and showy but unscented American hybrids (*L.* × *brownii* and *L.* × *tellmanniana*).

They all grow quickly and look nice if left unpruned to ramble on tall garden structures. This will give you a great number of flowers, which often come in more than one flush through summer, making the timing of pruning tricky. When plants become too unruly, they can be renovated at the end of winter or in spring for evergreen species; this will usually result in lots of new, more manageable shoots.

▶ Adult scale insects on a tayberry stem.

year and are unsightly, it may indicate that your climber is unsuited to its soil or location, or is very overcrowded by its neighbours.

The most common pests are aphids and scale insects. There are a few different species of scale insects, the most problematic of which is wisteria scale, found only in the South East of England. Vigorous climbers can usually cope with mild pest infestations. If treatment is required, try rubbing the insects off with your fingers or use an organic pesticide based on plant oils or fatty acids. For scale insects this will need to be done in spring when the young insects have hatched.

YELLOWING LEAVES

When leaves turn yellow, it can be a sign that plants are growing in soil which is too wet or dry or has the wrong pH, preventing the plants from taking up the nutrients they need. Climbing hydrangeas are very prone to developing yellow leaves with dark green margins (interveinal chlorosis), which is usually caused by the soil being too alkaline, perhaps because lime mortar is leaching out from a wall and raising the soil pH. If your climber is newly planted and suffering badly, it may be best to move it elsewhere, but if it is more mature and otherwise healthy, a dose of iron-rich fertiliser and plenty of water may help.

CHAPTER 7

SHRUBS & TREES

A WEALTH OF IMPORTS

Trees and shrubs play an invaluable role in gardens. As well as having intrinsic interest and beauty, they can be used to fill, frame or screen views, create privacy, break up open spaces and provide habitats for wildlife. In addition to many attractive native plants, there are innumerable ornamental species to choose from, thanks to centuries of worldwide plant-collecting.

Among the first imports to be planted in Britain were large conifers such as the cedar of Lebanon and the Corsican pine, some of which can still be seen in our landscapes. These were soon followed by a mass of flowering shrubs and trees more suitable for domestic gardens, including magnolias from North America, rhododendrons from the Himalayas and ornamental cherries from Japan.

The arrival of new woody plants from abroad led to changes in gardening fashion, from the creation of elegant shrubberies in Georgian Britain to the planting up of whole valleys during the Victorian era. In the 20th century, a passion for plant breeding led plantsmen to cross different species and select forms with better habits or showier flowers, giving rise to even more garden-worthy plants, many of them suitable for our smaller gardens.

Today we not only have easy access to this vast range of plants, we also have a wealth of information about how large they will grow, the soil conditions they need and how to prune and train them – knowledge our forebears often lacked. Few of our small gardens now have shrubberies given over wholly to woody plants, but many feature shrubs and small trees mixed into borders, planted within lawns or planted in large containers.

▶ Autumn colour provided by shrubs and trees in the Walled Garden at Wallington in Northumberland.

WOODY PLANTS

Shrubs and trees are long-lived plants with stems that become thick and woody.

Shrubs usually have multiple stems and range in size from under 1m to over 7m tall. Some small species such as lavender and sage only become woody at their bases and are known as subshrubs.

Trees generally have a single trunk, which branches above waist-height; most can reach anything from about 5m to over 18m. In horticulture we now have dwarf shrubs and trees, multi-stemmed trees and plants that are grafted onto the roots of other species to influence their growth.

Trees and shrubs can be deciduous or evergreen and a handful are known as semi-evergreen, meaning they may lose their leaves during a cold winter but can retain them in mild conditions. Most of the shrubs and trees popular for growing in UK gardens are adapted to cope with below-freezing temperatures (hardy), although some need shelter from winds and their blossom can be damaged by frost. In very sheltered gardens or those with large greenhouses, it is also possible to cultivate tender species.

COLETON FISHACRE, DEVON

When Coleton Fishacre was first built on its clifftop perch in the 1920s, the house must have looked rather bare and exposed and been buffeted by sea winds. Soon after, a belt of pines was established on the east side of the house to shield it from the winds, creating a far more sheltered garden and enabling a wide range of plants to be grown. Nearly a century later, the statuesque pines are still serving their purpose and the house nestles among very varied vegetation.

Rupert and Dorothy D'Oyly Carte, the owners of Coleton Fishacre, loved woody plants and records show that they tried many different species. Some of those that have really stood the test of time are the small *Luma apiculata* from Chile with peeling, cinnamon-coloured bark and *Cornus controversa* from Asia with flat,

open-stretched branches, as well as numerous rhododendrons, camellias and magnolias. A tulip tree planted on the lawn below the house in around 1930 is now 20m tall, far larger than the family must have imagined when they planted it under a treasured sea view.

THE TERRACES

Raised terraces built close to the house are very warm and sunny, supporting a huge range of tender shrubs including abutilons, Australian bottlebrushes, coastal rosemary, grey-leaved euryops, grevilleas, pineapple guava, winter-flowering *Correa alba* and the small tree *Acacia baileyana* 'Purpurea'. Senior Gardener Martyn Pepper, who has worked at Coleton for 18 years, recommends all these for experimenting with in similarly mild coastal sites, sunny town gardens

▲ *Luma apiculata* flowers in summer.

◀ A very architectural *Luma apiculata* growing in front of the house.

◀◀ Planting surrounds the house at Coleton Fishacre.

◣ Crimson bottlebrush (*Callistemon citrinus*) flowers in summer.

or against south-facing walls. Free-draining conditions on the terraces are key to their ability to get through winter, meaning that, no matter how much rain there is, the roots are never sitting in wet soil.

For gardeners with less sheltered gardens there is also plenty of inspiration from more hardy, sun-loving shrubs such as lavender, Russian sage, woolly Jerusalem sage, prostrate rosemary, rock roses, New Zealand daisy bushes, *Ceanothus arboreus* 'Trewithen Blue' and *Ceanothus thyrsiflorus* var. *repens*, which all lend a Mediterranean feel without being too fussy. For fuchsia enthusiasts there are six different species on display: hardy *Fuchsia magellanica*, tiny-leaved *F. microphylla*, striking *F.* 'Thalia', tree fuchsia (*F. arborescens*), beautiful *F. paniculata* and rare *F. boliviana*.

THE VALLEY GARDEN

Below the terraces a steep valley garden plunges down to the sea with paths winding between many choice shrubs and trees, including magnolias, Japanese maples, rowans, *Crinodendron hookerianum*, hydrangeas, witch hazels, tree ferns and corokias. In spring the Valley Garden is especially inviting, with colourful rhododendrons and camellias and sweet scent from *Azara serrata*. Many of the largest plants are very architectural, creating dramatic shapes on the sloping hillside, their branches laced with lichen thanks to the clean, humid Devon air.

NEW PLANTING SCHEMES

The gardeners at Coleton Fishacre regularly plant new trees and shrubs to keep the garden interesting and ensure that there will always be a good range in the future. They choose species that flower for many weeks, won't spread through the valley and feel right for the spirit of the place.

▲ The sheltered terraces are covered in exotic planting.

▼ A bridge in the Valley Garden.

◥ *Cotinus coggygria* 'Royal Purple'.

◥◥ *Cercis canadensis* 'Forest Pansy'.

▶ *Sambucus nigra* f. *porphyrophylla* 'Black Lace'.

A new area of planting leading from the entrance to the house displays a selection of rich, purple-leaved shrubs that are suitable for most gardens due to their manageable size and tolerance of most soils. These include *Sambucus nigra* f. *porphyrophylla* 'Black Lace', *Cotinus coggygria* 'Royal Purple', *Physocarpus opulifolius* 'Diabolo', *Cercis canadensis* 'Forest Pansy' and diminutive *Pittosporum tenuifolium* 'Tom Thumb'. These offer colour from the moment they come into leaf in spring and create a dramatic backdrop to the herbaceous planting in summer.

Exploring Coleton Fishacre shows us how important the role of shrubs and trees is in a garden, providing a setting for the house and for other, more ephemeral plants. Although it is less than 100 years old, the house feels as if it has always been here, nestled into a wooded garden that blends into its Devon hillside, despite being made up of species from all over the world.

▼ Mahonias can grow even in heavy soils and shade. *Mahonia* x *media*, seen here, has beautiful flowers and foliage, with flowers appearing in winter and providing a good source of nectar and pollen for bees.

CHOOSING SHRUBS AND TREES

All gardens need at least one shrub or tree to fill the vertical space and provide structure through the seasons. Choosing the right one needs careful thought as these are long-lived garden features and can take several years to reach their prime.

As with other plants, your choice will be constrained by practical considerations about the soil and aspect. Be guided by these factors as they are critical for plant health and healthy plants are essential for a gorgeous garden. It is possible to find shrubs suitable for every situation – even heavy clay soils in deep shade will support nice specimens such as mahonias, skimmias and sweet box.

Trees and shrubs are often used to fill or screen a view, so their sizes and growth habits will be key factors. You can work out the required height and width of a plant by creating a structure of tall canes tied together to form a 'T' and studying it from windows, seating areas and other important viewpoints, adjusting or repositioning it as required to fill the space. You'll find many catalogues list the mature heights and shapes of woody plants and sometimes the number of years they'll take to reach them. It's always worth ensuring that your garden can accommodate a plant's eventual size: it's a shame to have to chop them down once they have reached maturity and few plants will tolerate being held back – the constant pruning involved tends to spoil their natural shape and minimise flowering.

FOLIAGE AND FLOWERS

With soil, aspect and size established, it's time to consider details. Whether you need the plant to be evergreen is probably the first. Most gardens benefit from some evergreens to provide year-round structure, but deciduous plants are usually far more interesting, offering seasonal change. Many people are tempted by widely available, fast-growing species – such as *Photinia* × *fraseri* 'Red

TOP 10 SMALL GARDEN TREES

There are lots of trees that will stay below 8m, even when mature, without the need for pruning.

◀ *Acer palmatum* has many varieties, all with wonderful autumn colour. Best for neutral to acid soil.

◀ *Ilex aquifolium* **'J.C. van Tol'** makes a reliable, neat evergreen tree; this female holly reliably produces berries.

◀ *Amelanchier lamarckii* is a tough, reliable tree with lovely spring blossom, berries and colour in early autumn.

◀ *Malus transitoria*, a Chinese crab apple, has delicate, white flowers followed by abundant yellow fruit and good autumn colour.

◀ *Cornus kousa* is a little fussy but once happy it bears showy flowers and good autumn colour.

◀ *Crataegus persimilis* **'Prunifolia'**, a relation of common hawthorn, has a classic tree shape and nice blossom, fruit and autumn colour.

◀ *Euonymus europaeus* **'Red Cascade'** is showy with deep pink fruits and dazzling autumn colour. It can be grown as a shrub or tree.

◀ *Pyrus salicifolia* **'Pendula'** has a very elegant, weeping habit with lovely, silver-grey leaves.

◀ *Magnolia* **'Elizabeth'** is a small, neatly shaped magnolia with fragrant, pale-yellow flowers.

◀ *Sorbus vilmorinii*, a cousin of our native rowan, has unusual pink berries and wonderful autumn colour.

Robin', laurels, Leyland cypress or Lawson's cypress – but if you are prepared to shop around and be patient there are many other interesting plants available to you.

If flowers are important to you, consider when they will appear. Many woody plants flower in spring, making a splash before summer perennials get going. Others peak at the same time, adding to the effect. Some have delicious scents, which might be especially welcome near a door in the depths of winter (as with sweet box and *Viburnum × bodnantense*) or in early spring (*Osmanthus delavayi* and *Daphne odora*). For anyone choosing woody plants based on their spring scents, winter stems or autumn colour, it's wise to position the plants so that they catch the sun at some point in the day, as this will usually amplify the effect.

As with perennials, the foliage is a feature of your garden for far longer than the flowers. A number of shrubs, including lilac and mock orange, have lovely blooms that are short-lived and afterwards you are left with unremarkable foliage. Look for more striking leaves that are glossy, interestingly shaped, variegated, especially vivid in spring or exquisitely coloured before they fall. It's amazing just how many different shades of green there are and how much variation lies within gold, grey and purple foliage too – some of which will go far better with your existing planting, stone, brick or paintwork than others.

SHRUBS FOR A MIXED BORDER

Many shrubs and sub-shrubs work well in a mixed border among annuals, perennials, bulbs and even climbers. They add structure to the border and create mystery by obscuring parts of the planting from certain angles. Shrubs in borders work best if they are taller than neighbouring herbaceous plants and if their form enables them to cohabit well with the smaller plants. Those with fairly upright structures that allow light to reach plants nearby are ideal, including *Caryopteris × clandonensis*

▲ Shrubs in the mixed border at Lytes Cary, Somerset.

'Heavenly Blue', buddlejas, hardy fuchsias, Russian sage and *Hydrangea paniculata*, all of which can be pruned back hard at the end of winter. More rounded shrubs can also be successful, provided their neighbours don't swamp them. Popular choices include evergreens such as pittosporums, choisyas, box, hebes, *Euonymus fortunei* and deciduous shrubs like potentillas, spiraeas and polyantha roses.

BUYING SHRUBS AND TREES

Deciduous trees and shrubs can be bought bareroot, root-balled or potted. Most plants for sale in garden centres have been grown in pots and should have been potted on frequently to

SHRUBS AND TREES IN CONTAINERS

A wide range of shrubs and a few small trees will tolerate being grown in large pots, provided that they are watered regularly in summer. If your garden soil is alkaline, growing in containers gives you an opportunity to try camellias, rhododendrons, Japanese maples, witch hazels and other acid-loving plants. Always use a loam-based compost for plants that are to be kept in the same pot for several years. For acid-loving plants you'll need a loam-based, ericaceous compost.

ensure that their roots have not become too congested. Larger specimens at specialist nurseries are sometimes grown in bags or air pots instead, both of which are designed to create healthy root systems and plants that establish well.

Bareroot plants are grown in the open ground and then lifted for sale in winter when they are dormant. This method is ideal for young deciduous shrubs and trees. Plants are light and therefore cheap to transport and, provided that they have not been left sitting around for a long time, they establish well. Root-balled shrubs and trees have also been grown in the open ground, but they have usually been regularly cut beneath their roots with

machinery to encourage them to form a dense root system, which can be lifted with lots of soil attached and wrapped up in hessian for sale. This is a great way of producing a healthy root system and means that even relatively big specimens can be transported and established in a new site.

Experts often advise buying young plants and being patient for best results. This is certainly true for some species such as ceanothus and *Cercis canadensis,* which tolerate being moved only when very young. However, there will be times when you will want the instant effect of a bigger plant so just take care to source it from somewhere you trust and treat it with care.

PLANTING SHRUBS AND TREES

Tradition used to dictate that when planting a tree or shrub a very big hole was needed, filled with manure or compost. Now we know plants tend to do better if the hole is wide, but only as deep as the root ball and back-filled mainly with soil. This way the roots venture out into surrounding soil more quickly, anchoring the plant, and there is no risk of the manure underneath rotting down and causing the plant to sink. If your soil is sandy and poor, you could mix a little well-rotted manure or garden compost into the soil with which you backfill the hole. If your soil is heavy clay, take care to loosen the bottom and sides of the hole to help the roots find their way out.

Trees will always need staking for the first few years to stop them rocking about in the wind and dislodging their roots. There are several workable ways of staking a tree but, whichever you use, it's best to plan the position of the stakes and knock them in before placing the tree in its hole. Stakes need be only a third of the height of the tree and tied fairly low down on the trunk, just to stop the roots moving rather than the whole plant. They

UNDERPLANTING SHRUBS AND TREES

As trees and shrubs mature and their lowest branches lift off the ground, underplant them with bulbs and perennials. Great choices include *Cyclamen coum* or snowdrops, for a flush of interest in winter, and ground-cover plants such as lungworts, *Geranium macrorhizum* and *Epimedium* × *perralchicum* (shown below), all of which are tolerant of dry, shady conditions and spread quickly, smothering the bare ground.

should be on the side of the prevailing wind, so that when it is windy the tree is blown away from the stake rather than pushed into it, rubbing the bark.

Once you are ready to plant the shrub or tree, remove it from its pot or wrapping. If the roots are really congested, gently tease them out so they don't wrap around one another when they are in the ground. If lots of compost falls away from the root ball, fill your hole in a bit so the tree ends up at the right level in the ground: the soil should come up just above where the roots flare out from the trunk with none of the trunk buried. Overly deep planting is the cause of death for many trees.

As you backfill the hole it's a good idea to firm the soil with your feet, checking as you go that the plant stays at the right level. Once the hole is filled, water it to help the roots settle into the soil and then mulch around it with a layer of garden compost or well-rotted manure, covering the area above the roots but not letting it pile up against the trunk.

For gardens with rabbit problems, a tree guard or piece of chicken wire wrapped around the trunk may be needed. For gardens where deer are known to visit, or if planting in fields with cattle or sheep, a larger guard around the outside of the tree may also be required.

PRUNING SHRUBS

All shrubs have slightly different habits and their pruning will depend on what they can tolerate and what you want to achieve. Generally speaking, most look best when given space to express their natural habits and not constantly pruned to restrict their sizes (unless of course they are used for topiary or hedges, see Chapter 8). Some, such as *Viburnum plicatum*, azaleas, camellias, daphnes and hebes, achieve a nice shape with no pruning at all. Others have a tendency to get congested and twiggy or bare at the base with their flowers borne too high; for these, annual pruning is recommended.

If you inherit a garden with lots of unfamiliar shrubs in need of pruning, it may be worth employing an expert to show you what each species needs. Be aware that a properly trained gardener would never use hedge-trimmers to cut back all the shrubs to the same shape at the same time of year.

TIMING OF PRUNING

Evergreen shrubs such as box and yew, which are grown only for their foliage, can simply be clipped in summer, but for flowering shrubs, pruning needs to be timed to ensure potential flower buds for future flowers are not removed. Dense shrubs can provide places for birds to make nests so do check carefully before undertaking any work within the bird-nesting season, which starts at the end of February and runs right through until the end of July.

Shrubs which flower before midsummer

If a shrub flowers in spring or early summer, before much new growth has been produced, it stands to reason that its flowers are carried on stems that grew the year before. By delaying pruning until after flowering, you can be sure not to cut off potential flowers. Prune as soon after flowering as possible, giving the shrub the rest of the year to grow new stems, which can ripen ready to flower the following year. Examples include forsythias, Japanese quinces, exochordas, deutzias, kolkwitzias, mock orange and weigelas.

Shrubs which flower after midsummer

Shrubs that flower in mid- to late summer or autumn usually develop their flowers on shoots grown during the spring. By pruning them at the end of winter, there will be time for the plants to grow new shoots during spring and early summer and then flower. Examples include buddlejas, caryopteris, fuchsias, *Hydrangea paniculata,* indigoferas and Russian sage.

TIMING OF PRUNING

Broadly speaking there are three approaches to pruning: creating a natural shape, hard pruning and trimming (see p.148). Whichever technique you employ, always:

- Use clean, sharp tools.
- Treat pruning as the chance to find and remove dead and damaged stems.
- When you shorten a stem, cut it back to a bud or a side shoot, otherwise it will die back to that point, leaving a stub of brown stem.
- Try to remove branches that are either overlong or branching awkwardly towards the centre of the shrub, spoiling its shape.
- Remember that wherever you make a cut – whether it's close to the tip or right down at the base – you are likely to stimulate new growth from that point.

HOW TO PRUNE FLOWERING SHRUBS

Choose from these three approaches, depending on your shrub species and the effect you want to achieve.

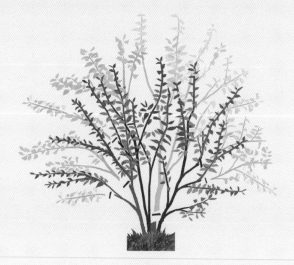

Method one involves removal and shortening of some branches to create a nice, natural shape and stimulate growth from the base. This is the best way to manage most of the deciduous spring- or early summer-flowering shrubs, such as forsythias, mock orange and weigelas, which have quite an upright habit. It stops them becoming bare at the base with all the flowers high up. Avoid removing more than a third of the plant's overall growth in any one year.

Method two involves cutting back hard to a framework each year. This is a great way to manage many of the deciduous shrubs, like buddlejas and fuchsias, which flower in late summer and autumn. It can also be done to elders and smoke bushes grown purely for their foliage and dogwoods grown for winter stem colour (it will prevent them from flowering, but generates bigger leaves and brighter stems).

Method three involves trimming the shrub over the top to remove old flowers and a few centimetres of foliage. This is suited to many bushy, rounded shrubs, both evergreen and deciduous, including choisyas, *Viburnum tinus*, *Potentilla fruticosa* and dwarf forms of *Spiraea japonica*. For mop-head hydrangeas, just trimming off the dry flowers in spring is enough.

Renovation pruning

If your shrub is really congested and if you don't mind losing a year or two of flowers, you may be able to cut it down completely. For deciduous shrubs this is usually done when they are dormant in winter; for evergreens it's in mid-spring. Many shrubs including elders, deutzias and berberis respond really well to this, sending up new shoots from the base so you have a fresh-looking plant within a year or two. Even mature camellias and rhododendrons will tolerate cutting back hard if they are strong and healthy. A handful of species, including ceanothus and rock roses, do not shoot readily from the base and old or weak plants may not recover so, if you don't want to take the risk, you may be better staggering hard pruning over a few years.

PRUNING TREES

Ideally, a newly planted tree will need only a little formative pruning in its first couple of years, to encourage a nice shape, and can otherwise be left to reach its mature size without any further pruning. However, if you inherit a tree that is too large for your garden and blocking views or light, there are a few options for reducing it sensitively without completely spoiling its shape. Since this usually involves a chainsaw or working at height, it is often necessary to employ a tree surgeon.

The options for pruning mature trees are: to shorten the longest limbs back to well-placed side branches, retaining a natural shape; to remove the lowest limbs altogether, letting light in underneath (crown-raising); or to cut all the branches back to a framework (pollarding). The latter is very brutal, only works for certain species and rarely looks right in a garden. Cutting the top off a tree is never the right approach and will ruin it.

Trees near buildings are often blamed for subsidence or structural damage and insurers may require them to be felled. Do seek a tree assessment from a fully qualified arborist before doing this. The majority of trees do not pose a risk to buildings and add much to the environment. Roots are unlikely to penetrate sound foundations directly and subsidence usually occurs only on shrinkable clay soils after periods of prolonged drought.

If you employ a tree surgeon to undertake any tree work, make sure that they are fully qualified, insured and registered with the Arboricultural Association. During consultation, they should consider the correct timing and technique for your particular tree and check birds are not nesting in it. Some tree species such as birches and magnolias are prone to bleeding sap if pruned at the wrong time and cherries can easily contract disease through open wounds. Trees contribute a lot to the local environment and may well be protected within a Conservation Area or by a Tree Preservation Order, so permission for work would need to be granted by your local council. Mature trees with holes may also be providing roosts for bats; it is an offence to disturb these so do have them checked by an expert before felling a tree.

DISPOSING OF WOODY DEBRIS

The advantage of employing a professional is that he or she may be able to take away the debris, chip up branches and even grind out stumps. If you are dealing with woody material yourself, it's best to chop all the green, soft bits into the compost and either burn or chip the thicker stems – or use them to make a woodpile for wildlife. Chippers can be hired and the resulting chippings are very useful for paths or left piled up to compost down for a few years. If you are able to have a bonfire in your garden safely without disturbing neighbours, the ash can be added to the compost heap.

MOVING SHRUBS AND TREES

Unlike perennials, woody plants resent being moved. It is very difficult not to disturb their root systems and the damage usually sets them back. The best chances of success are with young plants (good news for anyone realising they picked the wrong spot only a year or two before!) and with tough deciduous shrubs, like hypericums, potentillas and spiraeas. Among the least tolerant are rock roses, daphnes, tree peonies, ceanothus and any trees over about five years old.

If you do decide to move a mature deciduous shrub, do it in autumn, winter or early spring when it's largely dormant. Evergreen shrubs are trickier because they have to support leaves all year round – for them it's best to wait until early spring, when the ground is warming up and the roots can recover as quickly as possible.

Begin by digging a trench around the plant to investigate the root system. Starting about half a metre away all round and going at least one spade's depth should ensure that you leave plenty of roots undisturbed. Once you have exposed the majority of the root ball, you can usually slide a spade underneath and lift the plant, but for large shrubs you may need to dig down further and even cut through some of the thick roots with loppers or a pruning saw. Don't pull at the plant until it is loose as roots can tear badly. Have a plastic sack or tarpaulin nearby; once the plant is free you can drag the root ball onto it and wrap it up, so as to keep it out of wind and sun, with as much earth around the roots as possible.

You can replant the uprooted

REMOVING BRANCHES

If you need to remove a branch yourself, do it in stages to ensure that the weight of the branch does not cause it to fall and snap, leaving a messy wound. With your final cut, don't leave a stub, but also avoid cutting it too flush. Look for the branch 'collar', which should be left to enable the wound to heal.

plant right away or put it into a large pot and tend to it for a few months until you are sure that it is going to survive. Before, during or after moving it, you can prune the plant to make it easier to move or neater in its new position. Deciduous shrubs with healthy root systems can even cope with complete chopping down if required, but evergreens shouldn't have more than about 50 per cent of their top growth removed as they need plenty of leaves to continue functioning.

SHRUB AND TREE PROBLEMS

There are a number of insect pests that attack shrubs and trees, some of which are widespread (such as blackfly) and others that are specific to certain plants and don't pose a threat to others (the viburnum beetle, for instance). Most pests will cause damage only for a few weeks of the year and the plant can usually tolerate this, so treatment is often not necessary. Even when cotoneaster plants are smothered by the alarming-looking webber caterpillars, they will usually recover once the caterpillars stop feeding. Where unsightly problems persist year after year, check the plants carefully during spring and summer to identify the pest and then research the control methods needed to break its life cycle.

One of the most common symptoms of poor health in woody plants is their leaves going brown or yellow. It can often be hard to tell whether this is caused by stress or disease. Generally, if the discolouration is only at the tips or margins of leaves, or on just a few leaves, it is probably a reaction to stress such as drought, cold winds or lack of nutrients. For evergreen plants, it's normal for some older leaves to turn yellow or brown and be shed intermittently in spring and summer.

If leaves on an entire plant or a whole branch wilt and turn brown, it is usually an indication that there is an injury or canker on a main stem, or a disease affecting the roots, both of which inhibit water and nutrients moving around the plant. Common injuries include rabbit and strimmer damage, which can heal if not too extensive but may be fatal if the damage has girdled the trunk. A canker is a sunken, often weeping wound that occurs mainly in fruit trees and should be pruned out if possible. If the problem is with the roots, the most common

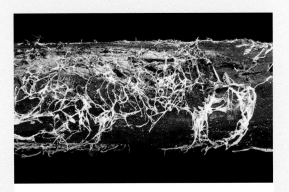

HONEY FUNGUS

You will not always see caramel-coloured toadstools around a tree or shrub infected with honey fungus. Instead look for cracked or soft bark at the base of a sick tree and peel some away. If the tree has honey fungus there will usually be white threads of fungus (mycelium), which smell very mushroomy.

If you are sure that honey fungus is the cause of the problem, remove the shrub or tree and dig out as much of its roots as possible, burning them or putting them in the general waste to limit the spread of the disease. If the tree is large, it's wise to get a stump grinder in to remove as much root as possible and to dispose of the grindings. When replanting with a new shrub or tree, research species thought to be less susceptible to this disease.

explanations are waterlogging, phytophthora root rot or honey fungus.

Good garden hygiene helps to minimise the spread of diseases, so do keep an eye on woody plants that are failing to thrive and inspect the roots of any that die, removing and burning them if possible. It's also wise to disinfect tools regularly, especially when pruning trees and shrubs, and to clean your gardening boots from time to time, especially if you wear them to visit other gardens or walk in the countryside.

▲ Viburnum beetle damage on *Viburnum davidii*.

CHAPTER 8
TOPIARY & HEDGES

LIVING SCULPTURES

Clipped hedges and sculpted shrubs have been a feature of European gardens since at least the 1st century BC. Records of Roman gardens reveal they had box topiary of all kinds, including neat hedges, geometric shapes and even animal forms. It seems that for as long as we have been creating ornamental gardens, we have been moulding and manipulating plants to suit our whims.

The art of sculpting hedges was popular in Tudor times, when knot gardens were created using low clipped plants arranged so they appeared to be woven together. Low hedging and topiary were also features of formal gardens during the Renaissance, when geometric, box-edged parterres graced every grand garden.

Formal fashions were swept away for many decades of the 18th century, but a love of topiary and hedged parterres was reawakened in the Victorian period. Around this time, gardening became an interest shared by people of all classes and neatly clipped hedges and topiary forms featured even in small cottage gardens. In the early 20th century, topiary was used in all manner of ways and a number of the playful shapes created in great gardens of the day can

still be seen, including the fox and hounds at Knightshayes in Devon and the Shamrock Garden at Mount Stewart in Northern Ireland.

The Arts and Crafts movement, which has influenced the design of many wonderful 20th-century gardens, relies on sharp hedges and topiary to enclose areas and create garden rooms. In these gardens, stone walls merge seamlessly into green ones, creating an architectural backdrop for loose, colourful planting. This contrast of formality and softness is a style for which British gardens have become renowned and something many gardeners strive to create.

PRUNING AND TRAINING

Topiary is the name given to both the art of clipping plants into shapes and the shaped plants themselves. First used in 1592, it derives from the Latin *Opus topiarium*, a term used by the Romans to describe their ornamental garden spaces filled with clipped box. Topiary can be sculpted into a huge range of shapes but, of course, columns, arches, spheres, cones and animal shapes are the most traditional. Yew and box, the classic plants associated with topiary, remain the best choices today, but it is possible to topiarise several other species.

Hedges are made up of shrubs or trees grown close together and cut as one to form a screen or boundary. They can be anything between 30cm and 3m high, with different species suited to smaller or larger hedges. Some are clipped tightly while others are left looser to allow for flowering. Wildlife hedges can even be 'laid', a process of partially splitting the stems of young trees so that they can be bent over, interwoven and left to sprout along their length.

◀ Box mounds surround the Lily Pond at Bodysgallen in North Wales.

▼ Long grass contrasts with sharp yew and box topiary at Hinton Ampner, Hampshire.

THE COURTS GARDEN, WILTSHIRE

The Courts Garden is an intimate garden, hidden behind tall hedges in the centre of a village. It is packed with interest, provided by colourful planting schemes, water features, magnificent shrubs and a wide range of clipped hedges and topiary. Although the garden is only four acres, each path presents a new and exhilarating view with exciting contrasts between large, architectural forms and ebullient planting.

The topiary and hedges play an important role, adding a wonderful, three-dimensional quality to an otherwise level site. The topiary structures vary in size, shape, colour and texture and include traditional spheres, cones and columns of box and yew, umbrellas of crab apple and silver pear and an arch of holly, as well as organic, bulging mounds of box. The range of hedges is also inspiring, with beech, holly, yew, laurel, box, berberis and rosemary. Some are clipped into perfect crescents or dead-straight walls. Others are shaped to represent the folds of linen or clouds floating above bare trunks.

PLANTS WITH PERSONALITY

Entering the garden through a gate, visitors are funnelled towards the house along a narrow pathway, flanked by pleached lime trees. Approaching the front door, they are greeted by four box sculptures which are the Head Gardener Paul Alexander's favourite. In the 1940s, these would have been conventional box balls in wooden

▲ Curvaceous and quirky topiary at The Courts Garden includes these lopsided Irish yew.

◤ The Sundial Garden with crescent-shaped hedge, clipped silver pear and topiary forms.

planters but, decades on, they have morphed into something much more interesting. Bursting out of their pots and rooting into the ground between the paving slabs, they have grown large and unruly but, rather than continually reining them back into balls, Paul and his team shape them gently to bring out the unique and curvaceous forms they are asking to become.

▲ A spiral form sculpted from an overgrown box bush.

◤ The curve of an Irish yew frames a view towards the house.

Paul loves the imperfect curves and lopsided tops evolving on some of the topiary, seeing them as signs that the plants are 'rebelling against our training to express their individuality'. But he knows that beauty lies in their contrast with the perfect forms elsewhere and so he is a stickler for keeping these crisp. He uses battery-powered hedge trimmers for almost all the pruning as they are light and sharp, making quick work of hedges and more complicated shapes. Having pruned these features for ten years now, Paul is usually able to follow existing lines, but for ultra-straight edges and perfectly flat tops he advises gardeners to use canes and string as a guide. To create topiary shapes from scratch, he recommends starting with a metal frame, which will look nice and architectural for several years before the plant fills it in.

HEDGE-TRIMMING

Hedge-trimming at The Courts Garden starts in early summer and continues through until autumn, ensuring everything is cut at least once in a year. Ideally, quick-growing species such as box get two cuts, one in late May or early June and another in July or August. Paul times these cuts to ensure the tender regrowth that emerges soon after pruning the box is not hit by late spring or early autumn frosts. The yew is slower growing and the team can often wait until August or early September to prune it. A single prune at this time is ideal for many of the hedges, including beech and holly, and will usually leave them looking neat for the rest of the year.

Because some of the shapes are really old, renovation pruning is necessary. In recent years Paul has tackled the yew crescents, cutting one side one year, the other side the next and finally the top. This

▲ Soft planting contrasts with crisp topiary and hedges.

staged approach lessens the impact on the plants and ensures that regeneration of each side has begun before the next side is hit. Hard-pruned hedges can look shockingly bare for a few months, but yew regenerates remarkably well. In the next few years Paul must tackle the huge Irish yew columns flanking a narrow path as they have not been renovated for over 20 years. Irish yews (*Taxus baccata* 'Fastigiata') are naturally upright but, to exaggerate this and prevent branches flopping out, mature specimens are encircled with loops of wire to hold the centres together and provide a structure onto which to tie the outer branches. Paul knows how to untie them and remove bare wood inside before wrapping them up again, but he is afraid that he will have to lose some of the highly characterful, lopsided tops that have evolved on these specimens. No doubt they will fight back and become quirky again in future years.

BOX BLIGHT

In 2014 Paul and his team found the dreaded box blight on some of their hedges. Not wanting to risk this spreading to other parts of the garden, they removed all the affected plants and their roots. They now spray the remaining box hedges with a specially formulated plant tonic containing a range of nutrients and trace elements, including copper, and so far have not experienced any more problems.

Being cautious, Paul plans not to buy in any new box plants to avoid reintroducing the disease and is researching alternatives should he need to replace box hedges in the future. He says some other suitable species, such as *Ilex crenata*, have the advantage of being faster-growing than box and he is happy to experiment with them if necessary.

DESIGNING WITH TOPIARY AND HEDGES

Topiary is an eye-catching addition to many gardens, providing year-round structure, creating focal points and accentuating corners or entrances. Simple mounds of clipped box, yew or pittosporum among other planting suit a garden of almost any style, whereas grand features like pairs of lollipops or spirals are usually best reserved for more formal situations, such as either side of a front door. Sculpting a dull privet bush into a classical or quirky form instantly gives your garden new character, while adding a potted box ball to a paved area greens it up in style.

Hedges are dependable features of many gardens, either forming the boundary to the whole site or a division between areas. They can provide shelter and privacy without adding hard lines and can also screen utility areas, roads or neighbouring gardens. They do take up far more space than a fence – and provide fewer planting opportunities beneath them – but in return you get a mass of green, possibly flowers and fruit, and you are also providing nesting places for birds. Added to this, the role of hedges in urban spaces is understood to be increasingly important: their dense vegetation helps to capture pollutants and clean the air. For those wanting more than just a green wall, evergreen hedges can be

◀ This unusual hedge provides the benefits of a boundary and the character of topiary.

pruned into undulating shapes or geometric patterns to provide the interest of topiary while still retaining a screening effect.

PLANT SELECTION

Hedges are usually a long-term investment, so it's worth doing plenty of research to find species that meet your needs and will thrive in your garden. Start with the fundamentals. Is the site soggy, free-draining or somewhere in between? Will the hedge receive sun or be in shade for all or part of the day? What height do you need it to reach? Do you want it to be evergreen or deciduous and do you plan to keep it tightly clipped or loose, perhaps with a flush of flowers? The leaf colour and texture of hedging plants is also worth exploring – you may be surprised at the very different effects provided by matt-textured conifers versus glossy, light-reflective foliage, or bright green leaves versus deep dark ones.

While a mix of species is perfect for country hedges, in gardens one type which will grow at the same rate usually looks best. Fast-growing species such as cherry laurel and western red cedar are very popular – but once they are established, they will continue to grow fast and require a lot of trimming each year.

With topiary, the choice of suitable plants is more limited as success usually requires small-leaved, evergreen species which readily re-shoot when clipped. For anyone seeking an instant effect, it is possible to buy a range of topiary pieces shaped and ready for display, especially if you seek out a specialist supplier. However, if you're happy to wait, it is fun and far more affordable to create your own, either growing them from young plants or – if you are brave – sculpting them from mature shrubs in the garden.

Plants for topiary

Box is undoubtedly the most versatile species for topiary, but a handful of other species also tolerate being shaped into complex forms, namely *Lonicera ligustrina* var. *yunnanensis*, common privet, Japanese holly and yew.

For fairly simple, rounded forms the choice is wider. Try native holly, bay, myrtle, *Phillyrea angustifolia*, laurel, white cedar, *Pittosporum tenuifolium*, *Viburnum tinus* and *Choisya × dewitteana* 'Aztec Pearl'. It's very hard to keep these species small and compact, so for low mounds try naturally small plants such as *Sarcococca confusa*, *Euonymus fortunei*, *Hebe*

PLEACHING

A handful of deciduous trees can be used to form 'hedges on stilts': ideal for planting beneath a wall to create a screen above it. Hornbeam and lime are most commonly used. Trained well, the branches will often fuse together, creating an especially architectural effect.

◀ A box spiral in a pot makes a highly architectural garden feature.

▶ A range of evergreen hedges can be seen at the magical garden of Plas yn Rhiw on the Llŷn Peninsula.

as well. Sage and rosemary are more tolerant of heavy soil than lavender; *Teucrium chamaedrys* and *T.* × *lucidrys* are neat and less vigorous than box, sending fewer roots into the beds; *Euonymus fortunei* 'Silver Queen' has bright variegation; hebes and potentillas offer pretty flowers; and spiky berberis can be used to keep people and pets away.

'Green Globe' or *Pittosporum tenuifolium* 'Tom Thumb' and 'Golf Ball'.

Deciduous plants including berberis and field maple can also be shaped into mounds, columns or even umbrellas, but their twiggy structure is not much to look at in winter. Beech and hornbeam work better than others, as their habit of retaining dead leaves over winter gives them lasting presence.

Plants for edging

Low hedges surrounding beds are a feature of many garden styles: grand formal parterres, Arts and Crafts gardens, potagers and even cottage gardens. They are a practical way of keeping people to paths, protecting beds and providing permanent structure in a garden.

Box and lavender are the most traditional edging plants, but many other species work just

ALTERNATIVES TO BOX

Common box and the dwarf form *Buxus sempervirens* 'Suffruticosa', which have been used as edging for centuries, are both prone to a debilitating disease known as box blight, as well as the destructive box tree caterpillar. Japanese box (*Buxus microphylla*) is less susceptible to blight, but for anyone wanting the traditional look without any risk, try *Ilex crenata* 'Dark Green' or 'Green Hedger' (shown above), *Lonicera ligustrina* var. *yunnanensis* 'Maigrün' or *Euonymus japonicus* 'Microphyllus'.

CLOUD PRUNING

Cloud pruning is the art of shaping trees so that their foliage forms cloud-like mounds at the ends of clear branches. It is a tradition originating in Japan and known as *niwaki*. Cloud-pruned trees can be bought ready-made: the large ones are very expensive but smaller pom-poms are also available. Common species to use for cloud pruning and pom-poms include Japanese holly, Japanese privet, juniper and pine. Daring gardeners who sculpt clouds from existing shrubs and trees have success with many other species such as holly, *Viburnum tinus, Osmanthus delavayii, Phillyrea latifolia* and holm oak.

Evergreens for hedging

For blocking out views of the road or unsightly buildings, a medium to large, evergreen hedge is often needed. Such hedges provide a permanent backdrop to other planting and green up a space when all else is bare in winter.

In addition to box and yew, there are a number of evergreen shrubs that form a dense hedge which can be kept clipped tight for a neat, structural effect. These include:

- *Elaeagnus* × *submacrophylla* can have silver or variegated leaves, is fast-growing and tolerant of most soils and salt-laden coastal winds.
- *Griselinia littoralis* also tolerates coastal sites, but needs free-draining soil and is best grown in the south of the UK. It can be kept narrow and has glossy, vivid green leaves.
- *Ilex aquifolium* (common holly) can be green or variegated, has berries in winter and grows slowly.

- *Ligustrum ovalifolium* (common privet) tolerates most soils, is healthy and grows fast.
- *Lonicera ligustrina* var. *yunnanensis* has small, dark green leaves, is tolerant of most soils and is fast-growing.
- *Phillyrea angustifolia* has elegant foliage, but needs a sunny, relatively sheltered spot.
- *Pittosporum tenuifolium* makes a light, elegant hedge, but needs a mild, sunny spot with free-draining soil.
- *Prunus lusitanica* (Portugal laurel) is fast-growing and shade-tolerant, with large glossy leaves that are more graceful than either cherry laurel (*Prunus laurocerasus*) or spotted laurel (*Aucuba japonica*).

FLOWERING EVERGREEN HEDGES

For looser evergreen hedges that are left to flower before pruning, there is a huge amount of choice.

◄ **Berberis darwinii** and **B. × stenophylla** are unfussy about soil conditions and fast-growing, with yellow or orange flowers followed by copious berries.

◄ **Choisya ternata** is fast-growing, with elegant, glossy leaves and wonderfully scented, white flowers borne in spring and autumn.

◄ **Hypericum × hidcoteense** 'Hidcote' is very hardy, fast growing and unfussy about soil or shade, but has jolly, yellow flowers for months.

◄ **Pyracanthas** have vicious thorns, but make up for this by being unfussy about soil conditions or shade and bearing masses of flowers, followed by yellow or orange berries.

◄ **Cotoneaster franchetii** and **C. simonsii** can be kept clipped into tight hedges, but still bear pretty flowers and a profusion of berries. They are usually evergreen but may lose leaves in a harsh winter.

◄ **Escallonias** are ideal for a sunny site and tolerate salty coastal winds. There are a number of cultivars with pretty pink or white flowers.

◄ **Osmanthus × burkwoodii** is slow-growing and a little fussy about drainage and shelter, but rewards you with very neat, glossy leaves and scented, spring flowers.

◄ **Ceanothus** 'Skylark' has glossy, dense foliage and brilliant blue flowers in summer and will make a dazzling hedge in a sunny, sheltered position.

◀ Redwings may visit gardens in winter.

▼ Beech hedging retains its rust-coloured autumn leaves throughout winter.

WILDLIFE HEDGES

Traditional, thick native hedges with a mix of species including hazel and blackthorn grow fast and can look quite messy between cuts, so they are best suited to large country gardens. For smaller spaces, a wildlife-friendly mixed hedge can still be created using a single row of the least vigorous native species, such as holly, field maple, hawthorn and guelder rose. Avoid wild rose and blackthorn, which are very thorny and unpleasant to handle. You can alternate the species you plant, group them into threes, or just plant randomly.

Deciduous shrubs for hedging

Deciduous hedges provide wonderful seasonal variation, from bright, tender new leaves and flowers to mature leaves, berries and autumn colour. Even in winter their dense twiggy structures can still act as screens. The best species to use are those which will respond to pruning with bushy growth. Shrubs like weigelas and mock orange, which become bare without strategic pruning, should not be used in hedges as repeatedly pruning the top and sides will result in congested and bare, woody centres (which look ugly in winter), sparse foliage on top, and few flowers in summer.

The very best deciduous hedges for neat boundaries are beech and hornbeam, both of which keep their old foliage through winter. Beech has the nicer foliage, but won't tolerate heavy or wet soils as well as hornbeam. If you like purple leaves, then purple beech or spiky *Berberis thunbergii ergii* f. *atropurpurea and B. × ottawensis* f. *purpurea* 'Superba' are effective. For autumn colour, field maple is exceptional and for a profusion of flowers try flowering currant, hawthorn or *Rosa rugosa*.

PLANTING HEDGES AND TOPIARY

Planting shrubs for hedging and topiary is pretty straightforward, but ensuring your soil is fertile and moisture retentive, and that plant roots are not dry or congested, will make all the difference in how quickly and evenly plants develop.

As with any shrubs or trees, topiary should be planted in well-prepared soil where there is not too much competition from nearby plants. Ensure that plant roots are buried at the right depth (just above where the roots flare out from the main stem) and mulch around them after planting. Stake tall plants to anchor the roots and prevent them from moving in the wind. Topiary is well suited to growing in containers, but do use a loam-based compost to keep plants healthy in the same pot for several years. Normal multipurpose compost will break down over time and lose its water and nutrient-holding abilities.

HOW TO PLANT HEDGES

Deciduous hedging plants are best planted when they are dormant in winter. They are usually bought bareroot at this time, meaning they have been lifted out of the soil where they were growing and sent out directly. Bareroot plants are affordable, they have big, strong root systems, are often grown using less fertiliser and water, are lighter to transport, and avoid the

need for plastic pots. Evergreens are not usually available as bareroot plants because they do not have a dormant period during which they can be lifted and transported without major disturbance. They can be bought root-balled or in containers year-round, but are best planted between October and April.

Bareroot hedging plants are usually one, two or three years old and are sold by height. Container plants are usually sold by height and pot size. While it's tempting to buy the biggest specimens you can afford for instant effect, smaller ones often establish better and are good value for money. Hedging suppliers will advise on the optimum spacing for the species and size of plant you are buying: three per square metre is fairly typical, but for small edging plants it may be twice this density.

Site preparation

To prepare an area for planting a hedge, mark out the line representing the middle of the hedge and clear about 30cm either side (wider if you are going for a thicker screen made of two staggered rows). If the soil is heavily compacted, you can dig it over. If it is impoverished (for example following

---

CONIFERS

Popular, cheap and very fast-growing Lawson's cypress (*Chamaecyparis lawsoniana*) and Leyland cypress (× *Cuprocyparis leylandii*) need regular pruning to keep them in check. If this is missed and they exceed the height you want, they cannot be reined back easily as hard pruning creates bald areas, which don't tend to green up. Better options are western red cedar (*Thuja plicata*) and white cedar 'Brabant' (*T. occidentalis* 'Brabant'), which are also fast growing, plus slower-growing Japanese red cedar (*Cryptomeria japonica*), all of which tolerate hard pruning.

UNDERPLANTING HEDGES

Once a hedge is established, the ground beneath it will become dry and shaded in summer. Fortunately, there are a number of ground-cover plants that will tolerate these conditions, including bulbs such as snowdrops, winter aconites and wood anemones, and perennials *Geranium macrorrhizum*, brunneras, epimediums, vincas, violets and many ferns. Use large groups of the same plants and repeat them for a unified effect.

the removal of a previous hedge), incorporate some well-rotted manure or garden compost. Otherwise, simply fork out weeds, roots and large stones and roughly level the soil prior to planting.

Planting

Smaller plants will be easy to plant individually along the line, digging holes with a trowel, or even just creating slits with a spade and slipping small, bareroot plants into them. For larger plants, it may be easier to dig out a trench all along the hedge line, position the plants – spreading out their roots if necessary – and then backfill. Most bundles of bareroot plants will contain some weaker specimens with few side shoots and small roots. This is no problem, but it's worth alternating them with more vigorous-looking plants for an evenly growing hedge. Many people choose to add a fertiliser and mycorrhizal fungi among the roots, but neither are crucial. As with other woody plants, it is important to firm the

soil gently around the roots with your feet, mulch with a layer of well-rotted manure or garden compost, and water in any prolonged periods without rain until they are established.

Low fencing on one side of a hedge can be useful for keeping pests out and pets in, until the hedge thickens sufficiently, but do this only if really necessary – such barriers will also prevent welcome guests like hedgehogs moving easily between your garden and the next.

PRUNING HEDGES AND TOPIARY

There are three types of pruning for hedges and topiary: formative pruning to establish a good shape, annual trimming to maintain it, and hard pruning to renovate old plants if needed. Formative and renovation pruning, which stimulate growth, are best done in winter for deciduous plants and in spring for evergreens. Annual trimming to keep plants in check is better done in summer.

A wide range of birds use garden hedges for nesting and may be nest building, laying eggs or rearing young from the end of February right through until the end of July. To avoid disturbing them, do your winter pruning before this time and summer pruning afterwards. If pruning within this time-window is needed, watch the hedge carefully for signs of bird activity beforehand and proceed only if you are confident there are no birds nesting.

FORMATIVE PRUNING

Formative pruning of young hedges usually involves trimming back long side shoots, to encourage bushiness, while leaving the tops unpruned, to allow plants to grow up and reach their desired height. One exception to this is hawthorn, which can be bare at the base and benefits from being cut down by half upon planting and again by about a quarter the following winter.

▲ Small topiary forms can be easily pruned
with shears.

PRUNING TOOLS

Sharp, clean secateurs or shears are usually
enough for formative pruning. Hedge
trimmers may be preferable for annual
trimming and loppers, a pruning saw
or even a chainsaw may be needed for
renovation. Hedge trimmers could be
petrol-, electric- or battery-powered. With
plug-in ones, take care that the cable is
positioned over your shoulder and out of
the way and always plug it into a circuit
breaker. With petrol-powered ones, read
the user guide supplied with the product
and take breaks as necessary. It's always
wise to wear goggles and thick gloves.

If you have tall hedges, it is unwise to
cut them from a conventional step ladder.
Instead, explore whether long-reach or
extendable-pole hedge trimmers could
allow you to cut comfortably from the
ground or invest in a wheeled platform,
platform ladder or tripod ladder, all of
which make working at height far safer.
For small topiary in pots, lifting them onto
a low table so that they are at waist height
can make pruning more comfortable.

Formative pruning of topiary is a little more
complicated and creating an elaborate shape will
take several years. As parts of the plant reach the
frame or desired size, lightly clip them to encourage
bushiness. Where you need a section to grow long,
perhaps to form the tail of a peacock, leave this
unpruned until it reaches the desired length. If
you are using a frame, it will act as an invaluable
guide and you can even tie shoots to it with string,
persuading them into the positions you want them.
If you don't have a frame, a few thick wires pushed
into the soil or compost, threaded through the
structure and bent into position can help, especially

for training stems horizontally. Any shoots growing
where bare stems are wanted should be removed
at their bases as soon as possible to save the plants
wasting energy on them.

ANNUAL TRIMMING

Once hedges and topiary reach the dimensions you
want, annual trimming is critical to keep them in
check. If this trimming is missed, stems become
woody and far harder to prune and lower parts
can become sparse. The ideal width at which to
maintain a typical garden boundary hedge is about
60cm with a height of 1.2–2m; anything taller

can cast shade and be a nuisance for neighbours. It's traditional to shape a medium-sized or large hedge with a 'batter', where it is a little wider at the bottom and tapering towards the top, thereby allowing light to reach the sides and snow to slide off. The top can be flat or curved, as you prefer.

Topiary and non-flowering hedges are best trimmed between late May and the end of summer, as needed (and depending on the presence of birds). Fast-growing species such as privet and *Lonicera ligustrina* var. *yunnanensis* may need two or three cuts during this period to keep them looking good. Less vigorous species such as holly, yew and beech may need only one in late summer, to last right through the year.

For flowering hedges, trimming needs to be timed to avoid cutting off potential flowers. For most species, including choisyas, escallonias and flowering currants, this would be straight after flowering in summer. If they carry lovely berries, such as cotoneasters and pyracanthas, you can delay trimming until winter, when you and the wildlife have been able to enjoy them. Roses and fuchsias, which flower on new stems, can be pruned in early spring. Very early-flowering evergreens, such as osmanthus, should not be trimmed until well into spring.

A sharp finish

For formal hedges or angular forms, you may wish to use canes and string to act as guides. Even simply using canes pushed into the ground to reach the desired height can help you to create a flat top. With topiary, you may be working to a frame or pruning freestyle. Either way, work slowly and stand back often, checking from all sides. When cutting flat surfaces, try to keep the blades of the shears or hedge trimmer parallel to ensure a level cut. When using hedge trimmers, upward sweeping motions from the bottom of the hedge work best, using the whole length of the blade and allowing the cut foliage to fall away. If you are using shears or a hedge trimmer for smaller curves and intricate details, you

will find it easiest to use just the tips of the blades for this type of work.

After trimming it's usually necessary to tap, rake or pick over the hedge or topiary to remove any cut debris lodged on top. This may result in a few uncut branches reappearing, which can be removed with shears or secateurs. Any rough or very visible cuts can also be tidied up with secateurs.

After cutting, topiary and hedges may have some browning where leaves have been sliced through and shrivel in the wind and sun. This is particularly unattractive on large-leaved plants such as laurel and you may wish to tidy them up a bit with hand shears or secateurs. However, all will recover naturally, often looking their best about six weeks later once a flush of new leaves has just appeared.

LAVENDER HEDGES

Lavender hedges commonly get rather leggy at the base and do not respond to hard pruning. To keep them bushy for as many years as possible, prune them straight after flowering, cutting off at least 3cm of the foliage as well as the flower stalks. If you prefer to leave the seed heads for goldfinches, prune in spring instead, just as the lavender starts growing; trim off a little foliage as well as any dead flower stalks.

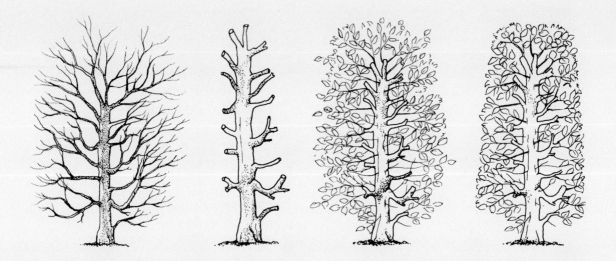

RENOVATION PRUNING

Many gardeners will inherit a hedge which has far outgrown the space intended and is casting a lot of shade. Fortunately, most species used for hedging will respond well to very hard pruning, either back to the height you want or right back to the base to start the hedge off again. If you are only reducing the hedge, rather than cutting it to the base, remember to cut about 20cm more than the eventual height and width you want, in order to leave space for new growth.

Species most likely to bounce back from hard pruning are beech, hornbeam, hawthorn, privet, box, holly, hypericums and laurel. The few that won't readily reshoot from old woody stems include hebes, lavender, ceanothus, Leyland cypresses and Lawson's cypresses. Old leggy hedges of these species usually need to be removed and replaced.

For valuable plants such as big yew hedges or those which may be old and weak, the impact of renovation can be lessened by doing one side each year. Feeding and mulching in the year before can also help to build up their strength. If strong new shoots don't appear within a year after pruning, it may be best to give up and replace the hedge altogether.

After hard pruning, it's a good idea to give the hedge a boost: feed in spring with granular fertiliser or chicken-manure pellets scattered over the root area and follow this with a thick mulch of well-rotted manure or garden compost to hold in moisture and deter weeds.

Topiary that has been neglected for a few years can also be hard pruned. Healthy specimens may respond to being cut right back and started again, but a less risky approach on simple shapes would be to hard prune one side each year (as with yew hedges). For complicated shapes that have lost their form, it may be safest simply to trim the green, bushy parts and gently shape them into whatever form is possible.

KEEPING HEDGES AND TOPIARY HEALTHY

As with all the plants, the key to healthy hedges and topiary is good care to prevent stress and addressing problems as soon as they are spotted.

Once established, hedges and topiary planted in the ground need little routine care besides pruning. Completely thorough weeding of hedges is not even necessary as most can support a few species at their base, but do remove vigorous weeds such as ivy, brambles and bindweed, which will steal light and water. Mulching every few years keeps a hedge looking tidy and deters weeds but isn't critical, especially for a deciduous hedge where leaves

are left to break down at the base of the hedge naturally. Feeding is also not usually necessary with established hedges on fertile soil.

Topiary in pots is more demanding, needing regular watering as well as liquid feeding two or three times each summer. Aim to repot plants into bigger containers every two or three years. When you reach a very large pot size and don't want to go bigger, you can tip the plant out, knock off the old compost, trim some of the roots and put it back in the same container in fresh, loam-based compost. In the years you don't repot, removing a few centimetres of compost from the top and replacing it with fresh compost can give plants a boost.

PESTS, DISEASES AND OTHER PROBLEMS

The shrubs and trees that make up hedges may incur a number of problems, ranging from fairly superficial pest or weather damage, affecting the foliage, to physical injury or disease, weakening roots and main stems. The most common serious diseases which result in the death of a hedge are honey fungus and phytophthora root rot. (For more information, see 'Shrub and tree problems', pp.150–51.)

New pests and diseases such as box tree caterpillar usually arrive in the UK on imported plants, so it is important to buy from reputable sources, keep an eye on new arrivals, and grow your own wherever this is possible.

Brown patches on conifers

Brown patches sometimes appear in summer on popular hedging conifers: Leyland cypress, Lawson's cypress and western red cedar. This can be caused by a number of factors including aphids, fungal disease and over-zealous pruning. If pruning is the problem, new growth should soon cover it up and can be tied in over a bare patch. If the cause is aphids, close inspection should reveal old aphid skins and black sooty mould growing where the aphids have left a sugary secretion. If this is the problem, sprays are available but, to be effective, you will need to monitor the hedge and only spray when live aphids are present. If the brown patches extend to whole branches or plants, they may well be fungal. There is no treatment available and if problems worsen, plants or whole hedges may ultimately need to be removed.

Holes in laurel leaves

Interestingly, the various pests and diseases that affect cherry laurels often result in the same thing: a hole forming in the leaf. If the holes are irregularly shaped with brown edges, the problem is likely to be powdery mildew. If the leaves are peppered with 'shot-holes', the problem is more likely to be a leaf-spot fungus or bacterial disease. The best course of action is to wait and see if changing weather conditions and plant growth relieve the problem; if not, there are fungicides which may tackle powdery mildew and leaf spot, but bacterial disease has no treatment and will need to be tolerated.

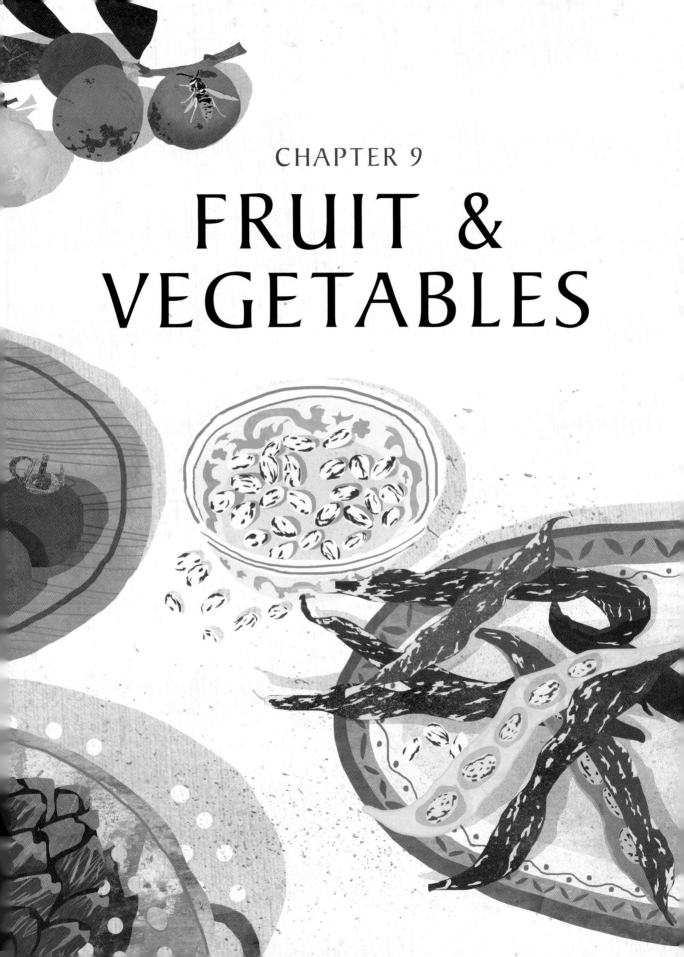

CHAPTER 9

FRUIT & VEGETABLES

THE ORIGINS OF OUR CROPS

Humans have been domesticating plants for food for over 10,000 years, gradually transforming tough wild species into succulent crops. Wild brassicas, for example, are bitter and stringy but from them descend today's cabbages, kales, cauliflowers, broccoli and Brussels sprouts. Most wild strawberries are tiny and time-consuming to harvest, but centuries of hybridisation have given us the large, delicious fruits we know today.

Iron-age Britons would have cultivated a few wild plants, picked hedgerow fruits and nuts, and farmed wheat, barley and peas. The Roman invasion extended the options significantly, bringing onions, leeks, garlic, apples, pears, plums and more. During the Middle Ages the range increased further, with monasteries cultivating extensive gardens and Norman settlers bringing horticultural skills from mainland Europe.

The Tudor period saw a surge of interest in horticulture and the discovery of new, exotic plants such as tomatoes, potatoes and runner beans from Central and South America. During the next 400 years, the kitchen gardens of large homes became bigger and increasingly elaborate. All manner of techniques were deployed to grow the widest possible range of crops, including heated walls, pineapple pits and – eventually – glasshouses.

Of course, few ordinary people were the beneficiaries of these impressive kitchen gardens and most grew what they could in their own small plots. A tradition of partial self-sufficiency was widespread right into the 20th century, with most private gardens having an area given over to vegetables and space set aside in towns for allotments. After the Second World War, growing your own gradually became the exception rather than the norm. Today, very few people rely on their own produce, but many take great pleasure in growing a few things for the table.

▶ The Potager at Woolbeding Gardens, West Sussex.

GROWING EDIBLE PLANTS

For success with fruit and vegetables, you ideally need a sunny, open position. Most average garden soils are suitable, but the ground needs to be thoroughly cleared of weeds and must not be dominated by tree roots. Most crops can be sown directly into the soil, although a sunny windowsill or greenhouse is great for starting off tender plants.

Vegetable gardens can take up as much time as you are able to give them, but even just two or three hours each week can yield satisfying results. The busiest period is spring when most seeds are sown. Weeding and watering need to be done throughout the summer and soil preparation is needed from autumn. Harvesting usually starts in May and continues through until October, possibly longer if you grow hardy, over-wintering crops such as leeks, kale or purple sprouting broccoli. March to May is often known as the 'hungry gap' because little is available for harvesting. Keen gardeners grow crops that can be stored for use in this period.

LAMB HOUSE, EAST SUSSEX

At the top of a steep cobbled street in the small seaside town of Rye is an elegant red-brick town house with a garden enclosed by tall walls. Originally built for James Lamb, a wealthy merchant and local politician, this house has been home to a number of renowned writers, including Henry James, E. F. Benson and Rumer Godden.

Plans of the site dating from 1878 show a well-laid-out garden with an area set aside for vegetables. Records from Henry James's time a few years later mention that he employed a gardener and took great pride in the crops from his garden, some of which were entered in local horticultural shows.

National Trust gardeners have recently taken on the maintenance of the garden and have converted part of the old vegetable garden into a small but prolific growing space. It's a lovely spot, sheltered by walls and hedges and it benefits from the sun throughout the day.

RENOVATING THE SITE

Work to convert the 10 × 15m area into a vegetable garden began in late autumn of 2017 with a view to producing a range of crops the following year. The area was thick with weeds, including brambles, docks and bindweed, so all the top growth needed to be cut down. Before strimming, the team had a good look for any shrubs and perennials that were worth keeping and found a blackcurrant, redcurrant, gooseberry and a large clump of horseradish. These were all lifted in order to clear their roots of bindweed, and the fruit bushes were cut down by half and put into pots ready for replanting.

After the weeds were cut to the ground, the whole area was dug deeply, each forkful being picked over for bindweed and other invasive roots. This can be back-breaking work but, luckily for the team, the soil here is quite light and easy to work, having been cultivated for over 150 years.

Small paving slabs found in the garden were used to make a simple path bisecting the space and four manageably sized beds were marked out. The beds were edged with boards sunk just above ground level to retain the soil and accommodate a thick layer of garden compost to be added annually. A layout like this is neat, attractive and allows for much of the work, such as hoeing and watering, to be done from paths without standing on the soil and compacting it.

At the end of the winter, the fruit bushes were returned to one of the square beds, along with some autumn-fruiting raspberries and three rhubarb plants. The horseradish was planted beside a bay tree in one corner of the plot, and another perennial crop – globe artichokes – were planted nearby.

MAINTAINING THE VEGETABLE PATCH

The garden is now up and running and, like many typical vegetable plots, must be managed with

▲ The Kitchen Garden at Lamb House in August.

limited time. The gardener and a dedicated team of volunteers work at Lamb House only one day per week and estimate they collectively spend about six hours on the vegetable patch. Watering is the main challenge: crops are vulnerable when they are first sown or planted but, once established, should last a week without water. A water butt on the small shed provides most of what is needed.

Within 18 months of starting the vegetable garden and moving the soft fruit, the bushes were yielding prolifically. The team have also grown potatoes, climbing beans, peas, carrots, onions, leeks, parsnips, beetroot, lettuce, celeriac and squashes, pumpkins and marrows. Many of the crops are sown directly into the soil, but any that need to be started off under glass are grown in the greenhouse at nearby Sissinghurst and planted out at Lamb House only at the end of spring.

Typical rows in this garden are 3.5m long and run north to south so that the tall crops don't shade the smaller ones. The squashes, pumpkins and marrows are especially rewarding as they need little maintenance but are very high-yielding.

Deterring pests

As in many town gardens, pigeons are a huge pest, not only eating crops but also pecking at young seedlings and dislodging them so that they wilt in the sun. For this reason, the team avoid growing cabbages and other related brassicas and put netting over peas and all their soft fruit. To avoid the netting becoming tangled with thorny crops and pea tendrils, it is strung over hazel poles topped with small terracotta pots, which look very attractive.

To ward against carrot root flies, carrots are sown in between rows of onions in the hope the smell

◀▼▶ Fruit and vegetables ready to harvest in the vegetable garden in August 2019.

of the onions will disguise the carrots. Flowers including Mexican marigolds and nasturtiums are also planted among crops to attract pollinating insects and distract pests. To reduce the likelihood of crop-specific issues building up in the soil, different crops are grown in different beds each year.

TIPS FROM THE LAMB HOUSE TEAM

- Get on top of the weeds before you begin to sow and plant. If you have bindweed or ground elder, delay planting until summer so that any roots left in the soil have a chance to show themselves and be removed.
- Add as much organic matter as you can lay your hands on, be it garden compost, well-rotted manure or spent mushroom compost. It will open up heavy soil, add body to light soil and provide nutrients to boost your crops.
- Slugs can cause terminal damage to a row of young seedlings. Try beer traps to tempt them away from precious plants, rather than resorting to poison.
- Start with quick and easy crops to set you on your way: radishes, beetroot, rocket and chard can all be sown directly where they are to crop and are reliable in most conditions.
- Don't be too eager to sow your first seeds in spring. Cold soil is the enemy of success, whereas warm soil allows for quick germination and growth.

PLANNING YOUR PLOT

While vegetable patches are best situated in the sunniest part of your garden, if this is spoken for, areas in light shade can also be productive. Set aside the largest space you can spare and feel able to manage. A traditional allotment of 250sq. m was once intended to feed a family of four, but many people today grow vegetables and fruit on only a third of this area.

It is practical to split plots into raised beds so that growing areas are defined, and foot traffic is kept to the paths in between. Brick and stone walls, new sleepers or wooden boards are all suitable materials for making raised beds, the last being by far the most affordable and simple to use (see overleaf). Avoid reclaimed sleepers, which may be heavily impregnated with creosote. Beds edged in box hedging look nice but the plants cast shade and their roots take up valuable space.

Open plots with long rows are also perfectly suitable for growing vegetables, but temporary paths across will be needed every few rows to give access for maintenance and harvesting. These can be made of stepping stones or simply trodden earth.

Group permanent plants together so you won't disturb their roots when preparing the soil for annual crops, and tuck them into a corner so they do not cast shade across the beds. Some, such as artichokes, will need a very sunny position, but much soft fruit is tolerant of light shade.

If you have south- or west-facing fences at the edges of your garden, these can be used for growing climbing beans and peas or training fruit. Most gardeners also create temporary structures for annual climbing plants – these look attractive but should be designed so they don't block the light from other crops. That said, a little shade in high summer can be beneficial for some crops, such as spinach and lettuce, keeping them cooler on hot days.

▶ A vegetable plot can be colourful and attractive, as well as productive.

MAKING RAISED BEDS

Raised beds are usually only about 1.5m wide so you can comfortably reach into the middle of them from either side. They can be as long as you want, but 2m is most comfortable for walking around without being tempted to take a shortcut across them. Paths need to be at least 60cm wide, to allow for kneeling on them, or pushing wheelbarrows along them. To make raised beds, 20cm-wide gravel boards (designed to go at the base of fences), attached to 5 × 5cm square stakes, are ideal. Both will have been pressured-treated with wood preservative (tanalised) to make them last even with soil against them.

STEP 1 Start by marking out your bed with string and canes. You may need to use a set square to ensure your corners are right angles. If you need to clear weeds or lift turf and dig the soil, do it now.

STEP 2 Knock posts into each corner, ensuring that they stay vertical. For beds over 2m long, it's best to put in additional posts along the long sides. The posts can be knocked in so they are the height of the gravel board or higher to provide support for netting. Place a spirit level on a board between posts to check they are the same height.

STEP 3 Cut the boards to the length needed and screw them onto the front of the corner posts, again using a spirit level to check levels. If you have dug the base incorporate garden compost or manure into the soil and rake it level; if not, simply cover the ground with a mix of topsoil and compost (this should smother any turf and prevent it re-growing).

PREPARING THE SOIL

Traditional preparation of soil for growing vegetables includes stripping turf and removing weeds, digging as deeply as possible and incorporating a 5–10cm thick layer of well-rotted manure or garden compost. Preparing clay soil is ideally done in the autumn, so that it is left exposed to frost and rain and is crumbly by spring, but sandy soils can be worked anytime through autumn, winter and spring. Digging like this can be very satisfying and, on sandy or loamy soils, will quickly give you a bed that's ready to sow into. However, it is back-breaking work, especially on heavy soil, and you may wish to save your strength for other tasks.

To convert weedy ground or turf into growing space without digging, cover it with some cardboard and a 10–20cm layer of garden compost or manure. You'll find this is easiest if the bed is edged with boards to hold in the compost. The cardboard and mulch will block out the light from any weeds, causing them to die back, but water will still able to permeate through and plants grown in the mulch layer will eventually root down through the cardboard and into the soil below. What you mulch with and how thick the layer is will dictate what you can grow in the first year. Courgettes, pumpkins, squash and potatoes will all be very happy growing in rough compost or rich manure and can easily send their roots down into the soil below. Crops such as carrots and salads, which are sown directly into the bed from seed, will do well only if the mulch layer is very crumbly and well-composted. They also need the mulch layer to be at least 15cm deep, as they may not be able to penetrate the compacted soil beneath. In the second year you should be able to grow whatever you want as the compost will have broken down, the cardboard will have rotted away and worms have begun to amalgamate the mulch and soil layers.

Maintaining the soil structure

Traditionally, vegetable beds are dug each year with another layer of well-rotted manure or garden compost forked in or spread on the surface. Digging allows for the thorough removal of weeds and debris from previous crops and the opportunity to break up clay, but it can also weaken the soil structure and disturb soil micro-organisms. Advocates of a 'no-dig' approach believe it is better to simply hand weed as necessary and mulch the surface, leaving the soil beneath undisturbed.

For most gardeners, a mix of techniques makes sense, depending on what type of soil you have, how well established your plot is, the quality and quantity of compost available, and what you're planning to grow. There is certainly no point in digging soils that are already friable and weed-free. At the very least, digging less often reduces the heartbreak of slicing through earthworms (which – contrary to popular myth – do not regrow). Conversely, sowing seed into a surface layer of rather lumpy garden compost is unlikely to yield great results so, if this is all you have, it may be best to fork the compost into the surface of the soil and use a rake to make a fine tilth.

(For details about making compost, see 'Looking after the soil', pp.247–48.)

▲ Well-prepared soil in long raised beds.

Green manures

If you can't produce enough garden compost and don't have a reliable source of manure, you can improve your soil by growing green manures. These are crops grown on bare ground either in spring or autumn and dug into the soil a few months later, to enrich it and improve the structure. The best, such as crimson clover (*Trifolium incarnatum*), have the ability to fix nitrogen from the air into nodules on their roots, which is then released into the soil as they break down. It's wise to cut down and dig in green-manure plants before they set seed, otherwise you may have seedlings appearing next year when you are growing other crops. On clay soils, bear in mind that deep-rooting, over-wintering green manures, such as grazing rye, can be hard work to dig in.

CHOOSING WHAT TO GROW

Traditionally, large vegetable plots often include a small fruit tree or two, a few soft-fruit bushes, a patch of raspberries, a strawberry bed, some perennial vegetables such as artichokes or asparagus, and lots of annual vegetables. However, there is no reason to grow this traditional selection of crops: focus your time and space on the things you really want to eat.

Gardeners with small plots could abandon currants and staple crops like potatoes, onions and cabbages, which take up a lot of space and are cheap to buy in the shops. Instead, they could concentrate on prolific cut-and-come-again salads, climbing beans and herbs. People with very little time might consider focusing on low-maintenance crops that yield harvests over several months with minimal effort; autumn-fruiting raspberries, chard and courgettes are good options. Winter squashes are also very useful as they can be stored for many months.

Once you have decided which crops to grow, the choice of varieties is endless. Look for those recommended for flavour, high yields and disease-

CROP ROTATION

Crop rotation involves grouping vegetables according to how closely related they are, or how similar their needs are, and planning to grow each group in a different bed each year. Cabbages and all their brassica relations are grown in one bed, for example, while root crops are grouped together as they have broadly similar requirements. This is thought to avoid a build-up of pests and diseases specific to certain crops and ensure plants with different rooting depths and nutrient needs grow in fresh soil each year.

Close adherence to this technique is not necessary in small plots, where most pests and diseases can easily travel a short distance between beds. It is better to focus your planning time on how much room each crop needs, how long it will be in the ground and what can follow it, in order to maximise the space you have. The elements of crop rotation to factor in as your plot develops are that potatoes break up the soil nicely and beans and peas add nitrogen, so it's good to grow them in different places each year for the benefit of the next crops. Also, if you do find a root disease such as club root on brassicas, don't grow them in the same spot again for several years.

resistance rather than the largest, firmest or best-looking, which have usually been bred for show or retail. You'll find many vegetables, including beetroot, carrots and courgettes, come in a wider range of colours than in the shops. When making your choices, it may be useful to know that 'F1' after a variety name relates to the plant breeding process and is often an indication of the quality and reliability of the seed. 'AGM' stands for the RHS Award of Garden Merit, proof that the variety has done well in trials held by the Royal Horticultural Society (RHS).

GROWING VEGETABLES AND HERBS

Most of the vegetables and herbs we grow are annuals or biennials, which are sown in spring for harvesting that year or early the following year. A few are perennials which can be established for cropping over several years.

▲ Lettuce 'Merveille des Quatre Saisons'

▲ Rainbow chard

ANNUAL CROPS

Annual vegetables originating from colder parts of the world, including cabbages, peas, broad beans, lettuces, carrots, parsnips, radishes and beetroot, can be sown directly into the ground in spring as the soil begins to warm up. Some of them can be started off in small pots in an unheated greenhouse if you prefer, but most root crops develop best if sown directly into the soil. Leeks are unusual in that they need to be started off in a bed of fine soil or a large pot of compost and then moved out into their final positions in midsummer once they are pencil thick. At this stage they can be dropped into 15cm-deep holes to exclude light from their stems, making them white and tasty.

Plants from warmer parts of the world, such as runner and French beans, tomatoes, cucumbers, courgettes and squashes, cannot be planted into the soil until the risk of frost has passed. These can be direct sown at the end of May but, for earlier crops, they are usually started off in pots indoors,

▲ Sugar pea 'Bijou'

▲ Climbing French bean 'Borlotto Lingua di Fuoco'

▲ Courgette 'Gold Rush'

▲ Flat-leaved parsley

or bought in as small plants. (For advice about raising seedlings under glass, see 'Sowing seeds under glass', p.208.)

Leafy annual and biennial herbs such as flat-leaved parsley, coriander and dill are well worth treating like vegetables and sowing in short rows, so that you have enough for cooking. Coriander can be fussy and run to seed at the slightest sign of stress, but parsley is very reliable. A spring sowing of parsley should give you plentiful harvests all summer and can even be over-wintered for a few spring harvests before it runs to seed. Parsley can take a while to germinate from seed so you can buy them as small plants (even supermarket plants split into a few sections should establish well). Parsley planted in spring often runs to seed in late summer; planted in summer it may last through the winter and into the following spring.

Direct-sowing seeds

There is no need to memorise the timings, sowing depths and spacings required by different crops; this advice is always on the seed packet.

If the recommended time-window for sowing outdoors is wide, bear in mind the earliest months are usually right for sheltered southerly gardens while the later months are best for northerly, exposed gardens or cold springs. You can touch the soil with your hands and feel whether it still has a chill to it or buy a soil thermometer. No seeds will germinate under 7°C. Clay soils, which hold a lot of moisture, are likely to warm up much slower than free-draining, sandy soils.

Rake the soil to a fine tilth before starting, removing any lumps from the surface. For best results do this when the soil is still moist after rain. To achieve nice straight lines, use a board the length of your required row; mark measurements on it as a guide for spacing seeds or plants evenly. To make a shallow drill for sowing fine seeds, simply run your finger alongside the board. For a deeper drill or trench, use a hoe or the corner of a rake. For a big open plot with rows longer than a board, use a string line tied to canes to mark the drill. When scattering seeds into the drill, tip a small amount into your hand first and don't return wet or dirty seeds to a packet, as they may deteriorate when you put them away for next year.

PERENNIAL CROPS

Many of our most popular herbs, including rosemary, sage, chives, thyme and mint, are long-lived plants that can be harvested for many months of the year in return for minimal care. These classics are all well worth making space for in even the smallest plots. Other long-lived herbs to try include sorrel, tarragon, lovage and fennel. One plant of each is usually enough for seasoning meals.

Only a couple of popular vegetables are perennials which, once established, will provide harvests for years: asparagus and globe artichokes. Asparagus is quite fussy and needs a raised bed of free-draining soil but, once you succeed, it will give you harvests in April and May for more than a decade. Globe artichokes are attractive and delicious but take up a lot of space and offer only small, intermittent harvests.

Jerusalem artichoke is a less common perennial vegetable that is very easy to grow, but worth being wary of. The plants have charming flowers, but can

▲ Freshly-picked rosemary, sage, basil and chives.

▶ Good King Henry (*Chenopodium bonus-henricus*).

▶▶ Whitecurrants are a form of redcurrant with the same flavour, requiring the same cultivation.

SUCCESSIONAL SOWING

Some quick-growing crops, such as salads, spinach and coriander, need to be eaten when their leaves are young and tender, before they begin to flower. To avoid having a glut followed by a shortage, sow them in short rows every three or four weeks.

Successional sowing is not necessary with most root crops, which sit in the ground well and can be harvested at different sizes, or fruiting crops such as courgettes and beans, which you pick every few days. However, since young plants are usually tastier and more prolific than mature ones, a second sowing of carrots, French beans and even courgettes and outdoor cucumbers, can yield great results, with harvests later into autumn. These later sowings have the advantage of being able to go into gaps from which earlier crops such as broad beans and peas have been cleared.

be quite invasive and the edible tubers quickly lose their appeal. Perhaps more deserving of space are the perennial kales (sometimes known as tree collards), which can be picked over for greens almost all year round. The young leaves are tasty and nutritious, if not as tender as annual kale. Other less common perennials to experiment with include tree onions, perennial leeks, sea kale and good King Henry, which gives spinach-like leaves for many months of the year.

GROWING FRUIT

Most vegetable plots or allotments have space for some soft fruit, which is relatively easy to grow, hardy and thrives in typical garden soils. Fruit trees are usually too large for average allotments or vegetable plots, but many can be trained flat against a wall or fence to take up less space.

CURRANTS AND GOOSEBERRIES

Blackcurrants, redcurrants, white currants and gooseberries can all be planted in partial shade if necessary, freeing up your sunniest spots for other plants. For those with very limited space, redcurrants, white currants and gooseberries can be trained as cordons or fans. Their only disadvantage is that the fruit is tart and usually needs cooking with lots of sugar. To get round this, try plump, sweet varieties of blackcurrant such as 'Big Ben' and allow gooseberries to ripen fully on the bush so that they become slightly soft before harvesting.

Pruning currants and gooseberries is fairly straightforward. Blackcurrants fruit best on young wood, so about one third of old stems are cut to the ground each winter, leaving younger (usually paler) wood to fruit. Redcurrants, white currants and gooseberries fruit on slightly riper wood, so can be allowed to develop a bushy framework of about five

main, upright stems and then have all the side shoots growing from this framework, shortened by at least half each year. For bushes, this is best done in winter but for plants trained as fans or cordons, summer pruning is needed too. In June, shorten the laterals to about five leaves, letting in light to ripen the fruit; then in winter you can shorten them further, to create spurs with only a couple of buds, which will carry flowers and fruit the following summer.

The jostaberry (shown below) is a very vigorous hybrid between a currant and a gooseberry. Treat these plants as you would blackcurrants, but accept they'll take up a lot more space. Blueberries are increasingly popular, but need to be grown in acid soil or large pots of loam-based ericaceous compost.

Autumn-fruiting raspberries in autumn, winter, and spring.

Summer-fruiting raspberries in summer, autumn, and spring.

RASPBERRIES

Raspberries are hardy, prolific and fairly problem-free. They will tolerate partial shade, but fruit best in a sunny position. There are two types: summer-fruiting varieties, such as 'Tulameen' and 'Glen Ample', grow long canes one year and then produce fruit on them the next summer; autumn-fruiting varieties, such as 'Polka' and 'Autumn Bliss', produce shorter canes that fruit at the top in the same year, usually from August until October.

Summer-fruiting varieties need a stout system of posts and wires to support the long canes over autumn and winter, ready for fruiting the following year. After fruiting, these canes are cut down and young ones that have formed are trained in their place. Autumn-fruiting raspberries don't need to be tied in individually, but the patch may require some wire around it for support in summer. Canes of this type are cut down completely in February and new canes grow up soon afterwards to replace them. If you have space for only one type, go for autumn-fruiting raspberries as pruning is so straightforward and fruiting goes on for several months. It is even possible to get them to fruit a little in summer by cutting some of the stems back by half in February instead of completely down to the ground.

STRAWBERRIES

Freshly picked strawberries can be infinitely better than anything available in the shops, especially if you track down varieties known for their flavour, such as 'Royal Sovereign' and 'Gariguette'. Most classic varieties fruit for a brief window in June but, to extend the season, try perpetual types, such as the delicious 'Mara des Bois', as well. These are not as prolific in June but will produce more fruit intermittently through the entire summer.

Late summer is the ideal time to plant strawberries, which can be ordered from specialist fruit nurseries. Young plants will establish quickly over the autumn and fruit the following year.

If you plant in spring, it's best to pick off the flowers that year so that they make better plants the following year. Strawberries like soil that has been enriched with plenty of garden compost or well-rotted manure and do need watering in dry spells.

Remove the leaves of summer-fruiting plants after fruiting has finished. The baby plants which form on long runners can be planted into gaps, removed or potted up to make new plants. Established plants tend to last about four years before they need to be replaced, less if they are perpetuals.

RHUBARB

Rhubarb is tough and reliable and can be grown in any soil in sun or light shade, producing stems that can be harvested from early spring onwards. It is best planted as dormant crowns in autumn and given plenty of space.

Don't start harvesting the stems or forcing them under cloches until the plant has been in the ground for at least a year and is well established. If flowers begin to form, cut them off to encourage the plant to put its energy into new stems instead.

TRAINED APPLES AND PEARS

Apples and pears lend themselves exceptionally well to training, with cordons and espaliers being the most popular forms. Cordons are created by buying young trees (known as feathered maidens) in winter, planting them at a 45-degree angle and shortening all their side shoots to a couple of buds, creating spurs. Espaliers take longer to establish as tiers need to be built up one at a time, but the finished effect is well worth it. Once you have achieved the desired shape, pruning is straightforward – you simply shorten all the new growth back to short spurs in late summer.

When choosing varieties, look for ones you can't get in the shops. If possible, visit an autumn apple day near you to taste many types and find out which you like best. There are dessert, or eating, apples for

▶ Harvested rhubarb and a terracotta rhubarb forcing pot at Felbrigg Hall in Norfolk.

▼ An espaliered apple tree in the Walled Garden at Erddig in North Wales.

eating fresh and cooking apples, which are sharp and usually make good purée. They may ripen early, late or in the middle of the season and some will store through winter. If you have space for only one, stick with an eating apple as you can always cook with them or go for a dual-purpose apple (which can be eaten fresh or cooked) such as 'Blenheim Orange'. Popular sweet and crisp eating apples include 'Kidd's Orange Red', 'Falstaff', 'Laxton's Fortune' and 'Sunset.'

Most apples need a different variety growing within 18m that flowers at the same time, so that bees can carry pollen between them, allowing for cross-pollination and fruit to set. If you don't have neighbours with apple trees, try to plant two varieties from the same pollination group. Pollination groups simply relate to the timing of when each tree flowers. Many popular varieties are in Flowering Group 3. Crab apples also act as good pollination partners for many varieties.

Apples and pears are always produced by grafting the selected variety onto the roots of a different plant that controls how vigorous it will be. For pears the rootstock options are limited to Quince A, which is suitable for most gardens, or Quince C for small, trained forms on fertile soil. With apples there are far more choices: MM106 is good for a small tree, while M9 or M26 are best for trained forms. M27 is the most dwarfing, but suitable only for very small forms, such as step-overs, and only in gardens with fertile soil.

CHERRY, PEACH, NECTARINE AND APRICOT FANS

Peaches, nectarines and apricots all flower very early, at a time when their blossom can easily be damaged by frost, so they do best trained against a sheltered, sunny wall. For peaches and nectarines, this has the advantage of allowing you to create a protective structure to keep them dry through winter and

PLUMS AND DAMSONS

Plums and damsons are hard to train into restricted forms and best allowed to grow into lovely garden trees that need minimal pruning. There is a wide range suitable for eating fresh, cooking and making jam. Particularly tasty varieties include 'Oullins Gage', 'Avalon' and 'Mirabelle de Nancy'. Most are partially self-fertile, but do best with other varieties nearby. The rootstock choice is either 'Saint Julian A', which is suitable for most purposes, or semi-dwarfing 'Pixy'.

◀ Plums ready for harvesting at Monk's House in East Sussex.

◀◀ A fan-trained fruit tree at Tyntesfield in Somerset.

◀◀◀ Apples on display for Apple Day at Barrington Court in Somerset.

spring when the fungal spores of peach leaf curl disease are in the air. Sweet cherries always need netting from birds and fan-training them flat against a wall makes this easier.

Fan-training of sweet cherries and apricots is an art that involves establishing a framework of about six main branches fanned out against the wall and shortening growth back to spurs in summer. The new growth is often very vigorous and spurs cannot be cut as short as with apples and pears, so it can be a challenge to keep them neat and flat.

Fan-training of peaches and nectarines (and also sour cherries) involves a different technique. They fruit best on young wood so pruning involves cutting out whole fruited sections and tying in new stems to fruit the next year. It's skilled work, but does mean they can be kept flat.

For all stone fruit, pruning needs to be carried out in spring and summer to avoid plants becoming diseased.

GROWING CROPS IN CONTAINERS

If you don't have anywhere to make vegetable beds or your soil is contaminated and unsuitable for growing food, you can still grow some fruit, vegetable and herbs in large containers. You can repurpose old tanks or troughs, or buy raised planters especially designed for growing vegetables (ideal for those with limited mobility).

Really large containers are best filled with a mix of soil and compost, or a loam-based compost. Smaller pots can simply be filled with peat-free multipurpose compost, but this will need to be changed each year as it loses structure and nutrients over time.

Plants growing in containers will need a lot of extra watering, so do try to have a water butt nearby. Organic liquid feeds in summer when the nutrients in the compost have been used up may also be necessary.

▲ Chillies of all types can be easily grown in containers.

Container crops to try

- **Herbs:** rosemary, sage, mint, chives, basil and parsley.
- **Fruit:** strawberries, blueberries and a small apple or cherry.
- **Vegetables:** lettuces, rocket, French beans, chillies, tomatoes and stump-rooted carrots.

MAINTAINING A HEALTHY PLOT

Fruit and vegetables are prone to pests and diseases. The keys to avoiding the worst problems are: having fertile, moisture-retentive soil; ensuring that plants aren't put under stress; protecting susceptible crops from pests; and understanding how to break the cycles of common problems.

AVOIDING PLANT STRESS

When growing plants from seed, try to ensure that seedlings experience the minimal amount of stress possible. If they are started off in seed trays, prick them out into individual pots as soon as they are large enough to handle. If they are in small pots and their roots can be seen through the holes at the bottom, pot them on promptly. Protect tender crops from cold weather, harden them off properly and consider using cloches or fleece if temperatures plummet soon after they've been planted out.

Regular hoeing and hand-weeding of beds is also important. Catch weeds before they mature to stop them competing with your crops for nutrients and light. Thinning out seedlings early and spacing crops according to the recommendations on the seed packets is strongly advised, so that plants don't compete with each other.

Watering is very important. It is best to sow seeds or plant out seedlings when the ground is moist after rain. If this is not possible, water the ground thoroughly before sowing or after planting. Seeds and newly germinated seedlings will need watering little and often in warm, dry weather if the soil surface dries out. However, once plants start growing, it is better to water them thoroughly but less frequently. Never just wet the surface as this discourages plant roots from growing down deeply. Once mature, plants such as courgettes benefit from a large watering can full about once a week in dry weather; plants in pots will need daily watering. Peas and beans may cope with minimal water while they are growing but will fruit more and for longer if watered when flowering and producing pods.

PROTECTION FROM PESTS

There can be no underplaying the war that vegetable gardeners wage with pests or the heartbreak of losing a precious row of seedlings overnight, but don't let it put you off. Slugs and snails are some of the worst enemies but simply keeping your vegetable patch tidy with minimal hiding places can make a big difference. Slugs and snails will lurk in long grass or crevices during dry spells, ready to strike vulnerable crops in damp conditions. Wooden edging and wood chip and gravel paths will slow them down.

One of the best weapons you can have is knowing which crops are vulnerable to attack from specific pests and putting up barriers beforehand. Carrot root fly, flea beetle and leek moth can be excluded by covering seedlings with a tent of fleece. These pests are common on allotment sites so this is well worth doing; however, they may not reach your garden so you could risk a year without protection.

Brassicas (cabbages, cauliflowers, kales and so on) are especially prone to pests, including whitefly and cabbage-white butterflies in summer and pigeons in winter. To keep pigeons off, pea netting draped between canes over the top of the crop is

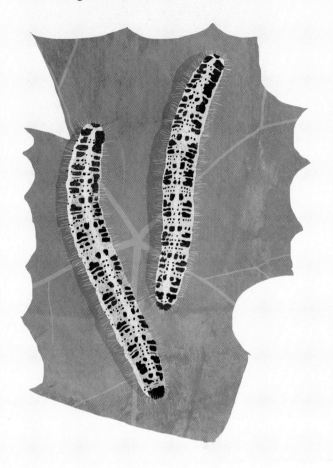

▼ Caterpillars of the large white butterfly, often known as the cabbage white.

BOLTING

Bolting is when a plant starts to flower before it is meant to. For leafy plants, such as lettuces, parsley, spinach and coriander, it is a problem as they stop producing edible leaves. Tips for preventing this are to direct-sow plants so that they don't experience the stress of being transplanted; avoid sowing too early as cold spells in spring can trigger flowering in summer; keep plants well-watered; and harvest them as soon as they are ready. For oriental salad leaves, sowing after midsummer is also helpful as the shortening days reduce the likelihood of bolting.

▲ A tomato plant infected with late blight.

▶ A cat wanders through the allotments at Monk's House in East Sussex.

POTATO AND TOMATO BLIGHT

Late blight affects potatoes and tomatoes, causing wilt and dark-brown patches on leaves, stems and fruit. Its spores are carried on moist air and are so prevalent across the UK in summer that they always seem to find their way to your crop, usually after a few days of warm, wet weather in mid- to late summer. Tomatoes grown indoors are safe but, for those without a greenhouse, it's wise to try resistant varieties or grow plants against a sunny wall with a canopy constructed above to keep them dry. This trick may not work for the whole season, especially in a wet summer, but it may keep the disease away long enough for you to get a harvest.

sufficient, but it takes a more closely woven net to stop cabbage-white butterflies laying their eggs, and tiny whiteflies need something really fine, such as horticultural fleece or enviromesh. If you don't want to invest in netting, you can try picking cabbage white caterpillars off the leaves, live with the damage, or simply grow something else.

If your soft fruit is not enclosed by a fruit cage, you can protect individual plants from birds with netting hung over canes. They can peck through the net, so pull it taut and well clear of the fruit. Brightly coloured fruits such as redcurrants, strawberries and cherries are usually the most popular, so make sure that you net the fruit before it begins to colour up.

BREAKING PEST AND DISEASE CYCLES

If and when problems occur, consider how to break the life cycle of the pest or disease rather than just how to treat it. For example, collecting rotten, shrivelled fruit hanging on a fruit tree over winter can stop fungal spores emerging in spring and reinfecting the plant. Removing a juniper plant that acts as a winter host for pear rust can eliminate the problem on your pear trees, as the fungus needs both species to survive.

If you do use a pesticide, for example to control scale insects on fruit plants, time the treatment to when eggs have recently hatched (usually late June to July), rather than targeting the tough eggs and

adults. Always read the label carefully for the most efficient use of any product and never spray plants when they are flowering, as you are likely to poison other insects, many of which are pollinators and a source of food for birds and small mammals.

Timing of sowing and planting can also help to avoid problems. Autumn-sown broad beans are often very well advanced in spring and fruit strongly before blackfly gets hold. Early potatoes are generally harvested before the spores of potato blight arrive.

If you have been unlucky enough to encounter fungal diseases that live in the soil and have no available treatments, such as onion white rot (which affects onions, garlic, leeks and other alliums), it's best to avoid growing any of these crops in the same patch or nearby again for several years.

Some vegetable varieties have been bred for resistance to certain diseases: potato 'Carolus', for example, has high resistance to potato blight; cabbages 'Kilaxy', 'Kilazol' and 'Kilaton' are less affected by club root; and courgette 'Defender' resists powdery mildew longer than other varieties.

CHAPTER 10

GROWING UNDER GLASS

THE EVOLUTION OF GLASSHOUSES

The first structures for growing plants indoors in the UK were built in the 17th century. They were called greenhouses or conservatories because they were designed to conserve evergreens, such as bay, myrtle and citrus, during harsh winter weather. As the fashion for exotics increased during the 18th century, it led to the construction of orangeries especially for citrus growing and smaller hot houses for pineapples and other tropical plants. These early buildings were not the sun-filled glasshouses we know today. Instead, they had partially solid walls and roofs and were heated by charcoal fires, making them dim and smoky.

During the 19th century, improvements in technology and an increasingly scientific approach to horticulture allowed for the design of far more complex structures, glazed all over with only thin metal or wooden bars. As the price of glass decreased and hot-water heating systems were finessed, a wide range of specialist structures was developed for growing specific crops, including figs, vines, tomatoes and peaches. Soon, every large kitchen garden had a range of well-stocked glasshouses and gardeners who worked round the clock to keep stoves burning and crops tended.

In the 20th century, as the wealth of the grand estates declined and garden teams diminished in size, many of these elaborate glasshouses were abandoned. At the same time, however, the popularity of gardening as a hobby had grown and many more people could now afford their own small domestic greenhouses.

Today the cost of heating, combined with the availability of cheap, imported fruit and vegetables and the mass production of seedlings for sale in garden centres, means fewer gardeners rely on greenhouses. But, for those with enough time and space, the opportunity to raise seedlings, grow indoor crops and overwinter tender plants will surely never go out of fashion.

▶ A restored 19th-century orangery at Peckover in Cambridgeshire.

SHOULD YOU GET A GREENHOUSE?

The decision about whether to install a greenhouse very much depends on your garden and gardening ambitions. If you need only to raise a few seedlings or overwinter a couple of tender plants, a sunny windowsill or cold frame may be sufficient. If you wish to raise a wide range of vegetables and flowers from seed, grow exotics or have a reliable crop of tomatoes, a greenhouse is a must.

All greenhouses need an open position that receives sun for at least six hours a day in summer. To be useful they are usually 1.3 × 1.8m or more. They come in a wide range of designs with very different price tags, from a basic aluminium structure to timber or painted metal made to look like traditional designs that can be seen at many National Trust gardens. Whichever you choose, they all provide a microclimate within your garden that will extend the growing season and open up your horticultural horizons.

GODDARDS HOUSE
AND GARDEN, YORK

The greenhouse at Goddards was built in the
late 1920s or early 1930s by one of the great
manufacturers of the time: W. Richardson & Co.
Ltd of Darlington. It was erected by the Terry
family, local chocolate magnates who designed
and built Goddards House as their family home
and lived there from 1927 for over 50 years. The
greenhouse would have played a critical role in
the running of the garden, supplying vegetable
plants for the kitchen plots and ornamentals for
the flowerbeds, as well as providing a place to
store plants removed from display.

Being wooden, the greenhouse requires regular
repairs and repainting and was last fully restored
by the National Trust in 2010. It repays the
effort in full, being highly attractive and a hub of
activity where Senior Gardener Tom Longridge

and his team of volunteers raise vegetable
seedlings, grow tomatoes, cucumbers and
grapes, overwinter tender plants and produce
bedding for the top terrace. The greenhouse is
open to visitors from February until December
and has permanent displays of pelargoniums,
aeoniums and a wonderful hardy palm
(*Trachycarpus fortunei*).

THE GREENHOUSE LAYOUT

The greenhouse is 5.2m wide by 12.4m long
and is set on waist-high brick walls, which are
excellent for retaining heat. It is divided into two
areas with an internal doorway; behind them is a
small brick potting shed. The whole greenhouse
was originally kept warm by a coal fire, which
heated hot-water pipes that ran around the
internal walls and through the adjacent cold
frames. The brick flue still stands and adds to the

▲ A partition within the greenhouse separates it into two spaces which can be heated differently.

◀ The entrance to the greenhouse is framed with troughs of flowers.

▶ The chimney from the original coal-fired heating system.

◢ Vines are trained inside the eaves.

character of the greenhouse. Today, to conserve energy, only the back section is kept frost-free, using a thermostatic electric-fan heater. The home-made potting bench has heated cables running beneath it, which provide warmth for germinating seeds and rooting cuttings.

Water is collected from the roof from where it flows into large, galvanised tanks inside the structure and two water butts outside – very convenient for watering and for helping to keep the greenhouse environment humid on hot days. Along each side are windows and in the roof are several vents, allowing for excellent ventilation. The front door is also kept open as much as possible in summer and Tom has stopped using sticky traps, as he wants as many insects as possible to come into the greenhouse to pollinate plants and eat aphid pests. He even grows flowers such as French marigolds to lure them in.

Plants in the greenhouse

Most of the floor area is smooth concrete, ideal for keeping it clean, but there are one or two beds for permanent plants to be rooted directly into the soil. The largest of these is in the middle of the first section where the palm greets you, surrounded by lush cannas and dahlias. Planted in the ground in the back section are two vines, 'Black Hamburg' and 'Regent', the stems of which are trained along the eaves to give a very graceful and timeless feel and dapple the light on sunny days.

Raised on benches around the walls of the first section are many more ornamentals for display. These are sitting on a few centimetres of water-retaining clay granules above a membrane, making them far less dependent on watering. Either side of the front door are deep troughs filled to bursting with startling, South African pineapple lilies.

In the second section, where the heated bench and vines are, Tom grows bedding plants for display on the terraces around the house and annual crops such as tomatoes, cucumbers and basil for use in the tea-room.

A YEAR IN THE GREENHOUSE

- **January and February** A telescopic brush is used to wash down the structure inside and out, keeping glass, paintwork and putty free of algae. Inside, surfaces and pots are also washed with a mild antiseptic solution to keep the whole area disease-free. Once completed, seed sowing begins with the earliest crops, such as peas, sweet peas, broad beans and peppers.

- **March and April** Dahlias that have been overwintered in the greenhouse are 'woken up' with light and water. There is much more seed sowing, including of basil, celeriac, leeks, tomatoes, runner beans, squashes, cucumbers and courgettes. Potted plants are repotted with fresh compost.

- **May and June** The greenhouse is overflowing with plants and as much as possible is moved into the cold frames to harden off ready for planting out. This makes space for cuttings of wallflowers, penstemons and germander to be taken. New growth on vines needs training in and tomatoes are guided up strings. Signs of pests and diseases must be monitored carefully as the weather warms up and weekly liquid feeding of greenhouse crops begins.

- **July and August** Everything needs constant watering and the concrete floors are sprayed with water two or three times on hot days to keep the temperature down and humidity up. Vents and doors are left open as much as possible. Tomatoes and cucumbers are harvested, grapes thinned and ornamental plants past their prime are moved from the display section at the front to rest in the back of the greenhouse.

- **September and October** The grapes are harvested, followed by the last of the tomatoes. Once the cold weather arrives, dahlias and other tender plants from the garden are lifted and brought inside.

- **November and December** Vines are hard-pruned and the canna is cut down. All tender plants in pots are moved to the second section, where watering is reduced and the heater put on a frost-free setting.

◀ A gardener damps down the floor on a hot day.

◀◀ Pelargoniums and other ornamentals on a bench lined with clay granules.

◣ Cucumber 'Socrates' does well in the glasshouse.

▼ Clary sage is easy to grow and has lovely, colourful bracts.

EASIEST GREENHOUSE CROPS

Tom recommends indoor cucumbers such as 'Socrates' and 'Emilie', which all do well for him at Goddards. Cucumbers are best out of scorching sun and like humidity and plenty of water. They can be grown in soil, pots or grow bags and trained upwards so that they don't take up too much space. Tom also recommends annual clary sage (*Salvia viridis*) as it is a cheap and easy annual to grow and carries its colourful bracts from June until September. He has been known to grow over 300 seedlings to fill the terraces. He starts seeds off in March and plants them out at the start of June, mixing them among permanent plantings of blue catmint and white penstemons. Mixed packs of clary sage with pink-, white- and blue-painted bracts are widely available, but Tom prefers sowing seeds of varieties with single colours, such as 'Pink Sundae', 'Oxford Blue' and 'White Swan', so that he can arrange them as he wants.

SITING YOUR GREENHOUSE

The most important consideration when looking to site a greenhouse is to try to find somewhere that has little or no shade cast on it from trees, buildings or hills. The worst obstacles are those to the south-east or to due south or south-west: the first blocks that all-important, low-angled spring sunshine and the last causes the sun to be lost early in the afternoon. It is also best to avoid areas that receive a lot of wind, weakening the greenhouse and cooling it in winter. A few, well-placed shrubs can help to reduce the impact of winds.

Orientation clearly affects the amount of sun reaching plants inside. In an open site, positioning it on a north to south orientation so that one long side faces east, to let in the morning sun, while the other faces west, to receive the afternoon sun, is ideal, especially for summer crops, which need as much light as possible. However, the alternative orientation (east to west) has advantages too: the long side facing south will receive maximum sun year-round, while in summer the north side becomes a slightly shadier place for seedlings and cuttings. In many gardens – where one side of the greenhouse needs to be close to a boundary fence or hedge – it may be best to position one long side against a northerly boundary so that the other long side is facing south and forms the main growing area in spring and summer.

Whichever position you go for, ensure that there is comfortable access to the door and around the structure for maintenance, as well as somewhere for a water butt to collect water from the greenhouse roof.

CHOOSING A GREENHOUSE

When you start browsing catalogues, you will see that there is a huge range of greenhouses available, varying in size, materials and design.

Generally speaking, it's best to get the biggest greenhouse you can afford and can fit into your garden, as keen gardeners usually find the range

of plants they want to accommodate just keeps growing and growing!

GREENHOUSE DESIGNS

Most modern greenhouses are free-standing but lean-to styles that can be erected against walls are also available. Lean-tos have the advantage that heat absorbed by the wall during the day is released into the greenhouse at night, helping to maintain an even temperature. Most domestic greenhouses are glazed all the way to their bases, which is good for growing crops at ground level. It is also possible to find highly attractive models that are glazed only part of the way to the ground and stand on a few brick courses, making them slightly warmer.

Small greenhouses need only one door, usually situated on a short side, leaving uninterrupted growing space on the long sides. Inside, a path running through the middle leaves enough width for a bench to sow seeds and take cuttings as well

as space for large plants such as tomatoes and cucumbers. Usually the minimum width for this type is 2m or 2.5m, unless you want a lean-to greenhouse with growing space on one side only. The width of the path should be about 60cm. If you want to bring a wheelbarrow or wheelchair inside, it should be wider and you'll need to ensure that the door is designed without a lip at its base.

The taller your greenhouse, the lighter and more ventilated it will be, with more space for working under the eaves. Greenhouses should ideally have roof vents on either side of the eaves, to allow for sufficient ventilation on hot days.

Greenhouse materials

For the frame, wood is attractive but a challenge to maintain against rain, sunshine, humidity and frost. If you do choose wood, avoid softwood and look for sustainably sourced hardwood. Painted timber will need regular repainting and unpainted frames

▲ A small, aluminium greenhouse in the garden at Budlake Old Post Office at Killerton, Devon.

◤ In this small garden, one end of the timber-framed greenhouse is sited close to the boundary hedge.

usually need treating with preservative. Aluminium is a more durable, low-maintenance option and can be made to look traditional if painted white, green or in other muted tones. Aluminium frames aren't glazed with putty, which saves time during the assembly and in the aftercare.

Horticultural glass is used for glazing most of the structure, as it transmits light well, retains some heat and is inexpensive and long-lasting. Since horticultural glass is thin, toughened glass is best for doors, which are more likely to get cracked. Polycarbonate is sometimes used to glaze structures as it is cheaper than glass, safer where children play and can hold in heat – but has the disadvantages that it does not transmit light well and becomes brittle with age.

◤ Newly germinated seedlings in the greenhouse at Hidcote in Gloucestershire.

◤◤ A thermometer in one of the greenhouses at Tyntesfield in Somerset.

▼ A greenhouse at Llanerchaeron in Ceredigion.

POLYTUNNELS

Where aesthetics aren't important, such as in a vegetable garden that is not visible from the house, a polytunnel is an affordable and less permanent option. Made from plastic sheeting stretched over a frame, they can create a suitably warm, humid growing environment for summer crops and provide a little shelter for winter ones. However, they don't let nearly as much light in as glass, are inefficient to heat and the use of plastic – which may need to be replaced every few years – is not very sustainable.

The greenhouse base

All but the smallest greenhouses need to stand on a base, to create a level surface and provide something to anchor the structure to. While a concrete base is an easy option, paving slabs laid onto a dry mix of sand and cement allow for better drainage. Alternatively, concrete footings just where the frame will be will provide a solid and level surface on which to attach the frame, while keeping the interior open for planting directly into the soil. Whichever base you choose, consult the manufacturers' instructions for the greenhouse you have selected, paying attention to the dimensions and how the structure will be anchored down.

Benches and shelving

Table-height surfaces are crucial for comfortable working, but need to be arranged so that they cast minimal shade on your crops. These benches are known as staging and are often slatted to allow light and air through. It is also possible to buy or make solid-topped staging, with a recess to allow for the installation of heated cables or for irrigation. Such heavy-purpose staging needs to be free-standing so as not to put weight on the greenhouse frame, whereas light staging and shelves that attach to the greenhouse frame are often available as an affordable extra from the manufacturer. The disadvantage of free-standing staging is that the legs take up space underneath, where you may want to store as many plants as possible, but the advantage

COLD FRAMES AND MINI-GREENHOUSES

Cold frames are solid or clear-sided boxes at least 1m wide and 60cm deep, with sloping glass or clear plastic lids. Placed in a sunny position, they provide wind, rain and a little frost protection to all sorts of small plants, especially those grown in the greenhouse, which need a slightly protected environment in spring prior to being planted outdoors. Mini-greenhouses are taller and usually plastic-covered, with shelves which are useful for raising seedlings. Their height also allows for growing one or two aubergines or tomatoes. By placing these structures against a sunny house wall, they can be kept warmer, enabling you to avoid spring and autumn frosts, if not winter ones.

is that you have the option of moving the staging in summer to make space for taller crops. Moveable staging is ideal for a greenhouse where almost all the sun comes from the long, south side, allowing you to grow seedlings on staging there in spring and then have tomatoes filling the same space in summer.

HEATING A GREENHOUSE

Greenhouses are not efficient structures to heat, so the decision about whether to install electricity and use a heater should be considered carefully. An unheated greenhouse provides sufficient protection for many things, including seedlings of hardy and half-hardy plants in spring; tomatoes and cucumbers in summer; cuttings in spring, summer and autumn; and slightly tender plants in winter.

To keep a greenhouse frost-free so that you can confidently overwinter more tender plants and grow on a wider range of plants raised from seed, aim for a minimum temperature of 3°C. The best choice is usually an electric heater with a thermostat plugged into the mains, although solar-powered products are available. For more tender plants, such as citrus, a minimum of 7–10°C during winter is necessary, but this uses a lot of energy and is usually the preserve of specialist growers.

If you do decide to heat your greenhouse, ensure the electrical work is carried out by a qualified electrician and that you use only equipment suitable for the damp, humid atmosphere. Try to restrict the space you heat by sectioning off an area and keeping all the tender plants in there.

SOWING SEEDS UNDER GLASS

While a sunny windowsill in your home is really useful for germinating seeds, if you try to grow seedlings there you may be left with leggy, leaning plants and a shortage of space long before it's time to plant them outdoors. Having a greenhouse with much higher light levels and lower temperatures will enable you to produce stockier, healthier plants in greater quantities.

TIMINGS AND TEMPERATURE

Spring is the traditional time for sowing most seeds, but autumn sowing can give some species a useful head start and take advantage of the greenhouse heat at that time of year. Seed packets will usually advise you on the best months for sowing. If they show a wide range of options, it's worth remembering that the earlier you sow seeds in spring, the more likely it is that they will need extra heat for germinating and even growing on, especially if you live in more northerly parts of the country.

Some crops, such as tomatoes and peppers, need to be started off in February if they are to reach flowering and fruiting size in summer. At this time of year, extra heat will definitely be needed to enable them to germinate and grow on strongly. If you don't have a heat source, it may be better to buy small tomato and pepper plants in mid-spring, when the greenhouse has warmed up. A lot of other annual vegetables, such as courgettes, pumpkins and runner beans, grow very fast. Starting them off early is a mistake, resulting in plants that get too big for their pots long before it's time to plant them outdoors. Wait until mid-April to sow them, by which time even an unheated greenhouse is likely to be warm enough for growing on, and possibly germination too.

Many popular flowers and vegetables, such as cosmos, French marigolds and celeriac, which are usually started off in March, need the extra heat of a heated propagator or sunny windowsill to germinate, but can be moved out to an unheated or frost-free greenhouse soon afterwards and kept there for the remainder of spring, ready for planting out when the risk of frost has passed.

PROPAGATORS

Propagators with lids can hold in warmth and humidity to aid germination of seedlings and rooting of cuttings. For guaranteed results, a heated propagator with an electrical element in its base is very effective, but requires a power source. The most expensive heated propagators have thermostats, which will switch the heat on and off as needed; simpler models will stay on all the time. Since many seeds germinate best at around 21°C and most need the compost to stay above 15°C, it may be best to use your propagator indoors in early spring when greenhouse temperatures are far below that. Ensure that your model has vents to open to avoid excess condensation building up.

▲ Cabbage

▲ Pot marigold

▲ Cornflower

▲ Lettuce

▲ Love-in-a-mist

▲ Peas

▲ Scabious

▲ Sunflower

▲ Sweet pea

HOW TO SOW SEEDS

Sow the seeds in seed trays, modules or individual pots. Pots are ideal for big seeds such as broad beans and courgettes, which grow quickly and prefer not to be disturbed. If you sow two seeds per pot and they both germinate, do make sure you remove one of them so that they don't compete with each other. For small seeds, sprinkling several in a small seed tray or wide, shallow pot rather than sowing them individually saves space on a windowsill or in a propagator. Once seeds have germinated and formed a pair of 'true' leaves, they will need to be gently pricked out and potted up individually to grow on (see illustration below).

Modules are trays made of very small pots and can be a useful compromise, taking up less space than pots but avoiding the root disturbance caused by pricking out. Peat-free, biodegradable fibre pots are another good option for avoiding root disturbance because the whole root ball and pot can be planted out and the pot will break down in the soil as the roots grow.

Fill pots, trays or modules and firm the compost down gently before sowing. Peat-free, multipurpose compost is suitable for most seeds, but may need to be passed through a garden sieve or have lumps picked out by hand, especially if sowing small seeds. Special seed compost, which is very fine-textured and drains well, also yields good results. The depth seeds should be sown at is usually specified on the seed packet: generally

HARDENING OFF SEEDLINGS

Plants grown under glass are usually soft and sappy and need time to acclimatise before being planted outside where they are exposed to wind and greater fluctuations in temperature. This is known as hardening off and is best done by placing them in a cold frame or sunny, sheltered spot during the day for two or three weeks. For the first week or two, either close the lid of the frame at night or, if you are not using a frame, move them back indoors.

speaking, big seeds go deeper while small seeds are covered with a very fine layer of compost, often sieved on like icing sugar. A few species including sweet alyssums and tobacco plants prefer to be on the surface where the light helps them to germinate. After sowing, water pots or trays gently, using a fine rose on your watering can.

TAKING CUTTINGS UNDER GLASS

Most plants have the capacity to form new roots from cut stems, sections of root, or even veins on cut leaves and leaf stalks. Propagating plants from these cuttings is really rewarding, but success depends on using the right technique for the species and caring for them well. Leaf and stem cuttings are vulnerable for several weeks until they have grown roots and begin to function as small

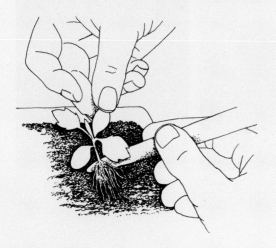

▲ Pelargoniums taken from cuttings in the nursery at Powis Castle, Powys.

plants, so protection inside a greenhouse will really improve your results.

STEM CUTTINGS IN SUMMER

Cuttings taken from stems are referred to as softwood, greenwood and semi-ripe cuttings, depending on the age of the stems being used. Very young, fleshy shoots often have the best capacity to root, but they are especially prone to wilting and rotting, while ripe stems are less vulnerable but usually slower to root.

Summer is a great time to take cuttings from many species including pelargoniums, lavenders, sages, rosemary, fuchsias and everlasting wallflowers. Many of these species are useful for bedding displays but are prone to getting leggy and need frequent replacement, so being able to grow your own is a real advantage.

In mid- to late summer, the warm conditions in a greenhouse enable most cuttings to root quickly without the need for any extra heat and to form decent-sized plants before temperatures and light levels decrease. Hardy plants will be able to stay in an unheated greenhouse over winter while pelargoniums and other tender plants will need it to be kept frost free or warmer.

HOW TO TAKE CUTTINGS OF EVERLASTING WALLFLOWERS

STEP 1 Prepare pots with sieved peat-free, multipurpose compost or special cuttings compost and water them. Select some non-flowering shoots that are soft at the tops, but firm at the bases.

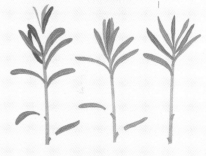

STEP 2 Cut each shoot just below a bud so it is 5–10cm long. Remove the lowest two leaves and pinch off the tip if you can see a flower bud or very soft, new leaves prone to wilting.

STEP 3 Insert the cuttings into individual pots, pushing them down about halfway, so that the remaining leaves are sitting just above the surface of the soil.

STEP 4 Place in a sheltered spot out of direct sun. A shady corner of the greenhouse is ideal. The cuttings will do best if placed in an unheated propagator with a lid or covered by a plastic bag. Check regularly and, if covered, lift the lid to ventilate.

By the following spring, plants should have good roots and plenty of top growth; they can be potted up into bigger containers or planted out in the ground.

FRUIT AND VEGETABLES UNDER GLASS

A greenhouse can extend the range of crops you can grow, but success depends on being able to make a daily or even twice-daily commitment to check on them. In early summer when the nights are cold but the days warm, doors, windows and vents will need to be opened each morning and closed in the evening. In high summer, when nights are reliably warm, this is less important but daily watering becomes critical.

WHAT CROPS TO GROW

Tomatoes are of course the classic choice. Grown in a greenhouse, they usually crop earlier than outdoor ones and keep going longer; the protection from rain also means that they rarely succumb to blight (a fungal disease that decimates outdoor crops). Cucumbers are another popular option: there are good outdoor varieties, but the thinnest-skinned, seedless ones usually need the protection of a greenhouse and flourish in quite humid conditions. Their close relation, the melon, does not thrive outdoors at all in the UK and is well worth growing indoors. Chillies, peppers and aubergines all need warmth too and rarely fruit prolifically outdoors so are a good use of greenhouse space.

In addition to the classic summer crops, you can use the greenhouse for leafy plants almost all year round. Sun-loving basil can be interplanted with tomatoes in summer, pea shoots will do well in spring, and cut-and-come-again salads can be sown right up until autumn (rocket and oriental leaves are especially hardy and may keep growing through winter). In frost-free greenhouses, keen gardeners even plant new potatoes in autumn for a midwinter crop or force mint into growth for winter roasts.

Greenhouse grapevines

For permanent fruiting plants, try home-grown dessert grapes. Traditionally grapes are planted just outside the greenhouse so that their roots stay cool

SUCCESS WITH TOMATOES

- Look for a variety known for its flavour, which can be trained as a single stem (these are known as cordon, indeterminate or vine tomatoes).
- Start the seeds off in February in a heated propagator and grow on seedlings in individual pots in a gently heated greenhouse. Alternatively, buy as plants in April or May.
- Once plants are 15cm tall and starting to produce flowers, plant them in large pots, grow bags or greenhouse border soil, spaced at least 45cm apart (or two per grow bag).
- Create supports with canes or vertical strings anchored into the ground.
- Water daily (don't splash the leaves) to avoid the compost drying out; feed, at least weekly, with a liquid fertiliser from June onwards.
- Pinch out side shoots that form in the axils between the leaf and stem (take care to distinguish between these and flowering shoots, which do not grow from the axils). Pinch out the top of the plant when it reaches near the roof of the greenhouse.
- In high summer, protect the plants from being scorched with some light shading, either painted on the glass or in the form of netting hung over the greenhouse.

▲ Grapes in the greenhouse at Lacock Abbey in Wiltshire.

▲ Colourful ornamentals fill part of the greenhouse at Lacock Abbey.

and moist. The stems grow through a hole at the base of the greenhouse so that they can be trained up inside; here they receive the early warmth needed to break buds and a longer, hotter ripening season for the fruit. If this is not possible, it is fine to plant grapes inside the greenhouse, but always put them into the greenhouse soil – container growing rarely gives them the space and moisture they need. Among the many amazing dessert varieties that simply won't ripen outdoors in the UK is 'Muscat of Alexandria', which is well worth the hours of training, pruning and tying in.

GROWING ORNAMENTALS UNDER GLASS

Greenhouses can also be used for growing and displaying a range of tender plants or for bringing bulbs, such as amaryllis and hyacinths, into flower before taking them into your home for display. To make space for these plants, plenty of shelving is advisable on both the sunny and shadier sides of the greenhouse.

Popular exotics are pelargoniums, aeoniums, agaves, oleanders and lantanas – all of which can be moved outside in their prime in summer and then moved back under glass to keep off the worst of the winter weather. Species that do well under cover all year round include scented pelargoniums, Cape primroses, African violets, kalanchoes and many cacti: some of these enjoy the brightest possible conditions, others prefer dappled shade. Many flowering exotics sold as house or conservatory plants, such as gardenias, gloxinias, hoyas and zantedeschias, will do far better in a greenhouse than in the home, as air circulation and light levels are usually higher. To overwinter them successfully, a minimum of 10°C is usually needed and that's where a heated greenhouse or fairly cool conservatory becomes very useful.

Plants growing permanently in pots will need regular watering, feeding and checking over for pests and diseases. Annual repotting is also important,

ALPINE HOUSES

These are small, usually unheated greenhouses with lots of ventilation that are used for growing and displaying bulbs and alpine plants which, while hardy enough to cope with frost, hate sitting in wet soil through the winter. Alpines offer a magnificent burst of spring colour and many can also be grown in conventional glasshouses, in pots outdoors or planted into very free-draining soil.

either into a larger pot or – once they are large enough – into fresh compost in the same pot after a light root trim. Many bulbs, cacti and succulents may need composts with added grit or sharp sand to improve drainage, while ericaceous compost will be needed for gardenias and other species that naturally grow in acid soils. During repotting, always check root balls for vine-weevil grubs and root aphids and remove any you see.

▲ Tender pelargoniums and succulents overwintering on a greenhouse shelf.

OVERWINTERING PLANTS UNDER GLASS

If your greenhouse is unheated, it can still provide some shelter and protection from cold and wet for slightly tender plants like *Melianthus major*, shrubby salvias, chocolate cosmos and evergreen agapanthus. These are all best grown in pots in most British gardens, so that they can be moved under cover at the end of autumn.

Keeping heated greenhouses frost free or warmer allows you to overwinter a wider range of plants, including pelargoniums, dahlias, cannas, bananas, pineapple lilies, cacti and succulents. To make best use of the heat, block up all spots that may let in a draught (such as louvred vents), insulate the glass with bubble wrap and partition off the smallest possible area to heat. Group plants quite close together, away from cold or damp corners, perhaps

lifting the most vulnerable onto shelves, wrapping them in horticultural fleece or covering with straw.

All overwintering plants do better if stored fairly dry. Fully dormant ones such as dahlia or begonia tubers, or pelargoniums that have been cut hard back, can be kept in completely dry compost to reduce the risk of roots rotting. Others, which are still partly active, such as cannas and evergreen agapanthus, should be kept fractionally moist with very infrequent watering. In a warm greenhouse where plants may continue growing during winter, more regular watering will be needed.

OVERWINTERING DAHLIAS

Dahlias make wonderful summer displays and cut flowers, producing a huge number of blooms. Looked after well, one tuber will multiply each year so that you can keep the same plant for many years and give away sections to friends.

STEP 1 In late October or early November, lift dahlias out of the ground or tip them out of their pots and cut stalks down to about 10–15cm. Knock as much soil off them as you can.

STEP 2 Prop the tubers upside down so that excess moisture drains out of the cut stems. Keep them somewhere dry, such as a greenhouse or shed.

STEP 3 After about two weeks, pack the tubers in pots or trays of dry, peat-free, multipurpose compost. Store in a cool but frost-free place; light is not needed. Check regularly for signs of mould or mouse damage over winter, but do not water.

STEP 4 In March, move the tubers into a sunny position that is kept frost free. If they are in pots, simply water to bring them into growth; if they are packed into trays, pot them up and begin to water.

By May dahlias should be in full growth and ready to harden off prior to planting out, once all chance of frost has passed. Keep a close eye out for slugs and snails.

A HEALTHY GROWING ENVIRONMENT

Maintaining a healthy growing environment inside a greenhouse can be a challenge, requiring daily attention in the growing season and good hygiene year-round.

Although greenhouses are all about capturing sun, do not be fooled into thinking that the more sun the better. The greenhouse effect converts light to heat which gets trapped inside – wonderful for amplifying spring sun, but a potential disaster for crops in summer, few of which can thrive in temperatures above 27°C. A thermometer showing the minimum and maximum temperature that the greenhouse has reached is a wise investment.

CONTROLLING THE ENVIRONMENT

On sunny days, good ventilation is critical. Automatic vents are useful, especially if you are away from home, but can be slow to respond and, as temperatures increase, the door and other manual vents will also need to be opened. Raising the humidity inside the greenhouse by spraying water on hard floor surfaces will help to cool the air. This is known as damping down and is especially beneficial for cucumbers, melons and grapes.

Keeping plants watered will help them to cope with heat. Installing drip irrigation or standing plants on capillary matting can take some of the pressure off, but there is no substitute for regular watering. Insufficient or irregular watering can quickly lead to problems, such as blossom end rot, which causes dark blotches on the undersides of tomatoes.

It may also be necessary to shade the south-facing side and roof slope in the height of summer to reduce temperatures and avoid damage to delicate plant tissues. Netting is ideal for this as it can be easily removed on dull days. Shading paints also work well, but need to be rubbed off in September to take advantage of autumn sun. Specially designed blinds are very attractive but may be costly to install.

CLEANING AND MAINTENANCE

Thorough annual cleaning of the greenhouse is crucial for keeping the glass clear and preventing pest and disease problems from building up. On a mild, dry day in autumn or winter, move all plants outside and then sweep out the greenhouse thoroughly. If you used shading paint, rub this off with a dry cloth. Clean the glass with a long-handled brush and proprietary window cleaner or slightly soapy water, getting in between any overlaps of panes with a plant label or knife. Use this opportunity to check over the greenhouse for rust, rot and cracks and clear the gutters. Oil any moving parts and, if you need to treat or

paint woodwork, do this on a dry, mild day. Wipe down surfaces with a disinfectant or detergent for household or greenhouse use, getting into corners where algae may grow or pests overwinter.

PESTS AND DISEASES

During the year it's important to look out for damage to plants and respond to pest or disease problems promptly because, left unchecked, they can increase rapidly under glass. You can remove a few aphids, scale insects, slugs and snails by hand or, if a plant is infested, it can be moved outside to stop the problem spreading to other plants.

There is also an increasing range of biological controls available to amateur gardeners, whereby an insect predator is released into the greenhouse to tackle a particular pest. The tiny parasitic wasp *Encarsia formosa*, for example, is often far more effective than pesticides at controlling glasshouse whitefly. Research the correct biological control for your situation thoroughly and follow the instructions about timing and temperature for best results.

A number of fungal diseases can occur in greenhouses and spread quickly if plants are too wet or overcrowded, or if the greenhouse is not well ventilated. These can be a problem for small bedding and vegetable plants growing on in spring and with germinating seedlings.

Damping off is a particularly common disease, caused by fungi which either rot seeds before they germinate or cause newly germinated seedlings to collapse. To avoid this, ensure that seeds and seedlings are not sitting around in cold and wet conditions, are not overcrowded or overwatered, and lids are lifted from propagating units so they do not get too humid. Using clean compost, pots, water butts and watering cans also helps to avoid spreading disease.

In greenhouses with beds for planting crops directly into the soil, growing the same crops in the ground year after year can impoverish the

GLASSHOUSE RED SPIDER MITE

This insect is the bane of many greenhouse gardeners' lives. Unlike the harmless velvet mite, which is sometimes seen in gardens (and should not be squashed), spider mites are not bright red and are hard to spot. The tiny mites suck sap from plants, making the foliage mottled, pale and dry. They are very common on cucumbers, tomatoes and aubergines and sometimes leave visible webbing on plants. Maintaining a high humidity and thorough annual cleaning can help to reduce problems with the mite, but once you have it, a well-timed biological control is your best bet.

soil and lead to disease problems. To combat this, consider swapping the topsoil with some from the garden or growing a green manure in between harvesting one crop and planting the next. Peas, beans and clover can fix nitrogen, while mustards are thought to have soil-sterilising properties.

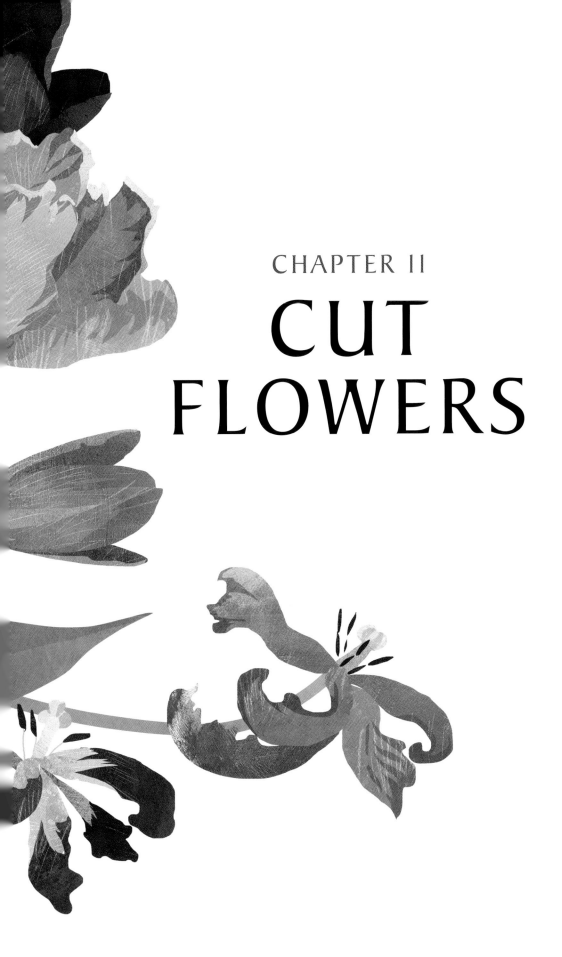

CHAPTER II

CUT FLOWERS

FLORISTRY FASHIONS

Fresh flowers played an important role in medieval Britain; they were used to decorate churches for celebration, mask bad odours in the home and were worn in small, scented bouquets known as nosegays. Many wild flowers would have been collected for this purpose but, by the 16th century, roses, larkspurs, pinks, sweet williams and snapdragons were all being cultivated especially for cutting.

Flowers became so popular in the 17th and 18th centuries that florists' societies were set up around the country. Florists at this time were people dedicated to growing and exhibiting decorative blooms, rather than those who sold cut flowers. Their favourite plants included tulips, carnations, garden ranunculus and anemones. Arrangements in grand homes often included these species and were very colourful, with patterned, speckled and bicoloured flowers being especially popular.

By the 19th century, head gardeners on large country estates were expected to produce enough fresh flowers to fill the house, as well as more to send to the owner's town house. Flowers for cutting were grown in kitchen gardens and whole glasshouses might be dedicated to single flower types, such as chrysanthemums or showy carnations. Flower arranging was a popular hobby, with competitions held at flower shows all over the country. Fashionable arrangements became more muted, with single varieties of one species displayed with their own or added foliage.

Cut flowers continue to be valued today. They make a room appear more welcoming and cared for and provide a lovely connection between the house and garden. Many people have to buy expensive, imported flowers, but keen gardeners know that, for several months of the year, exceptionally pretty, seasonal arrangements can easily be grown at home.

▶ The cutting garden in July at Hanbury Hall in Worcestershire.

GARDEN FLOWERS FOR CUTTING

The flowers that are most commonly sold in florists' shops today are selected for their long stems and ability to last well during harvesting, storage and transport as well as in the vase. Most of them are imported from countries with vast cut-flower industries and have often been grown under glass. Growing your own is a sustainable alternative. Many of the same species – including tulips, alstroemerias, gladioli and gypsophilas – can be grown, as well as many other garden plants that are rarely seen in shops.

Few people have gardens large enough to dedicate much space purely to cut flowers. Instead, shrubs and perennials for cutting can be grown in mixed borders, with a few pots or gaps in the vegetable patch set aside for prolific, repeat-flowering annuals, such as sweet peas, dahlias or cornflowers. Flowers for picking need not all be long-stemmed and perfectly groomed – a few blooms floating in a bowl or short sprigs in a tiny vase look delightful too. Summer provides the widest range of flowers for picking, but spring, autumn and even winter can yield plenty of cutting material.

COTEHELE, CORNWALL

The sunny, south-facing slopes around Cotehele House have a rich history of cut-flower growing. Daffodils, anemones and alstroemerias have all been cultivated in this microclimate and either shipped to market along the Tamar estuary or taken by train. The small quay at the bottom of the garden served as an important hub before the arrival of the railway and many bunches of flowers have passed through it.

Today at Cotehele a new tradition has emerged. Since the 1940s, flowers from the garden have been used to make a huge garland, which is draped through the cavernous medieval Great Hall at Christmas time. The garland is 20m long and features up to 30,000 dried flowers; every year over 35,000 visitors come to marvel at it.

THE CUT FLOWER GARDEN

The cut flower garden is made up of four beds, each about 3 × 2.5m in size, and it produces 20,000–30,000 cut-flower stems annually. The area is very neat and tidy, edged with low wire fencing to keep rabbits out. In summer it is the most popular part of the garden, with visitors stopping to admire the blooms ready to be cut.

◤ A gardener harvests everlastings in the cut-flower garden at Cotehele.

▼ Part of the garland of dried flowers made at Cotehele each winter.

◢ Strawflowers growing in the cut-flower garden.

The soil is an easy-to-work loam and the garden team add a thick layer of well-rotted manure to one bed every year, so that each section is enriched on a four-year rotation. They used to rotavate frequently, but to preserve the soil structure they no longer do this; they now sow green manures in autumn so that the soil is not left bare over winter.

Head Gardener David Bouch has been growing cut flowers here since 2004 and keeps meticulous records of which plants have been tried and how successful they were. When the team grows a new plant, they begin with only one or two rows before committing to more the following year if it's a success.

Annual maintenance
- **January** The team spend several days planning what to grow and ordering seed.
- **February** The first sowings of seeds are made in the glasshouse, including everlastings and strawflowers. They are sown into a mix of pots, modules and seed trays. The greenhouse has a heated bench to aid germination.
- **March** Any green manures are strimmed down at the start of the month and left to rot. As soon

◀ Newly germinated statice seedlings.

◥ Young plants growing in the cut-flower garden in spring.

▼ Stripping the leaves from everlastings prior to drying them.

as the beds are dry enough, they are dug over, raked level and firmed down by foot. The bed that has been manured simply has the manure forked in; beds with green manure have it turned in. The second sowing of seeds is done in mid-March and a third at the end of the month.

- **April** Any slight risk of frost has passed in this part of the country by now and the team spend the month planting out all the cut flowers. They plant in blocks created by 2–4 staggered rows next to one another, which knit together to form a mass of plants. Between each block is a gap at least 50cm wide to be used as a path for picking. They like dead-straight rows and use a wide plank to walk on so that they are not compacting the soil as they work.

- **May** The team begin feeding plants in the ground with a seaweed-based, liquid plant fertiliser, which they repeat every 10 days through the summer to get the best flowers.

- **June–August** Fresh flowers are picked twice a week and taken to the house for arranging. Flowers to be dried for the garland are gathered in sunny weather in bunches of 20 stems, stripped of leaves and tied with a rubber band. They are then hung up in a cool, dark, well-ventilated shed to dry for between 10 days and six weeks, depending on the weather. Any flowers that are spoilt by rain are picked and composted to encourage the plants to produce more blooms.

- **September and October** As blocks of flowers stop flowering, they are removed and a green manure is sown in their place. Manure is added to one bed when it is empty. Rows of perennial cut flowers such as astrantias are lifted, divided and replanted every few years.

BEST FLOWERS FOR DRYING

The garland is such a success that 70 per cent of what the team grows is specifically for this purpose. For any type of cut flower to work in the garland, they need 3,000–5,000 heads of it. The most reliable flowers are:

- **Everlastings** (*Rhodanthe chlorocephala* subsp. *rosea*, top left) are Australian and go by many names, including strawflower and the synonyms *Helipterum* and *Acroclinium*. They must be picked when flowers are fully open.
- **Hare's tail grass** (*Lagurus ovatus*, top right), with fluffy grass seed heads, is easy to grow and dries very well.
- **Pink pokers** (*Psylliostachys suworowii;* formerly *Limonium suworowii*, centre left) have pale pink flower spikes, which are lovely both fresh and dried.
- **Statice** (*Limonium sinuatum*, centre right) is an amazing flower for drying. Late summer rains can easily spoil the flowers, but picking them off will encourage more. The wide stems need to have their loose, leafy edges stripped off before drying.
- **Strawflowers** (*Xerochrysum bracteatum;* formerly *Helichrysum bracteatum*, bottom left) are similar to everlastings, but with larger flowers in more colours. They have a lovely, hay-meadow scent.

FLOWERS FOR FRESH BOUQUETS

From March until October, the garden team pick fresh flowers from the cutting beds and elsewhere in the garden twice a week. The cut stems are left in large buckets of water in a cool, dark room of the house which is set aside for flower arranging by volunteers. In March, a variety of daffodils from Cotehele's collection are used to decorate the house for the annual Daffodil Festival. As the season progresses, a wider range of flowers and foliage begins appearing, including astrantias, agapanthus, clary sages, cornflowers, cosmos, dahlias and pittosporums. *Alstroemeria* 'Princess Lilian' is an especially useful, compact variety, which is popular with the gardeners as it doesn't need staking.

CREATING A DEDICATED CUT-FLOWER AREA

Throughout the summer, most well-stocked borders will provide enough flowers to fill one or two vases in the house each week. For anyone wanting to pick more frequently or be able to gather the same combinations over several weeks, setting aside an area to grow flowers especially for cutting makes sense. If you have a vegetable plot, a part of this can be devoted to cutting flowers and may have the added benefit of attracting beneficial insects. Like vegetables, most cutting flowers do best in a sunny, sheltered position and you'll need good access for maintenance and picking.

Prepare the soil as you would for a vegetable garden, removing weeds and spreading a layer of well-rotted manure or garden compost the proceeding autumn, so that it is well broken down and ready for sowing or planting in spring. Arrange plants in blocks or short rows with plenty of space between for picking. It's a good idea to keep perennials and annuals separate, so that you don't disturb the roots of the former when cultivating the soil to plant the latter.

A good mix of species for a cutting garden could include:

- An evergreen shrub, such as a pittosporum or choisya, for foliage; the latter has scented flowers in spring and autumn.
- A row of spring bulbs such as daffodils or tulips. Go for early to mid-flowering species, rather than later ones, which bloom when plenty of other plants are available.
- A few clumps of long-flowering perennials, such as *Penstemon heterophyllus* 'Electric Blue', *Persicaria amplexicaulis* and *Achillea* Summer Pastels Group, plus a couple of frothy, white- or green-flowered species such as *Gypsophila paniculata* or fennel, which make useful fillers between more showy flowers.

▲ Flowers for cutting growing in the Kitchen Garden at Wordsworth House in Cumbria.

◥ Narcissus are some of the easiest bulbs to grow for picking in spring.

◥◥ Many perennials such as *Achillea* Summer Pastels Group make great cut flowers.

- At least three repeat-flowering annuals, such as *Scabiosa atropurpurea* 'Tall Double Mixed' (shown opposite), cosmos and cornflowers. Try to choose species that flower for a long time and will complement each other in a vase.
- Lastly, it's always worth including a few different dahlias, as they are exceptionally prolific and long-flowering. There are many different types, but those with smaller heads may be easier to combine with other flowers.

Cut-flower areas will need to be kept largely weed-free by regular hoeing between rows. Alternatively, to save on weeding, you can spread a layer of garden compost between rows after

planting or germination. If you grow hardy annuals such as nigellas, pot marigolds and cerinthes, they may set seed in future years, so it's worth learning to recognise the seedlings and leaving a few to mature on corners or the edges of paths.

Most plants of 50cm or more in height will need robust staking. Horizontal netting stretched taut between canes over plants when they reach about 30cm is ideal. For tall plants, a second layer at a height of about 60cm may be needed. Netting can be reused each year or you could look for a biodegradable jute product.

ANNUALS AND BIENNIALS FOR CUTTING

Annual and biennial cutting flowers are generous and respond to picking by producing more flowers. Annuals are generally sown in March or April or bought in as small plants in May for flowering that year. Biennials are sown around June or bought in autumn and planted in their final positions in early autumn for flowering the next year. They tend to flower earlier than annuals, so can be useful at a time when the main cutting flowers are not ready. Some short-lived perennials, such as stocks and *Euphorbia oblongata*, can also be treated as annuals or biennials.

The advantage of growing your own cut flowers from seed is the wide range available to you. If you prefer to buy in plants, it may be best to order online or look for specialist growers – a lot of the annual bedding plants for sale in garden centres are bred for containers and are not ideal for cutting.

If growing your own cut flowers from seed, note which need to be started off in a greenhouse, which need heat, and which can be sown direct.

SOWING WITH HEAT
Annuals that can't cope with frost need to be started off in a heated propagator or sunny windowsill in early to mid-spring and grown on in a frost-free greenhouse until the end of spring. They include cosmos (above, with zinnias), *Scabiosa atropurpurea*, French marigolds, cleomes, *Tithonia rotundifolia*, strawflowers, *Cerinthe major* 'Purpurascens', *Salpiglossis sinuata* and zinnias.

To be efficient with space in your propagator or windowsill, sow seeds into small seed trays or wide, shallow pots, probably using less than half the seed in a packet. Most don't need light to germinate but, as soon as they have germinated, they should be placed in a sunny position. When the seedlings are large enough to handle, you can prick out as many as you need into small individual pots (see also 'How to sow seeds', p.210). In the case of zinnias, which hate root disturbance, sow straight into small pots or modules and don't start them off before April as they need to be planted out into warm soil when still small.

SOWING WITH PROTECTION
A few fairly hardy annuals do really well if given a head start under cover in March and then planted out when the ground has warmed up a bit in April or May. This group should germinate satisfactorily in an unheated greenhouse or cold frame. They include *Visnaga daucoides* (often sold by its previous name *Ammi visnaga*), *Linaria maroccana*, sweet peas and China

asters (above left). Newly planted out, they tolerate cold but may need a little fleece protection if the weather turns freezing. Sweet peas should be sown individually into small pots, but smaller seeds can be sown into modules, small seed trays or pots, and either thinned or pricked out as needed.

DIRECT-SOWING SEEDS

Really easy, hardy annuals that do well if direct-sown where they are to flower include calendulas, cornflowers, clarkias (above), quaking grass, poppies, clary sages and love-in-a-mist. Sow them in fine, raked soil once it warms up in late March or April: if you sow them earlier, they might rot rather than germinate, but sowing later won't give them time to fatten up before flowering. It's wise to sow the seeds in rows or blocks marked with canes; that way, if other seedlings appear near the sown drills, you will know they are weeds and can simply hoe them off. As with direct-sowing of annual vegetables (see 'Direct-sowing

seeds', p.185) sow as thinly as possible. Once your seedlings appear, be brave and thin them out to the spacing recommended on the seed packet, usually somewhere between 25cm and 45cm, depending on the eventual size of the plant.

SOWING SEEDS FOR NEXT YEAR

Biennials, including wallflowers, honesty, hollyhocks and sweet williams (above), need to be sown the year before you want them to flower. Sow them in an unheated glasshouse, cold frame or sometimes direct into the ground between May and July. If sown earlier, they may try to flower weakly that same autumn; if sown later, they may not be big enough for overwintering. Once the seedlings germinate, grow them on in individual pots in a sunny place, sheltered from the hottest sun if they are in the greenhouse. Plant them out in their final positions in the garden by the middle of autumn for flowering the following spring.

GROWING SWEET PEAS

STEP 1
In September or October, sow peas in individual pots of peat-free, multipurpose compost, with the seeds about 1cm below the surface. Sweet peas have very hard seeds and some people suggest soaking or nicking them to help them germinate, but neither is strictly necessary. Place on a windowsill or in a greenhouse or cold frame. A sheltered part of the garden is fine too, but protect the pots from mice, which might steal the seeds.

STEP 2
Seedlings should appear within two weeks and can be left in a bright but sheltered place, such as the greenhouse or cold frame. Inside your home is probably too warm and will cause seedlings to get leggy. They need to grow slowly but steadily over autumn and then stop during winter.

STEP 3
In February, pinch the tips out of the plants to encourage them to become bushier. They should send up side shoots within a few weeks.

STEP 4
Once the soil has begun to warm up in March or April, plant the seedlings out into soil enriched with some garden compost or well-rotted manure. Provide support at least 1.5m high (canes with plenty of taut string, well-branched pea sticks or netting are suitable). Tie the sweet peas in as they grow to encourage them upwards.

STEP 5
Begin harvesting as soon as flowers start to appear, picking daily to keep up with them. Remove any flowers that have gone over and are beginning to produce seed pods, and water well in dry spells to keep them flowering.

A number of hardy annuals can also be sown in early autumn the year before you need them and overwintered as small plants in an unheated greenhouse, for planting outside in spring. This has several advantages: the greenhouse is reliably warm then; you may have more free time; and they will usually start flowering earlier the following year, giving you flowers when you need them most. Sweet peas and *Cerinthe major* 'Purpurascens' started off like this make far bushier, earlier-flowering plants and tricky species such as *Orlaya grandiflora* are more likely to do well. Some of the hardiest annuals, such as cornflowers and nigellas, can even be sown directly into the ground in late summer and will survive over winter as seedlings, just as they would do in the wild.

Breaking dormancy

A few annuals and biennials, including larkspur and honesty, need a period of cold to trigger germination. Some people sow these in small trays and store them in the fridge for a few weeks, before moving them into a propagator. If you don't want to use your fridge for this, you can sow them in autumn and leave them in a cold greenhouse or cold frame. They should germinate when they are ready in spring. Take care to label the tray – you may have forgotten all about it when the seedlings finally appear!

PLANTING OUT

Before planting seed-raised or bought-in plants outdoors, make sure that they are acclimatised to the weather by hardening them off (see 'Hardening off seedlings', p.210). If tender plants have become pot bound before it's time to plant them outdoors, pot them on into bigger containers. If they have become leggy, pinch the tips back. Most young plants are a favourite food of slugs and snails, which can wipe them out overnight, so keep a close eye on the young plants and consider putting down beer traps nearby during warm, wet weather.

CUT FLOWERS FROM BULBS AND TUBERS

Bulbs and corms are some of the easiest cutting flowers to grow, as they are far bigger and less fussy than seeds. Some bulbs, including daffodils, alliums, hyacinths, snowflakes and bluebells, will come back year after year and can be allowed to naturalise in an area of the garden. There are many wonderful alliums that make great cut flowers fresh or dry, including *Allium sphaerocephalon*, with its small, burgundy flower heads, and the large, starry-headed *A. cristophii*.

Gladioli and tulips, which make excellent cut flowers, can be left in the ground for a few years but, because many of their leaves are inevitably picked when the flower stems are harvested, they tend to lose strength and flower less well in subsequent years. If this is the case, replace them with fresh bulbs in the autumn. Lilies will come back year after year, but may be best grown in pots as they like free-draining conditions and protection from the worst winter weather.

The majority of hardy bulbs are planted in autumn for a spring display, but gladioli are planted in spring once the soil warms up for a summer display. Gladioli should be planted deep and usually flower reliably three months after planting.

▼ Daffodils ready for picking in the Walled Garden at Greys Court in Oxfordshire.

A handful of popular cut flowers have fleshy root tubers, which can be bought dormant but require good care to bring them into life for flowering and picking. Freesias, for instance, come from South Africa, where they are dormant in summer and need a period of heat to initiate growth. The most guaranteed way of succeeding with them is to buy 'prepared' bulbs, which have been heat-treated, and plant them outdoors in April to flower in summer. The tubers of *Anemone coronaria* can be bought pre-treated (soaked) for maximum flowering the following spring but, if planted in a sunny enough site, should come back year after year.

Highly reliable options are the deliciously scented chocolate cosmos and, of course, dahlias, both of which can be replanted year after year. One space-saving option is to plant dahlias into the spot from where you have just lifted tulips, and vice versa in autumn. This does require fresh tulip bulbs each year, as lifting them straight after flowering will mean that they haven't stored enough energy for flowering the following year.

▼ Gladioli corms ready for planting in spring.

GROWING DAHLIAS

Dahlias can be bought very cheaply as dormant tubers in spring. Pot them into peat-free, multipurpose compost, covering each tuber by a few centimetres (with the growing point – if you can see it – pointing upwards).

- Place the pots in a bright, warm position, such as a slightly heated greenhouse or a sunny windowsill indoors, and water to moisten the compost. Keep the compost just moist until new shoots appear.
- Dahlias grow fast but need to be kept under cover in a frost-free place until the end of spring, when they can be safely planted outdoors. If a plant starts to fill the pot before it's ready to go out, gently move it into a bigger pot, planting it a little deeper than before.
- At the end of May, begin to acclimatise the plants to the outside, taking great care to protect them from slugs and snails, which love the new shoots.
- Plant the dahlias outdoors in large pots or in borders (a little deeper than they were in their original pots, so that the tubers are not close to the surface). Keep slugs and snails away with copper tape around the pots, a mulch of gravel or sharp sand in the border and perhaps a beer trap nearby.
- Feed the dahlias regularly with liquid feed, especially if the plants are in pots, and provide supports for their tall stems.
- Flowering should begin in midsummer and continue until the first frosts. When you cut a stem, cut back to a pair of leaves, from which a new flower stem should emerge. Remove any spent flowers to encourage more.
- When you lift plants in mid-autumn, expect to find many more tubers than you originally planted. They can be overwintered under cover for more flowers next year (see 'Overwintering dahlias', p.215).

PLANTS WITH STRUCTURAL SEED HEADS

Architectural seed heads add much to summer bouquets and can be the mainstay of an autumn or winter display.

◀ *Allium hollandicum* **'Purple Sensation'** is a reliable allium with dense heads.

◀ **Honesty** (*Lunaria rediviva*), a biennial, has seed pods like transparent pennies.

◀ **Giant knapweed** (*Centaurea macrocephala*) is a huge perennial with gold-edged flower heads.

◀ **Poppies**, including annuals and perennials, have unique, fat, fluted seed capsules.

◀ **Greater quaking grass** (*Briza maxima*), an annual grass, has elegant, nodding heads.

◀ **Love-in-a-mist** (*Nigella damascena*) is an annual that will seed freely in the garden and bears beautiful, pink-tinged seed heads.

◀ **Chinese lanterns** (*Physalis alkekengi*) has delightful, papery, orange seed cases.

◀ **Drumstick scabious** (*Scabiosa stellata* 'Drumstick') is an annual with exquisitely structured heads.

PERENNIALS FOR CUTTING

A vast number of the hardy perennials we grow in our gardens make great cut flowers. If you want to be able to pick them freely, grow big clumps in your borders or set them aside in a cut-flower area.

Qualities to look for in a perennial cut flower include scented, spectacular or structural blooms, and a willingness to send up new flower stems over several weeks and the ability to last well in the vase.

Perennials are unlikely to be strong enough for large harvests in their first year and are best left to bulk up into big clumps before you pick with impunity. Most will need robust supports so that you get straight stems with flowers held gracefully on them.

As with produce from your vegetable plot, the first four months of the year are a 'hungry gap' for cut flowers. Perennials to get you through include sweet violets, *Euphorbia amygdaloides*, everlasting wallflowers, *Anemone coronaria* and as many bulbs as you can fit in, including snowdrops, snowflakes, grape hyacinths and daffodils of all types. Hellebores are also lovely in a vase, but be careful where you place them, as even their pollen can be toxic.

Once you get to May, different perennials come into flower almost every week and, with a bit of planning, you can have something highly pickable in your garden until October.

Late spring and early summer

The first, highly welcome perennials for cutting include geums – especially long-flowering varieties such as 'Totally Tangerine' – sanguisorbas, *Iris sibirica*, aquilegias, *Euphorbia epithymoides* and, of course, peonies. Pick peonies when the buds are just beginning to open for the longest-lasting flowers.

Midsummer

In midsummer, there is a vast number of suitable perennials to pick for the house, including *Knautia macedonia*, *Centaurea montana*, sea holly, scented *Phlox paniculata*, achilleas, *Alchemilla mollis*, *Anthemis tinctoria*, sweet rocket, bearded irises, pinks, lupins, scabious and oregano. Many people also pick delphiniums and astrantias, although the former can rarely be spared from borders and the latter are best used in small quantities (they can emit a slightly unpleasant smell).

◣ *Geum* 'Totally Tangerine' flowers from May until early autumn.

▼ *Alchemilla mollis* starts flowering in June.

◢ The flowers of *Physostegia virginiana* first appear in July.

Late summer and autumn

Many of the flowers that get going in midsummer carry on well into autumn. Try persicarias, penstemons, crocosmias, *Rudbeckia triloba*, agastaches, echinaceas, sedums and many asters, including *Eurybia divaricata*. *Physostegia virginiana* is not seen in bouquets as often as it deserves, despite its common name of obedient plant (a reference to how its flowers stay positioned just as you arrange them).

In addition to all these perennials, it's well worth picking and experimenting with anything else that catches your eye or smells delicious. Take care when handling anything new or unfamiliar, or displaying them near children, as a few have toxic sap, poisonous seeds or pollen that can stain.

SHRUBS FOR FLOWERS, FOLIAGE AND BERRIES

The rose, possibly the world's favourite cut flower, is of course a shrub. Hybrid tea roses give the neatest flowers, held on strong, upright stems, but old roses with bigger, blowsier blooms make magnificent displays too and usually have far more scent. English shrub roses, such as 'Gertrude Jekyll', have the qualities of an old rose but the ability to repeat-flower, so are ideal and well worth growing purely for cutting.

Other shrubs that can be successfully cut for their flowers include hydrangeas (*Hydrangea macrophylla* and *H. paniculata* are suitable both fresh and dried), spiraeas, forsythias, weigelas, Japanese quinces, guelder roses and buddlejas. Arrangements made using whole branches can be really dramatic and architectural. Those that are especially fragrant include *Viburnum* × *bodnantense* 'Dawn', *Osmanthus* × *burkwoodii*, *Daphne bholua*, lilacs and mock orange. Just a few sprigs of these can fill the house with scent, often in a subtler and more enchanting way than classic scented flowers like stocks or hyacinths.

▲ *Chaenomeles* × *superba* 'Fire Dance' (Japanese quince).

Shrubs with berries for autumn and winter displays include holly, hypericum (especially *Hypericum androsaemum* and *H.* × *inodorum*) and *Callicarpa bodinieri* var. *giraldii* 'Profusion'. Those with interesting stems include corkscrew willows and hazels, colourful dogwoods and pussy willows in spring. For evergreens to fill out wreaths, table decorations and vases, try *Euonymus japonicus* (plain or variegated varieties), rosemary and *Eucalyptus gunnii* (kept coppiced). *Viburnum tinus* is also useful, as it has glossy, evergreen foliage and flowers in the depths of winter, although in recent years it has become prone to viburnum beetle, which can make the leaves look rather ragged.

▲ Freshly picked zinnias are placed in a bucket of cold water until they are ready for arranging.

PICKING, CONDITIONING AND DISPLAYING

Floristry, like gardening, is both an art and a science, worthy of study and practice. However, for most gardeners picking for their own homes or for bouquets to give away, the key factors to consider are ensuring that stems are healthy and will last as long as possible.

PICKING

In summer, try to pick flowers in the morning or evening rather than the heat of day and pop them straight into a bucket of water, so that they don't experience any stress. Most blooms last longest if they are picked just as their buds are opening and beginning to show a little colour. On spikes with multiple flowers, ensure that the lowest flowers are fully open while the top ones are still in bud.

Don't cut stems right to the ground. Instead, leave some buds from which new growth can emerge. If picking from garden borders which need to stay looking good, try to take stems that are hidden from view or growing in a cluster with others. That way, you should be able to gather an armful of flowers and foliage without making a dent in the border. Tread carefully among existing plants – perhaps even place stepping stones in gaps for that purpose.

CONDITIONING

When you get indoors, strip the lower leaves from the stems so that none will end up below the water line in the vase and, for best results, recut each stem with sharp secateurs. Use a long, sloping cut for woody stems so that there's more surface area to take up water. If it's important that your arrangements last well, leave all the cut flowers in a bucket of clean water in a cool place for a few hours, or overnight, before positioning them in the warmth of the house. This also gives insects hiding inside the flowers a chance to relocate. For plants with soft stems and heavy flower heads,

such as tulips and peonies, support the heads by wrapping them in cones of newspaper while they are conditioning – they should be standing upright by morning.

A few species are prone to drooping and can be sealed by dipping the ends of the stems into recently boiled water for half a minute as soon after picking as possible. Cardoons, poppies, Japanese anemones, hellebores, *Smyrnium perfoliatum*, *Verbena bonariensis* and lilacs all respond well to this treatment. It also helps to stop euphorbias dripping their white, sticky sap, which can be irritating to the skin.

ARRANGING CUT FLOWERS

Arranging flowers is a completely personal thing. The guiding principles about complementary and contrasting shapes and colours, which apply to designing borders (see 'Flower colour and form', p.42) may be useful but, unlike borders, cut flowers can be easily rejigged until you achieve a combination you like. Sometimes as you wander around the garden, collecting flowers in your hand or a bucket, the perfect arrangement suggests itself. At other times, it will seem like a random assortment until you pad it out with

a mass of something green and frothy such as fennel fronds, euphorbias or foliage. Filler plants like these are crucial as a backdrop to flowers and, if they have rigid branches, as does sea holly, they can hold the other plants in place within the arrangement. If you don't have a vase that is the right size for what you have picked, then jam jars, teacups, empty bottles and jugs will all do perfectly well. If arrangements are small, consider making a group of them for added impact.

If you have plant food or can make your own (even a teaspoon of sugar will do) to dissolve in the vase, it can extend the plants' life even further. Ideally, try to place arrangements away from sunny windows or radiators, which will make them go over more quickly. Top up the water as needed and, if the display is lasting well, change it after a few days and recut the bases of the stems, removing any that are past their best.

CHAPTER 12
GARDENING SUSTAINABLY

THE WAY WE GARDEN

The last 100 years have seen major changes in the way we garden. The horticultural industry has given us access to a vast range of plants and equipment, making many jobs easier and quicker but also increasing our ecological footprint. Where gardeners used to raise their own plants in the open soil, wooden seed trays or terracotta pots, we now buy them in disposable plastic containers. Where we used to make our own composts or collect dung locally, we now buy what we need in thick plastic sacks. Technology has given us invaluable labour-saving tools, but today even the smallest gardens are managed using petrol-fuelled or electric equipment and weed control often relies on herbicides.

The role of gardens in the environment has also changed. As urban areas increase in size and farmland is more intensively managed, many gardens provide important refuges for wildlife, giving gardeners new responsibilities. Evidence suggests that declining species such as frogs, song thrushes and hedgehogs, which were once common in farmland, are now more abundant in domestic gardens. We can no longer assume that any creatures we deter from our gardens have space to thrive elsewhere. With this in mind, we need to think carefully before we call upon the arsenal of pesticides available to us, many of which are harmful not just to pests but to a range of other species that underpin the food chain.

Gardens in urban areas have an especially important role to play – not only vastly increasing biodiversity in towns and cities, but also cooling the air during heat waves, reducing pressure on drains in wet weather and boosting the health and well-being of those who use them. Since private gardens in British towns and cities make up half of the green space, as well as housing over 80 per cent of the urban tree stock, their collective contribution should not be underestimated.

▶ Teasel, foxgloves and ferns line a path at Snowshill Manor in Gloucestershire.

REDUCING HUMAN IMPACT

There is much gardeners can do to ensure that the benefits of our gardens far outweigh their ecological footprints. Simply by caring for mature trees and shrubs we can ensure that they continue to capture and retain carbon, cool the air and provide habitats for wildlife. By learning to select plants suited to our garden's soil, we can each avoid waste and lessen the need for watering. And by limiting our use of petrol, pesticides, plastic and peat we can cut down our demand on finite resources.

Small changes to the designs of our gardens can also make huge differences. Removing impermeable paving allows gardens to absorb more rainfall. Building ponds provides habitats and drinking water for a wide range of species. Reducing the size of our lawns lessens the need for mowing and can create space for richer habitats.

A sustainable, wildlife-friendly garden doesn't need to be messy; it simply needs to be gardened more gently to cause the least harm to its inhabitants. Timing of tasks is key. Before we prune a hedge, tidy up a border, cut long grass, empty a pond or move a pile of debris, we need to consider which species might be living there and when our actions would cause them the least disturbance.

NUNNINGTON HALL, YORKSHIRE

The gardens at Nunnington Hall are run on organic principles by a small but dedicated team of gardeners led by Nick Fraser. When Nick started out in horticulture 33 years ago he was taught very traditional techniques, but he was never comfortable using weedkiller or trapping pests. So he was delighted when he arrived 17 years ago at Nunnington, a place where he knew he could develop his ecological style of gardening.

Although Nunnington Hall is old and stately, it was always a family home with a family garden and the National Trust team who run it today try to maintain a relaxed, informal atmosphere. In the main garden area in front of the house, there are small orchards flanking the lawn. Carpeting the ground beneath the fruit trees is an ornamental meadow made up of native grasses and wild flowers, with a few bulbs such as blue camassias and pheasant's eye narcissus to add dramatic impact in spring. It is

unusual to see a meadow so close to a house, but it works really well, radically reducing the area of mown lawn and providing colour from spring until autumn. And it is buzzing with insect life.

BORDER LIFE

Beyond the lawn is a deep border planted with a mix of colourful perennials and shrubs for interest throughout the spring, summer and autumn. Garden borders like this can provide great hiding and foraging places for a wide range of insects, amphibians and small mammals. In summer, lady's mantle, hardy geraniums, foxgloves and red campions are followed by globe thistles and persicarias, then red-hot pokers, crocosmias, tall perennial sunflowers and deep blue monkshood. Long-flowering catmints line the steps, producing nectar and pollen for many months. Some of the hostas have been nibbled by slugs and snails, but Nick sees this as evidence that there is plenty of food around for the rescued hedgehogs that he

▲ *Astrantia major*, a garden plant highly popular with insects.

◀ The orchard, meadow and house viewed from the borders.

▶ *Alchemilla mollis* tumbles over the steps and paving through the old walled garden.

◢ Camassias and narcissus flowering under the fruit trees in spring.

releases into the garden. He suggests that if the damage cannot be tolerated, gardeners should try the large, thicker-leaved hostas, such as 'Sum and Substance', 'Big Daddy' and 'Halcyon' which seem to be far less palatable to slugs.

MAKING COMPOST

South-west of the house is the Cutting Garden, containing beds for cut flowers, a vegetable plot and a large compost area, which is often the busiest part of the garden for both gardeners and visitors. The compost system is made up of several large, wooden bays, which reveal all the stages of compost-making. In the first bay, the team are careful to chop up everything they add so that it begins to break down quickly. After four to six weeks, the contents of this bay are turned into the second one where decomposition happens fast, worm numbers multiply and lots of heat is generated. Another six to eight weeks later, it is turned into the third bay, by which time it already looks dark and well-rotted and the worm numbers are reducing. By the time it is turned into the fourth bin, it is dark and crumbly, has no

▲ Catmint lines the steps at the end of the main border.

▲ The vegetable garden in early summer.

unpleasant odour, is no longer very warm and the worm activity has slowed right down. This fine compost is then used in the vegetable and flower garden as a mulch over beds and as a fertiliser and soil improver whenever something new is planted. The vegetables are lush and healthy and the team never resort to pesticides or synthetic fertilisers.

Near the compost bays, several other methods of composting are also on display, including an enclosed tumbler, which composts food waste from the café, a wormery and a comfrey leaf-juice extractor, which produces rich, organic, liquid plant fertilisers.

ECO-FRIENDLY WEEDING AND MULCHING

Paths around the house and garden are a mix of gravel and paving, which of course harbour weeds but herbicide is never used on them. Instead, the gravel is raked regularly to disturb any newly germinated seedlings and occasionally hoed to remove any weeds that have taken hold. For the paved areas, a gas-powered weed-burner is sometimes used. Also, a couple of times a year, the team get down on their hands and knees to do some hand-weeding to remove any stubborn

species that have established between the stones. For mulching around newly planted orchard trees, sheep's wool is used – an entirely appropriate material for this sheep-farming area.

AVOIDING PROBLEMS

Having healthy soil and lots of biodiversity keeps pests and diseases to a minimum. Another precaution Nick takes is having a quarantine area where he keeps all new plants for a few weeks. Here he monitors them for signs of ill-health before planting them in the garden.

Checking over new plants is really important. It avoids introducing problems into our gardens and stops them spreading into the neighbouring countryside. Nick is aware of the invasive plants introduced to Britain through horticulture, such as Japanese knotweed and Himalayan balsam, and advises gardeners to be very cautious of using spreading plants such as bamboo or Russian vine, especially if your garden borders natural areas.

SUSTAINABLE ENERGY

Hedges are cut with rechargeable battery-powered equipment, charged by lithium batteries, which are carried in backpacks. Energy at Nunnington

▶ Grass clippings and other leafy waste on the compost heap.

◢ St John's wort, a British native, flowers in the garden.

▼ Plant labels made from hazel sticks.

is supplied by a biomass boiler fuelled with sustainably sourced wood pellets. Three water butts collect water from the greenhouse roof for watering inside. Plastic is avoided as much as possible or reused: plastic plant pots are stacked up and reused year after year; short hazel sticks are used to make plant labels; and even the garden games for children are made from natural materials such as rope and wood.

WILDLIFE AT NUNNINGTON

The garden at Nunnington provides a variety of habitats. The meadow and fruit trees offer food and egg-laying sites for a wide range of insects, as well as safe corridors through the garden for small mammals and amphibians. The river, which was diverted to pass near the house many centuries ago, has a man-made otter holt in its bank and these characterful creatures are often spotted by visitors picnicking nearby. Nick creates additional nesting, hiding and hibernating spots, including bug hotels and bird and bat boxes. He is a keen birdwatcher and loves to see a song thrush pop out from her nest between the wall and the trained peach tree to gather food for her young in the meadow. He is also enchanted by the spotted flycatchers that circle the courtyard and perch on the porch, unperturbed by the queue of visitors at the door.

In summer, regular bug-hunting events are held where you can see moths, butterflies, caterpillars, mayflies, leafhoppers, shield bugs and dragonflies. Nick is able to tell visitors all about these animals and how they assist with the natural balance of the garden. His joy in caring for the garden and all its creatures is palpable. He believes it's time for a change of mindset in gardening and wishes that we could all see plants as being there for wildlife, with their beauty simply as an added bonus.

REDUCING PESTICIDES

Despite much testing and legislation, weedkillers, slug pellets, insecticides and fungicides all have a potentially detrimental impact on the environment and their long-term effects are not always understood. If you are considering buying a product, read the label carefully to check the active ingredients and what warnings they carry. Consider whether the benefits of using it in your garden are really worth the risks. In National Trust properties, gardeners and rangers make these assessments whenever they need to tackle a problem weed or pest.

There are lots of non-chemical techniques for controlling pests, diseases and weeds, including hand-weeding, flame-guns, beer traps for slugs and clearing infected leaves as problems occur. In some instances, it might be worth just tolerating a little inconvenience. For example, rather than controlling plum moth, why not put up with some maggoty plums? It is rare that every single fruit will be ruined and most trees provide more than we can eat.

For weed control, hoeing of annual weeds is highly effective if done in mid-spring when annual weeds first appear, while the thorough digging out of perennial weeds usually has far longer-lasting effects than herbicide. If digging is too onerous, weeds can also be cut down and smothered with old plastic compost sacks or cardboard covered with mulch for a year or two.

COPING WITH SLUGS AND SNAILS

Slugs and snails are a fact of life in gardens, especially wildlife-friendly ones with plenty of hiding places. Succulent vegetable plants and leafy perennials such as delphiniums, lupins and hostas are always prone to attack. Many others are vulnerable when they are young, but become less palatable to the molluscs as they mature.

Avoid the worst damage by growing susceptible plants in pots (ideally with copper tape around the rims). Check plants and under pots on warm, damp evenings and remove any slugs and snails you find. Deterrents such as wool and crushed eggshells can also prevent slugs and snails from reaching vulnerable plants, while beer traps can lure them off course, but both will need regular replenishment. If slug pellets are used, look for ones approved for organic growing, which are least likely to poison other species. Metaldehyde was used for decades but is now understood to pollute water supplies and to be highly toxic to the creatures that eat poisoned slugs.

For established borders where slug control is not practical, choosing slug-resistant plants is often the best bet. There are a vast range of these, including many garden favourites such as hardy geraniums, astrantias, alliums, euphorbias, hellebores, Japanese anemones, eryngiums, penstemons and *Knautia macedonica*.

If you do decide to use a pesticide, ensure that you have identified your problem correctly and the product is suited to it, and follow the instructions carefully. Insecticides should never be sprayed on plants in bloom as this risks poisoning other harmless insects that are visiting the flowers. Herbicides should not be used near water or drainage channels as they may pollute water courses, causing damage downstream.

LOOKING AFTER THE SOIL

The key to healthy plants is healthy soil and this is achieved largely by adding organic matter, such as garden compost or animal manure. While synthetic fertilisers are widely available to add nutrients to the soil, they are energy-intensive to produce, prone to leaching into water courses and do not have any of the long-term benefits of organic material.

All types of soil benefit from organic matter. It helps to break up heavy clay soils and enriches light sandy or chalky soils, enabling them to hold more water. It can be added as a layer in autumn, winter or spring and either dug in or left on the surface as a mulch for worms and other soil organisms to incorporate into the soil. Mulching is the best approach for borders with plants already growing in them, but also works well around newly planted borders or on bare soil in beds left fallow for a period. Some vegetable gardeners also prefer to mulch rather than dig, in order to avoid disturbing the soil's structure or the worms and other organisms living within it.

◀ A bumblebee feeding from hedge woundwort.

▼ A volunteer gardener digs the Walled Garden in Penrose, Cornwall.

TYPES OF ORGANIC MATTER

The most sustainable form of organic matter is your own garden compost. Additional quantities of organic matter may, however, be needed and these can be bought from garden centres, council green-waste handlers, horticultural suppliers or local farms. If buying from garden centres, one bag is enough only for 1–2 sq. m and uses a lot of plastic, whereas buying loose compost avoids this. If buying in bulk, check with the supplier that they have tested and graded the material and, if it is for vegetable plots, check that manure has not come from fields that have been sprayed with herbicide. It is also worth noting that spent mushroom compost – a well-rotted manure that has been used to grow mushrooms commercially – is a great product for soil improvement, but it contains lime so should probably not be used every year as it may gradually make the soil too alkaline.

For especially hungry plants like roses and fruit bushes, organic fertilisers made from waste products including chicken manure can also be added to the soil in spring. For plants in containers, liquid feeds made from seaweed, comfrey or nettle leaves are ideal – and you can easily make your own.

MAKING YOUR OWN GARDEN COMPOST

Successful composting requires at least two bins so that one can be filled up and left to rot down while the other is being filled. The size of bin you need depends on how big your garden is and the amount of waste you produce – for most small gardens, metre-square wooden bays or plastic 'daleks' are ideal.

Bins should be placed on porous surfaces (such as soil or lawn) so that excess moisture can leach out and worms can find their way in. They are best positioned in a corner of the garden, under trees or beside a hedge, where you can access them but they aren't taking up valuable planting space. Ideally they should receive some rainfall but not too much direct sun, which can dry out the contents. Slatted sides allow for air circulation through the heap, while a lid keeps out excess rain

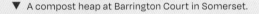
▼ A compost heap at Barrington Court in Somerset.

WHAT IS COMPOST?

The term compost is used a lot in horticulture, sometimes causing confusion. Potting compost, which you usually buy in garden centres, is a high-quality, expensive product for growing plants in pots. Professionals often call this a 'growing medium'. Various types are available for different uses, but the most commonly available is multipurpose compost. National Trust gardeners always use peat-free potting compost (peat extraction releases locked-in carbon and destroys habitats for wildlife).

Garden compost is a very different thing: it is the result of piling up garden and kitchen waste and letting it rot down to form a rich, dark, crumbly substance that is ideal for enriching your garden soil. It is usually too rich and lumpy to be suitable for potting plants directly into, but you can mix it with leaf mould, sharp sand and sieved soil to make your own potting compost.

and sun, but neither are critical and some gardeners compost successfully in open heaps on the ground.

The key to filling your bin is to add a good mix of materials – from soft, sappy, green stuff like grass clippings, weeds and vegetable peelings to thicker woody ingredients such as hedge trimmings, dry winter stems and cardboard egg boxes. Try to add these in layers, so that the woody material helps to add air and absorb moisture, while the green stuff softens things up and gets them biodegrading. If, at the end of a day's gardening, you find you are left with a big pile of hedge trimmings or grass clippings, put half in the bin and leave the rest to one side to add after something else has been put in. Never add cooked food as it could attract unwanted visitors, such as rats.

Turning the heap

Gardeners who chop everything up and are careful about adding a good mix of ingredients may get away with not turning their heaps, but most people find turning it once or twice is necessary to mix up the ingredients and help everything to break down quickly. If you have a plastic 'dalek' bin, you can do this by simply lifting it off and then standing it in a new position and forking the contents back into it. Once you have a good system going with two bins, you can use up the compost from one bin in autumn and then turn the contents of the other bin into it, mixing it in the process. Leave the full bin to rot down for a few months while you fill the empty one.

Weeds and diseased material

Many people are confused about whether they can put weeds and diseased material in the compost. Annual weeds are fine, as are most perennial weeds (which will be killed by the heat of the compost), but the roots of really pernicious ones such as bindweed may survive. These are best separated out during weeding and sent to the council green waste (where the heat of the huge composting

systems will kill them), left in the sun to dry out or soaked in water to rot, before being added to your compost.

Diseased material is a trickier subject. Many common problems such as powdery mildew or rose rust won't survive composting, but others such as black spot or canker in fruit trees are better burnt, buried or added to council green waste. Note that the highly invasive Japanese knotweed should never be put in council green waste or normal household waste, as this risks spreading it to new sites. Seek professional advice if it is present in your garden.

MAKING LEAF MOULD

Autumn leaves can be added to the compost heap, but are often generated in such big quantities that it's best to store them separately. Here they can be left to break down and form lovely, fine, low-nutrient leaf mould, which is ideal for using in home-made potting composts or top dressing plants in pots. A leaf-mould bin can be made using four posts with some chicken wire wrapped around them. It should not need to be covered, as rain is needed to soften the leaves and aid decomposition. If you don't have space for this, you can simply put your leaves in old sacks, pour in some water to soften them and leave to break down in a corner of the garden for six months or more.

USING FEWER RESOURCES

Caring for a garden can be highly therapeutic and bring us closer to nature, so it makes sense to do it in a way that respects the earth's limited resources, even if it costs a little more time and effort.

Petrol-powered equipment is very useful for large lawns and hedges, but often is not necessary in small gardens. Small, flat lawns can be satisfactorily mown using a manual mower; edges and hedges can be cut with sharp shears; sweeping leaves is often far simpler than using a leaf-blower and is a great workout for your stomach muscles! If you do use power tools, think about investing in rechargeable, battery-powered ones. Those designed for professional gardeners are very expensive, but there are lighter-weight models for domestic gardens. With petrol-powered equipment, consider trying aspen fuel, which is cleaner and better for engines, especially small ones such as strimmers that often sit unused for months at a time. With all manual and power tools, buy the best quality that you can afford and look after them, keeping blades clean, sharp and oiled in order to make them last as long as possible. Storing mowers over winter without fuel in them is best for ensuring longevity.

ECO-FRIENDLY PLANTS AND PRODUCTS

Buying plants from local nurseries or raising your own plants from seed and cuttings will reduce your garden's carbon footprint. (Most plants in garden centres have been raised under glass using peat-based compost, artificial fertilisers and lots of water and have often travelled hundreds of kilometres to reach you.) Favouring perennials and hardy annuals grown from seed is also more sustainable than using lots of bedding plants, which are grown for one season and then usually thrown away.

Some plant pots can now be put into household recycling bins, but it is still best to reduce the number you acquire, by buying trees and shrubs

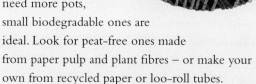

bareroot where possible and by asking garden centres and nurseries if they will take back their pots. Most home gardeners will recycle a small number for propagation. If you need more pots, small biodegradable ones are ideal. Look for peat-free ones made from paper pulp and plant fibres – or make your own from recycled paper or loo-roll tubes.

For plant ties, biodegradable jute string is ideal. It will need replacing annually, but this is actually good practice; plastic-coated wire left unchecked can cut into plants, damaging them. If you need to protect trees from rabbits, biodegradable types of netting are now available.

SAVING WATER

The storage, treatment and supply of clean drinking water direct to our homes is an energy-intensive process; using this 'potable' water in the garden is not ideal, especially when droughts loom. Many National Trust properties collect and store rainwater or water from local, untreated sources for use in gardens. In large gardens, this often requires boreholes or huge water-storage tanks and bowsers for moving water to where it is needed. In domestic gardens, the solution is to have as many water butts as possible to collect water from shed, greenhouse and even house roofs. The larger and more numerous the containers the better; this means you can collect water during heavy rains in autumn and spring for use several months later in summer.

It is also important to use water wisely within the garden. Firstly, try to select plants that are suited to your garden's soil and local climate, to minimise the need for watering them. Avoid watering established plants and lawns, as this only encourages surface rooting, making plants more dependent on water in the long term. Focus watering on vegetable crops, potted plants and anything newly planted and try to restrict planting of new borders to autumn or spring, ideally when rain is forecast. In

◀ Rainwater collection system on the shed at Stoneywell in Leicestershire.

▶ Piles of stones offering hiding places can help attract wildlife (see overleaf).

drought conditions, when hosepipe bans are in place and water butts have been used up, move pots and hanging baskets into the shade. If drought persists, you could stop watering annuals altogether and let them finish early. Alternatively, grey water from baths and showers can be diverted for use in the garden. The soap residues are usually not harmful, provided that they are used only for a short period.

As climate change threatens to put greater pressure on water supplies, National Trust gardeners are exploring sustainable solutions. For many drought-prone gardens, preparing for climate change may simply mean choosing more drought-tolerant species. For others it is more challenging, because plants may need to cope with excessive wet in winter as well as prolonged periods of drought.

ATTRACTING GARDEN WILDLIFE

Most gardens provide some shelter and food for wildlife, but there is much you can do to enhance this, increasing the range of creatures you attract and their chances of survival or successful breeding. Wildlife doesn't respect the boundaries between our plots and benefits most when gardens form a network of linked-up green spaces.

The first step to take towards making your garden more wildlife-friendly is simply to ensure that it has a mix of different perennials, shrubs and trees, including some more mature specimens, and to let some grass grow long. Another easy step is to provide shelter and nesting sites for invertebrates, amphibians and small mammals: leave piles of stones, logs, woody prunings or dry stems undisturbed, or even build a pile in a quiet spot that stays fairly dry. Introducing water, even just a tiny, shallow pond, will also benefit a wide range of creatures.

For more targeted habitat provision, specially designed bird and bat boxes and feeding stations can be erected and specific native trees and wild flowers introduced. Local wildlife enthusiasts may also be able to advise on which species are present in your area and likely to benefit from additional resources. For example, where swifts have been seen during the summer, putting up swift nest boxes under the eaves may encourage them to return and breed the following year.

INSECTS AND OTHER INVERTEBRATES

There are thousands of beetles, spiders, moths, butterflies, bees and other invertebrates that visit our gardens. Only a tiny fraction of these are problem pests. Many more are beneficial, because of their roles in pollinating flowers, keeping down pests or simply providing food for birds, bats and other creatures. It is therefore important not to kill a bug without knowing what it is and whether it causes any significant problems.

Research suggests that many garden flowers, even those from other parts of the world, can provide nectar and pollen for insects. Garden plants that flower very early or late in the year will

◀◀ A comma butterfly feeding on flowers in the garden at Coleton Fishacre, Devon.

◀ A log pile can be an attractive feature, as well as providing a great habitat.

▶ A young blackbird perches on a gardener's spade.

provide food when it is most scarce. Good options for early spring include crocuses, lungworts and mahonias, while Michaelmas daisies and sedums are good choices for late autumn.

In addition to nectar and pollen, insects need suitable places to lay their eggs. Solitary bees usually like holes in soil, wood, stems or masonry, but some species may be tempted to use specially designed bee-nesting boxes. Moths, butterflies and sawflies require specific host plants for their larvae to feed on. Many of these are considered weeds and are often removed from urban areas and farmland, so gardeners who let a few weeds flourish provide an invaluable service. A clump of nettles may host several butterfly and moth species. A little ragwort may draw in the cinnabar moth, while thistles support the painted lady butterfly.

Insect shelters

Many insects also need dry sheltering and overwintering sites and it is for this purpose that 'insect hotels' are built. They can be fun to create with children and can look attractive. However, simply leaving dry stems of herbaceous plants standing or piled somewhere over winter, and ensuring that potential hiding places are left undisturbed, will provide more of the right kind of habitat. If you do need to tidy areas of the garden in winter, work carefully. You may be surprised at what you disturb, such as a peacock butterfly, which can hibernate in our gardens for several months.

Another major requirement for some insects is dead wood, which few gardens contain. The optimum habitat is provided from dead and decaying branches, either left on trees or where

they fell. Mature fruit trees with peeling bark and some decaying wood are ideal, which is why old orchards are such important habitats. In most small gardens lacking very old trees, creating a log pile in a shady spot is a good substitute. It may attract a few beetle species, including the rare stag beetle, whose larvae feed on rotten wood for several years. Any unstained or unpainted wood is suitable, but big, natural logs are best, especially if they are partly buried in the ground to soften and decay.

ENCOURAGING BIRDS

Gardens provide food, water, nesting and resting sites for many different birds. Some of the species that breed in gardens during spring, including blackbirds, song thrushes and robins, live in the UK year-round and may even spend their whole lives in your neighbourhood. Others such as blackcaps and house martins are migrants, which come here from Africa or southern Europe to take advantage of the long daylight hours in order to raise their young. If conditions are good, they may return to your garden year after year.

PLANTS FOR BERRY-EATING BIRDS

Berry-eating birds particularly like small berries, which can quickly be seen, grabbed and swallowed. Many of the best choices are produced by beautiful, garden-worthy plants.

▲ **Common hawthorn** (*Crataegus monogyna*) is a native tree or hedging plant with lovely spring blossom and small red haws that persist long into winter.

▲ **Common honeysuckle** (*Lonicera periclymenum*) is a beautiful native climber that suits any garden. It has pinkish-cream flowers followed by succulent red berries.

▲ **Common ivy** (*Hedera helix*) is great for covering fences and walls. If left unpruned it will flower in autumn, providing food for insects and producing berries which are popular with birds.

▲ **Firethorn** (*Pyracantha species*) is a spiky, non-native shrub that can be trained against walls and fences and produces a mass of red, yellow or orange berries.

▲ **Guelder rose** (*Viburnum opulus*) is a native shrub with elegant white flowers, wonderful autumn colour and red fruits which appear early and are quickly eaten by birds.

▲ **Rowan** (*Sorbus aucuparia*) is native to the UK and has orange berries that are far more popular with birds than the white, yellow or pink fruits of its non-native cousins.

In winter, the birds in the garden will include species such as robins and dunnocks, which spend the cold months foraging alone in a small area, as well as more gregarious species such as tits and finches that gather in flocks and feed over large areas. A handful of birds, such as fieldfares and redwings, come to the UK in winter, having bred much further north; they may use your gardens as a cold-weather refuge once hedgerow food supplies have been used up.

Bird food and water

To meet the needs of the very different bird species, provide a mix of berry-producing shrubs or trees, seed-bearing plants such as teasels, knapweeds, lavenders and scabious, and plenty of habitats for insects. Insects are eaten year-round by birds, but are especially important for birds raising young in spring. In harsh weather, bird feeders hung with a good mix of ingredients, including seeds and fat balls, may be needed, particularly in late winter or early spring when berries have been used up. Make sure that they are kept clean and free of rotten food to avoid spreading disease. Birdbaths or shallow areas within garden ponds where birds can safely drink and bathe are a huge asset, especially if they are kept unfrozen in the depths of winter.

Nesting sites

For perching, cover and nesting, large shrubs and trees are needed, but some species may be tempted to use nest boxes as well, provided that they are placed at a suitable height and position. Bird feeders, birdbaths and nest boxes should always be made safe from predators such as cats and squirrels.

Evergreen or dense and thorny shrubs, such as berberis and pyracanthas, are especially popular as nesting sites. Nesting mostly occurs from early March to late July with the busiest months being April and May. In a good season, many species will raise more than one brood and vulnerable fledglings are often seen well into summer. It is an offence to disturb a nesting bird, so try to avoid cutting any hedges or dense vegetation during this period. If you do need to get on top of overgrown shrubs, cut them in February once the berries have been eaten but before they are needed for nesting. If you are a cat-owner and know that you have birds breeding in your garden, you could also consider keeping your cat indoors while chicks are fledging.

MAMMALS IN THE GARDEN

Unfortunately, many of the wild mammals we come into contact with in our gardens are considered pests. In urban and suburban gardens, they include grey squirrels, moles and foxes. In more rural areas, there may also be badgers, deer and rabbits. The presence of some of these creatures may mean that you need to protect individual plants or areas of the garden, such as the vegetable plot.

Hedgehogs

If you need to fence in your whole garden, do leave small spaces at ground level for visiting hedgehogs, which need to forage up to 2km every night. Hedgehogs will be attracted to your garden if there are plenty of beetles, caterpillars and worms to eat and long vegetation to sleep safely in during the day. Piles of dry leaves and branches left into autumn may even tempt them to hibernate in your garden, which is why it is critical to check through a bonfire pile before setting fire to it.

Bats

Bats are exciting visitors, living in holes in trees and buildings and sometimes specially designed bat boxes. British bats feed on a diet of insects, including midges, moths, mosquitoes and beetles, so anything you do to attract insects to your garden is good for bats.

Planting evening-scented plants such as honeysuckles, jasmines, sweet rocket, tobacco plants, stocks and evening primroses to attract night-time insects is especially beneficial for bats, as is providing a source of water. All bats are protected, so it is important to call in experts before making changes to places where they roost or are resident, such as mature trees or outbuildings; consider also keeping cats in at night in mid- and late summer while the bats are rearing young.

Other mammals

If foxes are seen in your garden, they may just visit to hunt or rest, but if there is a safe hole or hiding place beneath a shed they may breed there. Pregnant females choose where they will give birth in February, use the den for about four months and keep their young with them until August. So if you need to disturb a den in order to deter foxes, it is kindest to do it outside of these months. Badger sets are protected and so will need to be tolerated.

The damage badgers, moles and foxes can do to a lawn is frustrating, but is often restricted to autumn and spring when the soil is moist enough for them to dig for worms and grubs; it can usually be repaired before summer. If mole damage is too problematic, sonic deterrents can work in small spaces.

Other creatures known to visit gardens include the wood mouse, bank vole and common shrew, which all feed on a mix of insects, fruit and seeds and rarely harm our plants.

AMPHIBIANS AND REPTILES

Frogs, toads and newts may be found in gardens, where they feed on invertebrates including slugs. There are three native newt species and one of them – the great crested newt – has special legal protection. All amphibians breed in ponds during spring. Frogs and toads lay their spawn in the water, while newts lay individual eggs on submerged leaves, which they then fold over or wrap up.

▲ Tobacco plants, evening primrose and night-scented stocks all release their scent in the evening.

▼ Frogs and other amphibians breed in ponds in spring.

Amphibians spend summer and autumn largely on land – this is when they are most often seen in gardens without ponds – and then shelter over winter somewhere frost free, such as under stones, paving slabs, log piles, compost heaps or the muddy banks of a pond. Male common frogs are the only creatures likely to stay in the pond during winter. Amphibians don't hibernate and may forage during mild weather, so if you accidentally disturb a frog, toad or newt during the winter it should be fine.

Common lizards, slow-worms and grass snakes can also be found in gardens. Slow-worms eat slugs and snails, so should be especially welcomed. Grass snakes are harmless and easy to identify by their distinctive yellow and black collars. They may use ponds to hunt tadpoles and have also been known to enjoy the warmth of compost heaps for sunbathing and egg-laying.

BRITISH-NATIVE WATER PLANTS

It's best to restrict planting within a pond to mainly native plants; this ensures that you will have plant species that are great for wildlife and don't pose a threat to the environment if they escape into nearby natural watercourses. Source plants from places you trust so that you don't accidentally introduce unwanted species.

Plants to grow in wet soil in a bog garden, or in containers of soil on ledges within the pond, submerged up to 25cm, include:
- Flowering rush (*Butomus umbellatus*)
- Bogbean (*Menyanthes trifoliata*)
- Purple loosestrife (*Lythrum salicaria*)
- Yellow flag (*Iris pseudacorus*)
- Amphibious bistort (*Persicaria amphibia*)
- Marsh marigold (*Caltha palustris*)

Plants to grow in containers of soil in water that is at least 30cm deep include:
- Yellow waterlily (*Nuphar lutea*)
- White waterlily (*Nymphaea alba*)
- Curled pondweed (*Potamogeton crispus*)
- Common water starwort (*Callitriche stagnalis*)

CREATING A WILDLIFE POND

Any size or depth of pond will bring life to your garden and quickly be colonised by various invertebrates, including pond snails, dragonfly larvae and water boatmen. A pond for wildlife is best without goldfish and does not need water filters or pumps. Ideally it will be located in the sun to warm it up in spring. You can use a trough or rigid, preformed liners, but a flexible pond liner is better as it allows you to create your own shape. Rubber liners are the most long-lived.

STEP 1 Mark out and dig out the pond area. For amphibians to thrive, you'll need to dig out a space for your pond that is at least 1–2m wide and at least 50cm deep in places. Create one sloping, shallow side and some level ledges about 20cm wide and deep for plants.

1. Shelf for marginals
2. Sand and lining
3. Marsh marigold
4. Water forget-me-not
5. Watermint
6. White waterlily
7. Purple loosestrife
8. Yellow iris
9. Ridged hornwort

STEP 2 Line the base with a layer of sand to protect your liner from sharp stones, which could puncture it. Place the liner on top and smooth out the creases as much as you can. Now let your pond fill naturally or with rainwater collected in water butts. If you must use tap water, wait a few weeks for some of the chlorine and nitrate to dissipate before planting. Cover the liner around the edges with flat stones or turf.

STEP 3 Plant a mix of marginal and submerged aquatic pond plants (see previous page) in baskets or bags filled with soil (compost is too rich) and sit them on the ledges. Oxygenating plants, such as rigid hornwort (*Ceratophyllum demersum*) can simply be placed in the water to float about.

If you already have a pond, the best time to do major work to it is autumn, when the least number of creatures are using it. If you need to remove the silt from the bottom, put it in a bucket to return it afterwards, as it may well have eggs and larvae in it. During the rest of the year, pond care should be confined to gently scooping out fallen leaves, duckweed and blanket weed. Pile any material you remove beside the pond for a day or two, so that any creatures can crawl back in, then put it on the compost heap. In prolonged cold weather, it's best to de-ice ponds to stop harmful gases building up in them; this can be done by sitting a pan of hot water on the ice to melt it gently.

FURTHER READING

Blacker, Mary Rose, *Flora Domestica* (National Trust, 1999)

Brickell, Christopher and David Joyce, *RHS Pruning and Training* (Dorling Kindersley, 2017)

Brickell, Christopher (Ed.), *RHS Encyclopedia of Gardening* (Dorling Kindersley, 2012)

Buczacki, Stefan and Harris, Keith, *Collins Pests, Diseases and Disorders of Garden Plants* (William Collins, 2014)

Campbell, Susan, *A History of Kitchen Gardening* (Frances Lincoln, 2006)

Campbell-Culver, Maggie, *The Origins of Plants* (Headline Book Publishing, 2001)

Edwards, Ambra, *Head Gardeners* (Pimpernel Press, 2017)

Grant, Fiona, *Glasshouses* (Shire Publications, 2013)

Hadfield, Miles, *A History of British Gardening* (Penguin, 1985)

Hobhouse, Penelope, *Borders* (Pavilion Books, 1991)

Hobhouse, Penelope, *Plants in Garden History* (Pavilion Books, 1999)

Lacey, Stephen, *Gardens of the National Trust* (National Trust Books, 2016)

Lancaster, Roy, *The Hillier Manual of Trees and Shrubs* (RHS, 2019)

Masset, Claire, *Cottage Gardens* (Pavilion Books, 2020)

McVicar, Jekka, *RHS Seeds* (Kyle Caithie, 2012)

Mikolajski, Andrew, *How to Grow Roses* (Lorenz Books, 2017)

Raven, Sarah, *Grow Your Own Cut Flowers* (BBC Books, 2002)

Roach, F.A., *Cultivated Fruits of Britain* (Wiley-Blackwell, 1986)

Stuart Thomas, Graham, *The Art of Planting* (J.M. Dent & Co., 1984)

Toomer, Simon, *Trees for the Small Garden* (Timber Press, 2005)

Van Wyk, Ben-Erik, *Food Plants of the World* (CABI, 2019)

Willes, Margaret, *The Gardens of the British Working Class* (Yale University Press, 2015)

PLACES TO VISIT

Coleton Fishacre
Brownstone Road
Kingswear
Devon
TQ6 0EQ

Cotehele
St Dominick
Near Saltash
Cornwall
PL12 6TA

Goddards House and Garden
27 Tadcaster Road
York
North Yorkshire
YO24 1GG

Hinton Ampner
Near Alresford
Hampshire
SO24 0LA

Lamb House
West Street
Rye
East Sussex
TN31 7ES

Lytes Cary Manor
Near Somerton
Somerset
TA11 7HU

Nunnington Hall
Nunnington
Near York
North Yorkshire
YO62 5UY

Monk's House
Rodmell
Lewes
East Sussex
BN7 3HF

Packwood House
Packwood Lane
Lapworth
Warwickshire
B94 6AT

Sissinghurst Castle Garden
Biddenden Road
Near Cranbrook
Kent
TN17 2AB

The Courts Garden
Holt
Near Bradford on Avon
Wiltshire
BA14 6RR

Tintinhull
Farm Street
Tintinhull
Yeovil
Somerset
BA22 8PZ

INDEX

References to illustrations are in *italics*.

▼ The Rear Courtyard at Stoneacre in Kent.

PICTURE CREDITS

© National Trust Images

Caroline Arber p.16 above, below, p.18, p.19, p.122, p.124, p.191 left, p.195, p.237 below left, above right; Mark Bolton p.31 below far left, p.77, p.94 right, p.113 right, p.158 right, p.207 below right, p.209 below left, p.214 below left, pp.240–241; Tracey Blackwell p.47; Charlotte Brey p.211 above left; Jonathan Buckley p.31 above far left, above far right, p.66, p.95 left, p.118 right, p.119 above, below, p.121, p.220–221; Andrew Butler p.31 below centre, above right, below right, p.44 left, right, p.53, p.63 above right, p.78, p.80, p.81 above, below, p.83 left, p.100, p.101 bottom left, top right, p.102, p.103, p.118 left, p.120 centre left, below left, pp.144–145, p.155, p.156, pp.156–157, p.158 left, p.159, p.168, p.251; Tom Carr pp.136–137; Brian & Nina Chapple p.205, p.242, p.244 above left, p.270 below; Rob Coleman p.254 below right; Val Corbett pp.14–15, p.226; Stuart Cox p.232 above right; Derek Croucher p.138, p.161; Hilary Daniel p.246 above left; Sarah Davis p.207 below left; David Dixon p.254 below centre; James Dobson p.17 above, below, pp.18–19, pp.20–21, p.27 right, pp.76–77, pp.198–199, p.206 right, p.214 above left, p.223 above left; Arnhel de Serra p.22 below, p.171; Carole Drake p.10, p.46, p.52 above, p.139 below left, above right, p.140 left, p.222, p.224 above left, centre left, below left, p.225 above left, centre left, below left, above right, p.227 above left; Fisheye Images p.189 above left; Peter Greenaway p.108 bottom right; Peter Hall pp.190–191; Paul Harris p.31 below left, p.243 above left, above right, p.244 above right, p.245 centre right; Ross Hoddinott p.9, p.252 left; Neil Jakeman p.145; Chris Lacey p.27 left, pp.34–35, p.37, p.39 above, below, p.58, p.59, p.140 right, pp.176–177, p.178 above left, above right, below left, p.179 centre left, below left, above right, p.186, p.243 below right, p.247, p.257 left; Andrew Lawson pp.6–7; Marianne Majerus p.120 above left; John Millar p.8 above, p.88, p.210 above right, p.248 below left; John Miller p.3, p.8 below, pp.154–155, p.189 below right, p.200, p.201 above left, above right, below right, p.202, p.203 above left, above right, p.206 above left; Sam Milling p.62; Paul Mogford pp.78–79; Robert Morris p.110, pp.138–139, p.245 above right, below right; Hugh Mothersole p.169, p.231 below right; NaturePL/Colin Varndell p.167 right; Clive Nichols pp.56–57; Mel Peters p.223 above left, p.225 below right; Alex Ramsay pp.116–117; Stephen Robson p.31 above centre, p.61 below left, pp.174–175; Mike Selby p.36; William Shaw p.190 left; Joe Wainwright pp.98–99, p.163; Clive Whitbourn p.254 above left

© Alamy Stock Photo

Bailey-Cooper Photography p.216 below right; Blickwinkel/Dautel p.61 below far right; Nigel Cattlin p.132 below left, p.151 right; David Chapman p.254 below left; CTK p.63 below far right; Clare Gainey p.63 above left; Robert HENNO p.233 above left; Paroli Galperti p.60 (above left); Kateryna Pavliuk p.256 (below right); Premaphotos p.73 (below right); RM Floral p.63 (above far left); WILDLIFE GmbH p.63 (above far right).

© GAP Photos

Maxine Adcock p.61 above right; Thomas Alamy p.41 centre right, p.72 right, p.132 above right, p.184 above centre, below right; Matt Anker p.63 below right, p.83 right Design: Alexandra Noble Design; Lee Beel p.209 below centre; Pernilla Bergdahl p.41 below right, p.63 below left, p.209 above left, p.228 right; Dave Bevan p.48 centre left, p.187 below right, 232 below left; Richard Bloom p.209 above right; Mark Bolton p.38 above right, p.126 below centre, p.164 top left, p.234 below left; Elke Borkowski p.41 bottom right, p.51, p.129, p.184 below centre, centre right TRIB; Jonathan Buckley p.43 below Garden: Pettifers Garden, Oxfordshire, p.48 below left, centre right, p.71, p.72 above left, p.105 below right Design: Sarah Raven, Perch Hill p.126 above left Design: Sarah Raven, p.143 above left Design: John Massey, Ashwood Nurseries, above right Design: John Massey, Ashwood Nurseries, bottom right Pettifers Garden, Oxfordshire, p.164 top right, p.184 above right, p.209 centre right, below right, p.227 below right, above right, p.228 left, p.229 right, p.234 below ccntre, p.236; Tomek Ciesielski p.166; Sarah Cuttle p.254 above centre; Julie Dansereau p.38 below right; Paul Debois p.90; Frederic Didillon p.164 above left; Carole Drake p.123 top right, p.141 above left Garden: Broadwoodside, Owners: Anna and Robert Dalrymple, p.214 centre right Garden: Rustling End; Owners: Julie and Tim Wise; Designer: Julie Wise; Heather Edwards p.209 centre left, p.233 below left, p.252 right; Liz Every p.141 above right, p.151 below left; Ron Evans p.146; FhF Greenmedia p.41 bottom right, p.63 below far left, p.184 centre; Victoria Firmston p.48 above left; Tim Gainey p.70, p.106 below right, p.126 below left, above centre, centre, below right, p.143 bottom left, p.203 below left; GAP Photos p.52 below, p.65, p.106 top right, p.126 centre right, p.143 top left, p.233 top left; GAP Photos/BBC Magazines Ltd p.111; Suzie Gibbons p.143 below right; John Glover p.73 above left, p.94 left, p.95 right, p.233 top right; Annie Green-Armytage p.25 above, p.162 left; Jerry Harpur p.106 centre right; Marcus Harpur p.24, p.123 below right, p.160; Carrie Herbert; Michael Howes p.106 above right; Martin Hughes-Jones p.38 above left, p.41 centre left, p.106 bottom right, p.123 bottom right, p.143 below left, centre right, p.164 bottom right; Jason Ingram p.143 top right; Lynn Keddie p.92, p.141 above right; Geoff Kidd p.73 above right, p.123 top left; Joanna Kossak p.41 below left; Fiona Lea p.43 above, p.182, p.259; Jenny Lilly p.123 centre left, p.163 right; Robert Mabic p.38 below left, p.41 top left, above left, p.104; Fiona McLeod p.61 above left, p.89; Zara Napier p.254 above right; Clive Nichols p.187 above right; Brian North p.91; Nova Photo Graphik p.60 below left, p.61 below right, p.123 above right, centre right, p.164 below left, p.164 below right, p.233 bottom right, p.248 above right; Sharon Pearson p.126 centre left,; Fiona Rice p.123 below left; Howard Rice p.22 above, p.31 below far right, p.60 above right, p.72 below left, p.73 below centre, p.84 Design: Carrie Herbert, p.123 above left, p.126 above right, p.128 Madingley Hall, Cambridge, p.133 left, right, p.164 above right, p.165 John Drake, Hardwicke House, Fen Ditton, Cambridge, p.167 left, p.217 above right; Abigail Rex p.28; Stephen Robson p.61 above far right; S & O p.194, p.249; J.S. Sira p.209 above centre; Gary Smith p.30 below, pp.180–181; Jan Smith p.41 above right, p.234 below right; Martin Staffler p.48 below right; Nicola Stocken p.25 below, pp.28–29, p.61 above far left, p.82, p.105 above, p.109 above left, pp.112–113, p.125, pp.204–205, p.225 centre right; Friedrich Strauss p.48 above right; Graham Strong p.109 above right, p.192; Maddie Thornhill p.30 above; Ian Twaites p.233 below right; Visions p.61 below far left, p.143 centre left, p.162 right, p.164 bottom left; Juliette Wade p.187 above left, p.212 above left, p.229 left, p.233 bottom left, above right; Rachel Warne p.109 above centre Credit Jane Stevens, Railway Cottages London NGS; Jo Whitworth p. 49, p.209 centre; Rob Whitworth p.41 top right.

ACKNOWLEDGEMENTS

To the whole National Trust gardens community, in particular Mick Evans at Packwood, Paul Alexander at The Courts Garden, Damian Mitchell at Lytes Cary, John Wood at Hinton Ampner, Helena Hewson at Tintinhull, Nick Fraser at Nunnington, Guy Pullen at Lamb House and Sissinghurst, Martyn Pepper at Coleton Fishacre, Tom Longridge at Goddards and David Bouch at Cotehele, as well as the Gardens Consultants and other experts who helped with specific chapters: Annette Dalton, Alison Pringle, Patrick Swan, Simon Toomer, Kate Nicoll, Simon Ford, John Lanyon, Jacq Barber and Ian Wright.

Special thanks go to Claire Masset and Jenny Bevan who have read every single word of this book several times over and given me such encouragement and support.